The Bostrom Conspiracy

Visit www.booksurge.com to order additional copies.

The Bostrom Conspiracy

The True UNTOLD Story of America's Top Motorcycle Racers Ben Bostrom & Eric Bostrom and Their Crime Family

J. Y. Johnny

2007

The Bostrom Conspiracy

This book is dedicated to JAMES DUCK

Because he didn't give a FUCK

Introduction

This book is a true story of events that took place during the last twenty five years in the lives of Dave Bostrom and my step-father while they created the racing careers of Ben and Eric Bostrom.

A story of the Bostroms' tight knit motorcycle racing family based on a secret background of drugs, stolen cars and stolen motorcycles which helped fuel their meteoric rise straight to the top of the motorcycle road racing world.

This book tells a story full of deception and lies, leading up to international fame and fortune and ROC star status.

Ben and Eric Bostrom have fans all around the world who line up for their autographs and they all want to know how to be like a Bostrom, how to ride like a Bostrom and how the Bostrom brothers became America's number one motorcycle road racers.

J. Y. Johnny

9-1-1983

September 1st, 1983, Thursday, it was a typical cold and foggy San Francisco summer morning. It was finally here: opening day.

This was the fulfillment of my new step-father's dream of one day opening a motorcycle shop, a dream shared by most people who have been around motorcycles all their lives. He was around motorcycles his entire life, in the San Francisco bay area since the 1940's and through the '50's, '60's, '70's and up through the present day: a true "lifer" in the motorcycle world. His idea at the time was to open a store in which customers would buy used motorcycle parts in an over-the-counter shop environment instead of the standard "dealership" type of shop, like the majority of motorcycle businesses in the bay area.

Going ahead with his thinking, he applied for all the necessary licenses and permits and proceeded to embark on finding an ideal location for his store. Many weeks of preparation took place during the application process. This involved purchasing a small number of 1970's Honda parts and parts bikes from an older individual in the San Jose area. This man owned a small repair shop and was going out of business due to spending too many years bent over, working on the old bikes; he said he wanted to retire and become a farmer. Since this old fellow was willing to deal, my step-dad was able to snatch up all his old junk and a little bit of shop equipment for only $6,000. We rented the necessary truck to get the parts moved up from San Jose to the place he located for his new business in the San Francisco bay area.

My step-dad said he already spent a good amount of time driving around scouting for the perfect area in which to open his shop. He didn't want to step on any toes by opening in another shop's territory as was the custom at the time. He seemed to think shop competition wasn't really a problem since he was opening a used parts store and not a dealership. One day he came home and said he found the perfect place in an old warehouse in the industrial area of South San Francisco. It was 5,000 square feet of inside storage with a yard in the front of the building and a sliding locking gate. He said it would only run him $1,500 a month in rent and it would make the ideal setting for his vision of his shop.

I couldn't wait to see the place. The following morning he and I jumped into his truck and drove to an industrial section of South San Francisco. We wound up in an area of many auto body repair shops and commercial buildings with a giant warehouse which was used as an old steel fabrication company. It had been in business during the 1930's. The place was huge and covered close to four acres and consisted of several separate buildings. When we arrived, the landlord was already waiting for us in front of the place in order to show us the space my step-dad was considering leasing. My step-dad stated to the landlord he wanted street frontage for his new motorcycle shop so customers could ride up to the entrance and buy parts and do business.

The landlord thought he had the perfect spot in the building that would work for the motorcycle shop. He took us to the corner of the property and walked us through a large sliding metal door that must have been 20 feet high. Inside the place you could have put a Boeing 707 airplane. There were men working in the warehouse, putting up partition walls to separate the vast open space into smaller units of about 5,000 square feet each for different renters in different types of businesses.

The landlord told us the space with corner and street frontage could be ready for us to move into in a week's time. I thought it was a little bit rough for a motorcycle shop. I already visited many bay area motorcycle dealerships with my step-dad, and they were in newer buildings with new shiny bikes and displays. By contrast, this warehouse was very cold and didn't have any amenities such as heat, or even a bathroom. He seemed to think the place was wonderful, especially after the landlord said, "I can have my workers frame you up a bathroom over in the corner for free if you sign a lease for five years." My step-dad jumped at the opportunity and signed the lease right in front of me.

My step-dad was busy with a whole series of things going on in his life during this time. He still was dealing with his first family of four children and an angry ex-wife he divorced six years earlier right before he married my mom in 1977. He now had a new family of four children that consisted of me, my two brothers and my sister with a new wife who was my mom.

He and my mother were both in their mid-forties when they met and first dated. He was short and walked slightly hunched over, always complaining of back pain from of all his years of riding. His skin was tan all year long because he enjoyed water skiing and other outdoor sports. His hair was thin and grey around his ears and the top of his head was bald, shiny and brown. His hands were never clean and he always had grease under his fingernails. He didn't like to shave or wash much and he was missing some teeth. I wondered what my mom ever saw in him because he was not an attractive man.

He was also a fireman for the Daly City fire department. Since he was at the firehouse half the week I did most of the work moving all the parts to the warehouse from the San Jose sale. Even though there were now eight children in the family, I was the only motorcycle rider besides my step-dad. I was twenty one years old at the time and the only one who put out the effort or enthusiasm to work at the new shop.

Some firemen he knew moonlighted in different areas of the construction trade. His moonlighting expertise was in something much more technical and required trade school training in Dayton, Ohio. This was the home of the National Cash Register Company and he attended their training program years earlier. He became an expert in the repair and service of most of their machines and therefore had a side job in the San Francisco bay area that included all of the motorcycle dealerships that needed to have their cash registers serviced on a regular basis. My step-dad made many stops along his routes, stretching for miles. He serviced many drinking establishments and restaurants, with their shiny chrome cash registers, as well as the motorcycle dealerships. He was known throughout the bay area as Cash Register Charlie.

Charlie was a very popular guy in the motorcycle community and was for a long time. He was always invited to the special weekly lunch get-togethers with the bay area motorcycle dealership owners at a pub in San Francisco called the Mad Hatter, on Geary. The owners all met in a room in the back of the pub, where everyone would eat sandwiches and drink beer while talking loud in their own environment. Everyone had a good time, always discussing business and riding their bikes.

Charlie's friends weren't your typical biker types. They were a different kind of motorcyclist who thrived on going around corners fast and playing café road racer. Most of his friends grew up in the bay area in the 1940's and 50's and rode fast on many roads including the Marin County coast roads which they favored most. They eventually called it the Sunday Morning Ride. These guys took a lot of chances over the years and had the injuries and the stories to back it up. The older fellows in the room owned the bay area motorcycle dealerships and spoke about business. The younger ones were the wild and crazy kids of the owners, who rode fast and bragged about their fast riding.

Charlie couldn't go to the lunch every week because of his commitment to the fire department which involved 24-hour shifts three days a week. When Charlie was off from the firehouse, he would take me to various motorcycle dealerships on his cash register service route and introduce me to the owners as his new kid. He serviced the registers for the shop owners, while I checked out all the different variety of motorcycles on the dealership floors. Current models available at that time included Honda's CB750F and 900F and KZ1000s and XS1100s from Kawasaki and Yamaha. The dealerships also had many used bikes in great condition from the mid 1970's, as well as new bikes of the early 80's. However, given the financial difficulties of the early 1980's, business at most dealerships wasn't very good. Unknown to me at the time, some dealerships in the bay area were owned by the parents of Ben and Eric Bostrom.

In the beginning, Charlie thought it was best that his shop was open between the hours of 9 A.M. and 6 P.M., Tuesday through Saturday. Sunday and Monday the shop would be closed. He thought it was important to be open on Saturdays because people with motorcycles worked during the week and some could only come to the shop for their bike needs on the weekends.

When the warehouse was in the final phases of completion, there wasn't much inventory in the building, which left a lot of open space, so it didn't look much like a motorcycle shop yet. Charlie decided it was best to have an office and a wooden counter. Recently I acquired some basic construction skills at a local trade school, as well as some on-the-job training in carpentry so Charlie put me to work building the counter and office of his shop and went back to his duties at the fire department.

I never attended any type of motorcycle mechanics school, but I thought enthusiasm would be enough to get things started. I knew I could learn about the bikes as time progressed, because Charlie had vast knowledge of motorcycle mechanics. From the time he married my mother, when I was fifteen years old, he impressed me as a man who knew everything about motorcycling and everyone involved with it in the bay area; he was literally a celebrity among his motorcycle friends. I knew from watching him in his motorcycle world I could learn from him all I would ever need to know how to ride fast like him and learn the skills needed to run a motorcycle shop.

Charlie's shop was open for a couple of weeks and not much was happening. When he opened the doors, nothing besides the wind blew through. Business was slow in the beginning because we didn't have any inventory or any customers banging down the door for the parts we did have. The warehouse was cold with no heating. The ceiling was almost 40 feet high and most of our electric heaters didn't work very well in this environment. The only form of heat that was any good was found inside the small office, which was now completed and measured 15x15 feet with one door and no windows and a ceiling eight feet high.

Charlie didn't want to spend much money on expensive furniture, so he found a giant wooden spool used for industrial wire down in the community yard of the warehouse property. When the spool was flipped on its side it made a round table. Charlie had many friends who were willing to get rid of things like used furniture and desks, so he acquired two free metal desks and an old refrigerator. With a little used carpet the office was completed; it was the only place to warm up in a cold, empty warehouse.

With the office completed, I then built the counter. It was twenty feet long and located next to the entrance of the shop. One of the many friends of Charlie's who floated in the shop to check things out stated he had a couple of old glass display cases from a bakery that closed down. He said Charlie could have them for free and they could be used with the wooden counter I built for display cases to show motorcycle parts.

Business was slow while Charlie was at the firehouse half of the work week. He thought it was best to bring in an employee to help things run more smoothly. He wanted a guy who already possessed skills in working on bikes. Charlie said it would motivate more customers to come through the door by having a person with expertise. One of his friends had a son whom Charlie believed would fit the mold perfectly so Charlie told me his new employee would stop by the shop to start working with me.

The next morning, after I parked my truck in front of the shop at opening time, I was alarmed by the sound of a rear wheel of a motorcycle skidding and screeching to a full lock slide stop right behind where I was standing. An energetic tall thin rider in his late twenties with messy red hair jumped off a 1978 Yamaha XS750 Triple and said he was the new employee. His bike was like none I had seen before. There were all sorts of extra lights and wiring for loud horns. The one thing that stood out the most, aside from his riding skills, was that he had two clutch levers mounted on the left handlebar. Curious because I never saw anything like this before, I asked him while pointing to the clutch lever, "Dude, what's that extra clutch lever for?"

He replied quickly and arrogantly, "That's the rear brake, kid."

I had never been called "kid" before by anyone except Charlie, but since he seemed to look older than me by a few years and seemed to have vast knowledge of bikes, I figured I would play along and see what he had to say. He proceeded to tell me the way you set up motorcycles to go fast is to put the rear brake function from the right foot to the second clutch lever mounted on the left handlebar. You did this by routing a cable through the bike from the second lever to the rear brake, eliminating the foot braking parts.

The end result is you can lean the bike far over on the right side, further than anyone who doesn't have this special setup can lean it. He said his family invented this device from years of flat track racing, going back to the 1960's. He stated his family had roots deep in dirt track's Lodi Cycle Bowl in central California. I didn't know what he was talking about because I never heard of the place, but he said the Lodi Cycle Bowl was a breeding ground for up-and-coming riders in the California dirt track scene.

After he was done bragging about his skills, he stated he would come in and start the next day as the new mechanic because he had things to do and still wanted to eat. He fired up the Yamaha and proceeded to yank the bike straight up in the air on the rear wheel with total control and confidence. He rode the wheelie all the way down the street and out of sight, going 60 MPH in a twenty five zone.

I opened the shop the next morning at 9:00 a.m. but there was no mechanic to be seen. 10:00 came and went and still no mechanic. I started to wonder who Charlie hired. Even though I was dazzled by his skills and daring moves on a motorcycle, I wasn't so impressed with his ability to show up when he said he would.

Around noon, I noticed a van pulling into the driveway, one of those 1970's surfer vans with spoilers and horns and sirens mounted all over the vehicle. It was painted a strange faded blue color. Out of the van jumped Charlie's mechanic, as if he was getting to work on time and it was nine in the morning. He told me Charlie said it was okay for him to park the van in the yard in front of the shop. He would live in it and be a mechanic/security guard. He also said he would bring all the rest of his tools and tables later and set up his mechanic area inside the shop. I didn't say anything to him or express any dissatisfaction because it seemed as if it was what Charlie wanted.

The next day on a warm afternoon, when Charlie and the mechanic were working on a bike, I saw the mechanic up close a little better than I had previously. He was wearing a sleeveless shirt, and I noticed he had a very slender build and what appeared to be scarring on his forearms. Later in the day, I asked Charlie what the deal was with the scars on the mechanic. Charlie claimed the old flat trackers said the mechanic was a druggie from the old days and that he shot speed and heroin.

Charlie said the mechanic was known to everyone as Pin Head. I asked Charlie how anyone came up with a name like that and he told me it was because when Pin Head was very young in the dirt track scene he had a head that was shaped like the head of a pin. Charlie said that Pin Head was on drugs for many years even though he rode like a madman and carried the racing license of an AMA expert/pro. He said Pin Head could road race as well as he dirt tracked and said Pin Head would shoot speed and then race in classes at Lodi Cycle Bowl in dirt track and at Sears Point Raceway in Sonoma for road racing.

After several weeks working, there wasn't much mechanical work taking place at the shop, so Pin Head wasn't needed all the time. It seemed as if it was a part-time work deal and part-time social deal for him since he was living out front in his van. Pin Head asked Charlie if he could bring in a couple of his race bikes to store and work on them in the shop during his off time. Charlie said yes, and the stuff was moved in.

Pin Head had a bad drug problem, and he was messy in his mechanics and shop lifestyle. His crap was thrown around everywhere while he would work on his race bike to prepare it for an upcoming race at Sears Point. He was very proud of his road racing bike. He bragged it was something special nobody else had for racing in the single cylinder class. He said it was a Lillie Thumper 680cc bored out from the stock engine size of 500cc. In stock form this bike was known as the Yamaha SR500 single cylinder, but there wasn't anything stock about Pin Head's race bike. The trick items on the bike included the strange two-clutch levers mounted on the left handlebar, which he said worked well in road racing and dirt tracking alike.

One day while Charlie and Pin Head were prepping his race bike, I was working with a customer in the front yard. The customer just finished buying a small part for his motorcycle and took off driving down the street.

As he turned right at the stop sign and vanished from sight, a black high-performance Porsche 930 came blasting around the same corner with the rear end hanging out sideways in a controlled slide. The driver brought the car to an abrupt pit stop halt right in front of me. The driver jumped out, wearing sunglasses. I never saw him before, and I never saw a car like his before. He was a tall slick talking Chinese guy in his late twenties, about the same age as Pin Head. He spoke as fast as he drove. The driver inquired if this was the place where Charlie opened the new motorcycle shop. I answered him yes, but I couldn't stop staring at the Porsche 930. As he walked toward the shop, he stopped in his tracks, spun around and said, "Hey, kid, you like that car?"

I was taken aback because he called me "Kid" in the same fashion Pin Head had the day I first met him. I told him his car was nice as he responded quickly, "If you play your cards right, kid, one day you can have one of those cars and play with the big boys just like me." He dashed into the shop, while I stayed outside looking at the car.

After a few minutes, he came out of the shop and walked over to the car. He opened the door and jumped into the sleek black leather interior. He started the engine, and it fired with a roar while he rolled down the window and said to me, "Hey, you're Charlie's kid, right? Well, if you really like this thing, I can get you started in one for $20,000; that's how much you need to play with us big boys. I build these cars, so I know all about them." He shoved the car into first gear and dumped the clutch and did a burnout all the way down the street until he was out of sight. He was gone as quickly as he arrived. I was relatively new at the cycle game and wasn't really sure about what I just witnessed, but he looked like the kind of guy who could be trouble.

I walked back into the shop to take care of the counter and see how things were going with Pin Head and Charlie. Pin Head was having a huge shit fit, throwing tools around and complaining yelling, "Fuck, I can't make this stupid part fit on my race bike to have it ready by this weekend."

Charlie went into the office to give Pin Head some time to cool off, and I went in as well. I said to Charlie, "What's the matter with Pin Head?"

He answered, "Oh, he's all fucked up on drugs, and throwing a temper tantrum because he can't get something to work."

While I absorbed that, I asked him, "Charlie, who the hell was that guy outside with the Porsche?"

He answered, "That's Ed Woo; he's the Porsche guy, and he's a racer too." Charlie said that Ed Woo was racing at Sears Point the same weekend Pin Head was, and it would be a good show to attend.

A few days passed in preparation for the upcoming weekend race. One early afternoon while I was working in the back of the shop, stocking some parts on the shelves, Charlie became excited in the front of the shop because another one of his friends came in to visit him at his new place. I looked up front to see what all the commotion was about. Charlie was with a man I never met before. Even though this man appeared ten years younger than Charlie, they seemed to be communicating about motorcycle things on the same level. While Charlie and this guy talked about the new shop, I noticed he brought three young boys with him, ranging in ages between eight and twelve. The boys were occupied with playing among some of the old bikes and wandering around the warehouse while their father went into the office with Charlie and closed the door behind them.

A few minutes later, Charlie and the man came out of the office, and Charlie had a big smile on his face. The man, without saying anything to me, collected his boys and proceeded outside with Charlie. I stepped around the counter and looked out the door to see the man getting into the driver's seat of a black Porsche, while the kids all tumbled in the back and passenger side. He started the car, back out of the driveway and drove away.

When Charlie came back in, he didn't have anything to say about the man, only that work in the shop was progressing and things were getting done. I, on the other hand, was wondering who the man was so I asked Charlie and he answered, "That's Davey Bostrom and his three sons. I knew Davey since he was just a little kid." Charlie went on to say when Davey was a little boy, Charlie taught Davey and his two friends, Mikey and Petey, how to ride motorcycles. They grew up in the same neighborhood Charlie lived in years ago near Daly City. Charlie bragged, "Davey's smart and he buys houses and puts them in his boy's names so he doesn't have to pay taxes." Charlie then looked at me with a smirk on his face boasting, "Hey, Davey does it right; Dave gets it done."

I took a moment to think about what Charlie said. I always knew Charlie complained about paying taxes and said smart people knew different ways to get around things like that. I got the impression you had to be a well-connected person with many friends to get away with something like not paying taxes. I wanted to question him further about taxes and money, but a customer walked into the shop. Charlie said, "Hey, don't worry about my business; just take care of the customers that need help so we can get the fucking rent paid around here."

The customer needed a used tire installed on his bike so I found one and told him it would take a few minutes to get it installed. I would have to do the work myself because it was very close to the race weekend, and Pin Head was busy working on his race bike. He was ready to test ride it on the street in front of the shop. When I went into the back to get the work started on the tire, Pin Head said confidently, "Hey, kid, are you going to come out to Sears Point Raceway this weekend to see me win?"

I answered yes I was planning be there to see him go around the track. As I worked on the customer's bike, I watched Pin Head roll his race bike out the back door and fire it up with a loud roar from its open exhaust pipe. It felt strange because he was supposed to be the mechanic, and I was supposed to be the counter man but I was doing all the work because he thought it was more important to go racing.

When I finished the repair, I rolled the bike up front and noticed a police car with its lights on outside. It turned out Pin Head had been riding 50 MPH wheelies the entire length of the quarter-mile street on the rear wheel testing his bike out. He was engaged in a heated exchange with the officer because Pin Head had no driver's license. It was suspended multiple times, and he never paid any of the fines to get it back. The race bike he was testing also had no registration or lights or even a license plate.

The officer was about to arrest Pin Head and impound the bike for the violations when Charlie came outside to see what was going on. He walked over to the officer and within a few minutes Charlie and Pin Head rolled the bike back over to the entrance of the shop. The officer jumped into his patrol car and drove off down the street. When they rolled the bike over by me, I asked in amazement, "I thought Pin Head was in trouble. What the hell happened?"

Charlie looked at me and answered arrogantly, "Hey, I'm in the fire department. Did you forget?"

Perplexed, I said back to him, "How does that get Pin Head off the hook?"

Charlie said, "I just told the cop that Pin Head's my kid and he's racing this weekend so he was testing the bike out. It's no big thing."

Inside the shop toward the end of the workday, I sat in the back with Pin Head and asked him how he lost his driver's license so many times before. He answered that after years of getting in chases and blowing off the cops on the Sunday Morning Ride he received his share of tickets. He bragged that he could elude the police by hiding his bike in bushes and ditching down side roads.

He said riders would meet at 7:30 a.m. in Marin County and ride at high speed north up Highway 1 to Point Reyes Station. Pin Head said he was one of the fastest riders and would always arrive there first. I asked him if he was getting another driver's license and he said he would obtain one in another name because it was the easiest way to get around his suspensions. He bragged he had many friends from the ride who all had different driver's licenses with different names and ages because many of them lost their licenses. I asked him how was it so easy to do and wasn't it illegal? He said all you have to do is have a phony copy of your birth certificate and it was easily done at the DMV by lying about your age and name. Pin Head boasted, "I even have a friend who's name is Don Williamson, and when he lost his license, he grew a beard and then changed his name to Don Beard on his new phony driver's license." I tried to inquire further on the subject, but he was excited because the race bike was finished and ready to be loaded into his van for the trip to Sears Point on the weekend.

It was a hot sunny morning on race Sunday. Charlie's shop was about 40 miles from Sears Point Raceway as I drove to the track alone to see the racing and to see Pin Head win. When I arrived, there were race bikes everywhere, but Pin Head was nowhere to be seen. After a while, I located Pin Head's faded blue van parked up at the far end of the pits near the dry hillside, where no other racers were pitted. I walked up to the end of the parking lot and banged on the van door. He was in the van getting into his leather suit and smoking a joint. I noticed he had a large scar the full length of his right leg and he said it gave him a lot of problems. I asked him where the scar was from, and he told me that a year ago, before Charlie opened his shop he was in a head-on collision. He was injured while riding the passenger seat backwards on his friend's motorcycle holding a movie camera, attempting to make the first film of the famous Sunday Morning Ride. He said today would be different because he was ready to win.

It was now mid-morning, and the announcers called Pin Head's race to the starting grid. I asked him as he was putting on his helmet, "Why do you park all the way up here when all the other racers are parked down by the starting line?"

He answered, "There's a lot of assholes who run this race organization that don't like me or my family. They say we ride too fast and we're too crazy for this organization." He fired up the bike and took off for the grid. When the green flag dropped, the bullshit stopped and Pin Head shot to the lead of the singles group. Races were about eight laps long, and sure enough, by the end he was in the lead and riding real fast. As he predicted, he won the race and brought back a trophy to where I was standing by his van. He tore off his suit, threw his helmet and trophy in the cluttered van and lit up the rest of his joint to finish it up with pleasure. He said his friend was coming out in the next race, which was the formula one class and it was the most exciting race to watch.

The racers filled the grid for the next race. When the green flag flew, the racers all came through turn number one and up the hill in a huge bunch. Exiting turn two, I could see a black TZ750 Yamaha with a rider wearing a black leather suit and a black helmet surge to the lead of the group as the pack of bikes quickly disappeared out of sight over the dry hot mountain-side. Because the track was so hilly, I didn't see the bikes until they came around for the next lap. When the pack raced by on lap two, I saw that the racer on the TZ750 had gapped the field rather far and I noticed on the back of the rider's black leather suit three very large red letters: WOO.

I turned to Pin Head and asked him if that was his friend. He said yes, and he was the same guy who came into the shop last week with the black Porsche. We watched the TZ750 pull away smoothly through the entire race, all the way to the checkered flag to win. I said to Pin Head, "Dude, do all you guys smoke weed and still race and win?"

He said, "Fuck yeah, kid. We can ride on drugs or not on drugs. It doesn't even matter; we just like to go fast." I asked him if his friend Ed Woo also smoked weed and raced. He answered Ed didn't smoke, he had a whole different appetite for stimulants. Pin Head pointed to his nose smiling and said, "Ed Woo is into the cocaine scene. You get the picture, don't you, kid?" The exciting day started to wind down by the late afternoon and a few beers were pulled out by Pin Head when the races were over.

The following work week, Charlie was on the phone with an insurance company to purchase some salvage bikes for the shop. The way the business was supposed to work, is he would get in a wrecked motorcycle for parts and the process would be to dismantle the bike and sell the parts individually over the counter. Before this could be done, Charlie must fill out and submit to the DMV paperwork to state the cycle was being dismantled. Following the rules was a very important part of the procedure, according to the DMV. The process was called salvage.

Charlie hung up the phone that morning and told me that he made a deal with an insurance adjuster for two wrecked bikes. The first one was a 1983 Honda CB650 SC Nighthawk, and the other one was a 1983 Suzuki GS550ES sport bike. Since the bikes were crashed, they would be delivered by a tow truck later.

When the bikes arrived, they were wrecked and in poor condition. Pin Head and I pushed the motorcycles into the back of the shop, where they would be stored until the paperwork was cleared by the DMV.

A few weeks went by while the bikes sat in the corner of the shop. Charlie came out of the office one day and said the bikes cleared the DMV and was ready to be taken apart so he could sell the parts. Pin Head said he thought more money could be made if the bikes were fixed up with new parts and sold as running bikes. He said his friend could get the parts real cheap because the cost of the dealer parts to fix up the bikes were too expensive. I felt it was a little strange because I thought we were supposed to be selling parts and doing repairs to make money, not selling whole bikes.

The following morning, after the shop opened, I saw an old black Dodge van from the 1970's pull up in front of the shop. I thought it was a customer, but it turned out to be Ed Woo. He stepped out of the van and said hello to me and told me he had two bikes for Charlie while he quickly walked past me to find him. After a few minutes, Ed came back outside and jumped into his van, he backed up to the rear entrance to met Charlie there while I walked over to see what they were doing. Charlie and Ed, along with Pin Head, swung open the van's rear doors and rolled out two nice new condition motorcycles of the exact same brand and color as the two wrecked bikes from the insurance company.

The three of them stood around the four bikes and talked about taking all of the parts off the nice bikes Ed brought in, and then put those parts on the wrecked bikes to fix them up to make both of them like new again. Since I had no experience working on any current-year motorcycles—the only experience I had was working on simple two stroke street bikes like the bike I owned, which was a 1972 Yamaha R5—I stood back and watched to see how they undertook this task.

The color of the Nighthawk 650 was burgundy, and the Suzuki sport bike was blue and white. Not only were they the same bikes, but the color schemes matched perfectly with the wrecked bikes. Ed and Pin Head were on fire from the get-go. Tanks, seats and bodywork were off the bikes in a matter of minutes. Next, they took the wheels and forks out and soon they had the engines removed from the frames and on the floor. Before you knew it, both motorcycles were completely taken apart.

The disassembled pile of parts on the shop floor all came from the complete bikes Ed showed up with just forty minutes earlier. Their next task was to take all the broken parts off the insurance bikes. In a few minutes, the Ed Woo parts were assembled onto the insurance bikes and soon they were completed and running with both the insurance motorcycles in perfect condition.

Pin Head said he wanted to test the Nighthawk in front of the shop so he fired the bike up, zoomed out the front door and took off down the street. After waiting one or two minutes and thinking the worst happened, into my sight came the Nighthawk on the rear wheel, heading toward me from down the street. Pin Head slammed the front end down at 60 MPH, then proceeded to lock the rear brake and skid the motorcycle sideways for a hundred feet, before coming to a stop in front of me. With a big smile on his face he said, "This thing's a happy motorcycle, kid. This bike still has good life left in it after the accident it was in; it loves to wheelie."

I asked Pin Head, "Doesn't riding like that break or damage things on a street bike?"

He replied, "All motorcycles love to wheelie; you just have to know how to do it."

Charlie came outside yelling and said to get the motorcycle back in the shop before the cops show up and take Pin Head to jail. He barked, "Get your asses back inside here and get to work, and stop fucking around!"

During the first year of business, Pin Head did most of his living in his van, located in the yard in front of the shop. It was behind the locked chain linked gate, so the police would not bother him at night for living in his vehicle. It also made the perfect small hideaway for privacy when he was juicing himself up on speed. The problem was on some days when the shop was opened, Pin Head wasn't available to work because he was up for days on speed.

The problem was compounded one morning when Pin Head came in and I thought he was in a bad fight the night before. His face had many open wounds that looked like cuts, but they were self-inflicted picking wounds that came from Pin Head when he was wired up on speed. Charlie said to me that morning, after seeing him, "Pin Head's all fucked up on drugs again, and he's picking his face himself." I was amazed someone could have that type of a problem because I was not familiar with drugs of that sort.

A couple of hours passed, and I was on the phone with a customer when a very skinny female walked into the shop. She had thin straggly dirty hair and looked about as bad as Pin Head did in the face sore department, maybe a little bit worse. She demanded to know if Pin Head was working. I said he was in the back. She walked passed me raving with anger looking for Pin Head while complaining about children, child support and all sorts of crap he was supposed to take care of on the family front. I never saw her before, and I didn't even know Pin Head had a family. It turned out she was his wife. She was also very upset at him because she apparently found out he had a new sex object and speed partner living in the van with him. Pin Head's wife was yelling and screaming in the shop making a big scene, saying she was finished with him and all his crap. I thought to myself, I too also had enough of Pin Head.

While all this was transpiring a customer walked in the door. He was looking for parts for his old Norton motorcycle and said his name was Steve. He was a young guy about my age of twenty one with brown hair tied in a foot long ponytail. He said, "Dude, who's that mechanic you have working in the back? He's crazy and people don't want to see that kind of crap working on their bikes. Dude, who's that psycho chick yelling at him? You've got to get them out of here."

After the fiasco with Pin Head and his wife blew over and she left the building, Charlie told Pin Head it was best if he took some time off and moved his van out of the yard—one reason was because drug people had been coming around and socializing with him during shop hours and at night. Pin Head was angry he couldn't work at the shop anymore, but his wife threatened to get a lawyer to make Charlie attach Pin Head's wages for child support and alimony. Charlie's deal with Pin Head about his pay was cash under the table. He didn't have him on any kind of payroll that Charlie would be responsible to pay taxes for and Charlie did not want to get caught.

Pin Head loaded his tool box in his van and managed to stuff in the Lillie Thumper 680cc race bike too. While he was driving out of the yard, he leaned out the window and said to me, "I'll be back, kid. I've known Charlie from riding at Lodi Cycle Bowl since I was just a little kid myself. Charlie's just mad, he'll get over it."

A few days passed since Pin Head was fired, and it was quiet around the shop. Charlie was at the firehouse half the time, so I was alone at the shop several days out of the week and felt that I could use some help running things. Steve, the long haired dude with the Norton, came around more often now and said he was currently not working and would like to work at the shop.

Steve said he also knew how to work on bikes. He told me that it was better in the shop now and quieter without the Pin Head show going on for all to see. When Charlie returned the next day, he said he thought Steve would work out as a good employee, so it was a done deal as long as it was cash under the table.

As time went on, more customers came into the shop. Steve and I worked the counter and phones, while Charlie was in the office doing paperwork part-time and worked at the firehouse when he wasn't at the shop. More and more people wanted to have repairs done on their bikes, so the need for a new mechanic started to arise. Steve said Charlie would be crazy for bringing back Pin Head and he knew the perfect guy to fill the spot. Steve told me his friend was young and strong and eager to work and had mechanical experience from working at a local Honda dealership, setting up new bikes for sale. I told Steve I would talk to Charlie about his friend.

Saturdays were usually the busiest day of the week, and this Saturday was no exception. A few customers were in the front when I heard that old familiar screeching sound coming from outside. I looked outside to see Pin Head dazzling the customers with all of his knowledge and riding skills. Steve was not too happy to see Pin Head because he thought it was a replay of the same old bullshit but Pin Head said he was only visiting.

Outside, Charlie was not upset at all to see Pin Head because across the street a large silver motor home pulled up and Dave Bostrom with his three young sons were standing around it. Dave was taking his sons dirt bike riding and stopped by to say hello with the boys before they left. Charlie came back in the shop, where Steve and I were, accompanied by the Bostrom bunch and Pin Head. He stepped around the wooden counter and took down a bunch of oil bottles from the stock shelf and handed them to Dave and his sons. He turned to me and said, with an ear-to-ear grin, "Hey, we sponsor the Bostroms."

The boys were allowed to stretch their legs running around the shop while Dave and Charlie went in the office and closed the door. Steve was in the back, working on a motorcycle, and I was in the front trying to get a part to fit on a customer's bike when Pin Head came over to me and said he would help. The long dark haired middle boy of the Bostrom gang walked up to the front of the shop to watch what we were doing. Pin Head fixed the problem on the bike rather easily and in front of the small Bostrom boy, he boasted, "In order to fix anything quickly on motorcycles you have to remember to KISS, meaning keep it simple, stupid." Pin Head then turned to the young boy and asked him, "You're Dave Bostrom's kid, right? Which one are you?"

The boy answered, "Ben...Ben Bostrom. I'm a racer just like my dad"

1984

The New Year brought new changes to the shop, as well as a new era in motorcycling with the introduction of the Kawasaki Ninja 900 in the United States. Honda also was involved in the new sport bike wave with its Interceptor line of V4 engine performance motorcycles. Suzuki also introduced a sport bike line, as did Yamaha. Manufacturers realized a sport bike with fairings would be all the rage, based on the popularity of the factory sport bikes in the AMA racing series.

Most of the customers who came around the shop didn't have the new sport bikes, but a few took the plunge and made the big purchase. Those customers only came to the shop to buy oil or gloves; since their bikes were new and only needed to be ridden.

Steve was working out well with us, and he made the customers happy with his skills, helping them tinker with their bikes. I spoke to Charlie some time back about bringing Steve's friend in to help out on the mechanical end of things but Charlie said he didn't want to spend too much money on another employee. He was constantly complaining about paying the bills and getting the rent paid. He thought it would be putting out too much cash on a weekly basis.

One Saturday, when the shop was busy with customers, and backed up with a couple of tire changes and tune-ups, Steve said his friend would stop by and they were going out to lunch together. Around noon a guy on a blue 1977 Yamaha RD400 pulled up and came inside. Steve told me the guy was his friend he mentioned for the mechanic job and his name was T. Steve said together they will get the backed-up work finished before they headed out for lunch. I asked T if that was his real name and he answered, "Yes, that's right. Just like the letter, one 'T' honestly."

He was a big strong guy about eighteen years old who wore a backwards baseball cap over his thick black curly hair. He displayed a good amount of mechanical knowledge and skill considering he was just out of high school. Charlie was amazed at the process and thought it was absolutely wonderful work was getting done in such an accelerated fashion. When T and Steve returned from lunch, Charlie decided he wanted T to become the new mechanic, so it was a done deal.

One afternoon, Dave Bostrom came into the shop, went into Charlie's office and closed the door. T asked me, "Hey do you know that guy?"

I said, "No, not really."

T returned with, "That's Dave Bostrom. I used to work for him at his Honda dealership in Daly City."

Steve added, "Yeah, and you know what? He's tight with that Ed Woo guy too."

After Dave left, Charlie came in the back to make sure everybody was working and told us he was leaving for a while. When Charlie left, Steve talked about Dave. Steve said he and T used to work setting up bikes at Dave's Honda dealership and said Ed Woo was in the dealership all the time because Ed and Dave do some sort of business on the side.

I asked Steve what he was talking about and he replied, "Dude. Everybody knows that guy Dave is all white."

I said, "What do you mean?"

Steve smiled, "What do you think I mean?"

Before I could answer him, with T laughing in the background, Steve said, "Cocaine dude. Dave's from Brisbane and all the big drug dudes come out of Brisbane." Steve said it was a pretty wild time working at Dave's shop while he was there and Dave Bostrom had a series of lieutenants working there who were younger than Dave and a lot wilder. Steve said, "Legend has it, if you want to get some white powder for your nose, that shop is the place to score." At first, I didn't know what to say.

Drugs and freedom were more available to me after my mother met and married Charlie. My younger sister had friends who, as early as high school, were dabbling in nose candy, so drugs were not frowned upon around my home since Charlie moved in.

Charlie was hardly the disciplinarian type dad. Everyone was free to do whatever they wanted and he was okay with the freedom as long as you didn't get caught by the police. As young teenagers we could smoke pot and drink as much alcohol as we wanted and drive cars fast. The best father advice Charlie would give was, "Do whatever you want as long as you don't get in my way or touch my stuff. Just don't get in trouble because only stupid fucking idiots get caught."

Charlie had many friends who liked to party. Some would have a beer and a little smoke of weed after their work days were finished and some would grow weed in their backyards for their own consumption.

One of these guys was Charlie himself. He purchased a house with my mother in a sunny area on the San Francisco bay area peninsula after they were married, and he didn't wait long before his own marijuana plant was growing in the back. He named the plant Gertrude and we all had a great time drinking beer and smoking up with our new dad. I was 16 years old at the time.

My mother had been married to Charlie for five years before Charlie opened his motorcycle shop. They used to go out on dates with Charlie's friends in and around the Brisbane area. They said they met at a bar called the 23-Club in Brisbane. Charlie never took me to the 23-Club to fix any cash registers during his rounds, so I never knew where the place was or had ever been there.

Charlie thought the shop was no place for marijuana smoking because it was a business but T and Steve thought differently since they had experience smoking weed and partying. Steve said T had friends who could get him a quarter pound of weed, he could easily sell most of it and smoke whatever was left over for free. T and Steve had many friends on the Peninsula, so they knew a big network of people who would always score weed from them. I got the impression all of this was happening long before Charlie opened his shop.

Steve said T had a couple of joints rolled up, and since Charlie left for a while he wanted to fire one up. They asked me if I would like to join them. I figured since Charlie was coming back soon to start his end-of-the-day ritual of bitching about the bills and rent along with work needing to be done, what the hell.

Later on, Charlie came back to close down the shop and lock up. While he emptied out the register he said, "Hey, it smells like dope in here. Were you guys smoking dope in here?" Before anyone could answer, he hustled into the office with his money saying, "No dope smoking in the shop."

After we locked up, T and Steve took off for the day and I went into the office to change out of my work clothes, I said, "Charlie, I didn't know that Dave Bostrom owned a Honda dealership."

While sitting at his desk counting his money, he replied without turning to me, "Naturally. Everyone knows he owns Daly City Honda on Mission Street at the top of the hill in Daly City."

Charlie folded up the day's receipts and left to go to his Thursday night pizza dinner with all his motorcycle cronies. With a slam of the iron door and a click of the giant padlock I was done for the day.

A few weeks later, Charlie said he was going to make a deal to get some more bikes in the shop because we had a large warehouse with a small amount of parts in it. Since T was good at getting old crap bikes running and there was so much room in the shop, we were able to make an oval-shaped racetrack to race around the bikes inside the warehouse which also went outside the front door and back in the rear door. Charlie always yelled at us while we raced around the track, complaining, "No work is getting done. Stop fucking around on my bikes; you assholes are going to break something on good bikes we can sell to the customers."

Charlie was eager to make a deal on buying more used bikes because he figured if he filled up the warehouse with motorcycles, there would be more dismantling going on and much less time for fucking around. Generally, most racing around the oval track was done during off-peak hours or around closing time. We always had a great time. You could wheelie out the front door down the steep driveway and back into the narrow rear door at the end of a short straightaway. There was lots of bumping and banging going on between the riders. Customers would even join in on their own bikes after watching us go around the track.

Charlie came in the shop one afternoon and said he made a deal on a bunch of used bikes and parts. He said he was bringing the first load of stuff and he told us to be ready to unload it when he returned. Charlie was very impatient and wanted to get the parts moved right away. He drove away and said he would be back quickly. Since Charlie was gone and the rest of the day would be spent loading and unloading used motorcycle junk, T asked if I wanted to smoke a quick one before Charlie came back. I thought since Charlie said no more dope smoking in the shop, we could step outside and smoke near the rear door. The three of us had a quick toke while waiting for Charlie to return.

About two hours later, Charlie returned with a bunch of parted-out rolling chassis bikes on his pickup truck, along with some motorcycle racks and pipes from 1970's-vintage Japanese bikes. The load weighed enough to completely compress the suspension on his pickup truck down so the tires were all the way up in the wheel wells.

He parked in front of the shop and yelled out, "Hey, you idiots get your asses out here and get these parts unloaded off my truck, real quick-like." We went outside and saw the junk load.

Charlie said, "This is the stuff for parts. I'm going back to get more parts and some bikes that have engines so we can sell them as running bikes." We unloaded his truck and pushed everything inside for dismantling. Charlie said he would return with the next load. He took off again, and we retreated into the back for another much-needed marijuana smoke break.

Charlie came back with a second load of the Honda Hawk series motorcycles. These bikes had engines in them and appeared to be running bikes that were only missing some of the more minor parts.

We quickly unloaded and were checking the bikes out as Charlie yelled out, "I have a few more loads to pick up at the place so I will be back soon."

When Charlie returned, he was irritated when he noticed all of the bikes and parts were situated so you could still maneuver a motorcycle around the giant piles of parts and bikes, thus forming a series of turns now added to our racetrack. We just spent a few minutes testing out the new track when Charlie said again, "You guys are supposed to be working on this shit and not fucking around, riding my bikes."

After Charlie complained about the racing, we stopped, parked the bikes and went in the office. T asked Charlie, "Hey, where did you get these Hondas from?"

Charlie answered, "Dave Bostrom's shop, naturally. I paid Dave $6,000 cash for all the loads." I said to Charlie, "That's a lot of money for this old stuff. Can we sell these old parts?"

Charlie barked back, "Hey, this is a good deal I made with Davey on this stuff and you only need to concentrate on dismantling it and selling it to pay the fucking rent around here."

He went on to say with a growling look on his face while waving his left arm towards the office door, "Why don't you three lob cocks get the hell out of here and get back to fucking work and mind your own business." We all looked at each other with rolling eyes and left the office.

While T was working on a tune-up he said to me, "Dude, your step-dad Charlie is kind of a dick, honestly." T thought Charlie was nice some of the time, but the rest of the time he was a grouch and hard to work around. T said he preferred the days Charlie worked at the firehouse because the environment in the shop seemed easygoing and not stressful. I agreed, and so did Steve.

A couple of months passed, and Charlie's deal with Dave didn't bring in a very good return on his investment. Charlie purchased old parts that many customers didn't need for their bikes. He did have one good thing going for him in that T repaired several of the motorcycles into running bikes with potential to be sold.

One afternoon a tall, slender young guy about my age came into the shop and introduced himself to me as Chris Crew. He told me about his new business he opened in San Francisco: a motorcycle messenger delivery service. Chris said since he started a business he didn't have to go to college like his dad wanted him to. He said he was looking for some cheap running motorcycles because the employees he hired didn't have dependable bikes to ride. He wanted to buy bikes which his business would own and his employees could ride. I told Chris the shop had some cheap bikes for sale that might fit his need so I took him to the back of the shop and showed him three Honda CB400T Hawk motorcycles T had running with all the lights working.

Chris said the bikes looked good and asked if he could test them out. He jumped on the first Hawk and rode it out the door as I went outside to watch him. He took off down the street and cranked the bike up on the rear wheel and rode it out of sight. As I watched him, I thought to myself: that dude can really ride.

He returned safely and said the first bike had good power and a good clutch for the hills in San Francisco. He said the way you test these bikes is if they ride wheelies well. He tried out the other ones, and the results were about the same. Chris thought the bikes would work for him while I told him Charlie wanted $1,500 for them.

Chris came back later with his father to see the bikes. They decided to take them, and his dad wrote a check for the three bikes. Chris looked over at me and said, as he handed me some of his business cards, "Thanks for helping me get my new business off the ground." Chris said the name of his new business was called Lightning Express.

Charlie was happy to get the money because the rent at the time was $1,500, so when he received the check, he said, "Hey, that's good, now we can pay the fucking rent around here." Charlie was in a good mood because he thought he was getting money out of the Dave Bostrom parts deal and it was profitable after all. Charlie said he made other deals like the one he made with Dave with other bay area dealerships that wanted to clean out their old stock.

Some time later, one of the big dealerships in San Francisco was going out of business because the owner had died. This shop was a Kawasaki dealership and sold motorcycles for many years to customers who lived in the city. This included many new sport bike riders who were in the process of updating from the older Kawasaki's to the newer Ninja line of sport bikes.

News of the shop closing was followed with the announcement of an auction that would be held for all the new and used motorcycles still left on the premises. Charlie and I went down to see the shop; as usual he knew the people who were putting on the auction, and they let him in a day early to see the inventory. I was amazed to see many bikes and tons of parts and used junk everywhere. There were many of the new Kawasaki Ninjas and many leftover GPZ's in stock that were on the showroom floor at the time the owner died. Charlie thought the Kawasaki's were nice bikes and we might get a good deal on some of them.

Because the auction was advertised for a couple of months there was a huge turnout on sale day. Charlie sent me because he already made a deal for the used parts and junk at the Kawasaki shop and wanted me to attend the auction. He said he already agreed to pay $6,000 for all the parts left over in the shop after the auction, and said as I was leaving, "Don't spend too much of my money on anything." I agreed and drove off to San Francisco.

When I arrived at the dealership, which was located on Valencia Street in San Francisco, it was hard to find parking because of the crowds that turned out for the auction. I parked three blocks away and walked to the shop. There were new street bikes lined up by the dozens in the showroom area, and so many bikes they overflowed all the way through the shop and into the service area. Every motorcycle was given a stock number with a tag on the bike, so everything in the place was inventoried. There were many local customers there from the city that used to go to the shop in the past. They thought as well as everyone else, you might get a good deal on a new or near-new Ninja.

When the sale began something strange happened: The auctioneer would sell one lower-line model motorcycle and then he would skip over the next motorcycle in the line that was a new model bike, saying, "There's a bank loan against this one, so we can't sell it; this one isn't cleared." The auctioneer then proceeded down the line of the bikes, one after another, and continued to skip most of the high-line sport bikes. When he passed on a good bike, he continued with the same statement about the bank loan and the bike was not available for sale.

People in the crowd started to think the sale was bogus because none of the good bikes were selling and only the older junk bikes were available for auction. One of the customers standing next to me said out loud to his group of friends, "Damn, they ain't even selling none of the good shit. A black brother can't get no ride for shit up in here." After hearing him say that, I watched him and his friends walk out the door disappointed, without buying anything.

When the sale ended, I didn't purchase any bikes either. Most of the new sport bikes were not sold. I walked down the street and climbed in my truck and headed back to Charlie's shop. When I returned, I told Charlie I didn't get anything at the sale and all the old junk bikes sold for too much money. I also told him the new bikes I thought were going to sell didn't because the auctioneer stated some of the bikes had bank loans against them. He didn't seem to care.

As the year progressed into the summer months, the weather started to get nice for motorcycle riding in Northern California. One hot summer day during the week Dave Bostrom and his three sons came by the shop. Dave and Charlie went into the office for one of their frequent private meetings with the door closed.

It was close to lunch time and Steve, T and I just finished up a small bike racing session around our track. The Bostrom boys wanted to see us ride around the track again, so we started up our bikes and began racing around. The boys were enjoying themselves watching our newly-named 'Salvage Squad' speeding around the track, which was very tight and challenging. We raced about four laps, turning and sliding on the oily, gravel-covered parking lot.

Charlie had a total shit fit when he saw that we were riding his shop bikes and not working. He yelled out, "Hey, you assholes get your asses back to work and cut out that riding shit in my shop or take it out onto the street." The Bostrom boys all laughed because Charlie appeared funny to them while going through his temper tantrum. Charlie said he and Dave were leaving for lunch with the kids and we'd better get back to working on bikes and stop fucking around. He said we had dismantling to do and customers to help. Dave and Charlie rounded up the boys, and they all took off in two pickup trucks.

After Charlie left with the Bostroms, business around the shop was a little slow. T and Steve went down the street to pick up something to eat and I was in the shop alone. I thought about Charlie saying to take the racing out on the street and I knew the road went all the way through the large complex our warehouse was part of. I was thinking since it was half dirt and half pavement it would make a great track for riding.

After making sure there were no customers up front, I fired up the nearest small bike and took off out the front door. I raced down the street and turned a hard right into the giant parking lot. I raced across the dirt yard past several businesses in our complex. After another gradual right turn, it emptied into a short straightaway down an alley, between parked semi-truck trailers. Another right turn put me back on the street, where traffic was flowing. I rode on the street for about 200 feet then took another hard right turn to put me back in front of the shop. I thought to myself, this is a good track for us. Once back in front of the shop, I realized there were no customers and the phone was not ringing, so I decided to see how fast I could do five laps on the new track.

About halfway through the five laps, I noticed a man stood outside one of the businesses in the yard watching me racing through. I was worried that maybe he was upset but instead, on the next pass through the yard, he was standing there with a big smile on his face and gave me a thumbs-up with one of his hands. With one more lap left to complete I came through the yard even faster than any of my previous laps. When I did, I could see the man was still watching and as I passed by, I noticed he stood under a large sign for an Insulation company.

I finished the last lap and rode the bike back to the yard in front of the shop. As I climbed off the bike, I turned around and noticed Ed Woo pulling up in a black Porsche. I walked over to him as he stepped out of his car and he asked me if I was saving my nickels and dimes for one of his special Ed Woo Porsches. I told him I was only making $300 a week and it would be a long time before I could ever save $20,000 to buy a car from him. He gave me a big smile and walked around the front of the car to get something out of the trunk. He popped the hood and reached into the car and pulled out a duffle bag and said he was here to meet up with Dave and Charlie.

While I was looking at the car and asking him questions about how it drives, Ed told me to take a close look at the firewall area because that was where he made the special modification. I looked in the trunk area at the firewall while he pointed with his finger to a more exact spot where the VIN number was located and said, "This is where you do the changing; you take the number out of one car and you put it on the car you want to build up."

He told me to take good look at the quality of the welding while saying, "You can't even tell where the old number was removed and where the new number was installed." He also boasted that the condition of the welding work was so good and smooth the cops would never be able to see the VIN number was changed. He told me to stand back while he slammed down the hood bragging, "Like I said, kid. I build many of these cars and I even built the one Dave Bostrom is driving." I told him Charlie and Dave left for lunch a while ago and I didn't know when they were coming back. Ed said he needed to drop off some stuff for Charlie and Dave so he would leave it in the office because he was busy and couldn't wait for them to return.

Ed went into the shop with the duffle bag and then came out with it and told me he would stop by in a few days to see Charlie. As he opened the door, he threw the bag in and jumped into his Porsche, he grinned, looked at me, and said, "Like I told you before, kid. You'll have to really think about scoring one of these cars from me because this is what you need to drive if you want to learn to hang with the big boys." He fired the engine up and took off down the street at a high rate of acceleration. I could see the rear tires twisting from the torque of the engine as he sped away out of sight.

I walked back in the shop and answered a few calls from customers when T and Steve returned from lunch and started to work on some projects. I told them Ed came by and he was looking for Charlie and Dave. Steve said to me, "Dude, that guy Ed Woo is all white too. Every one knows he's the hook up on cocaine just like Bostrom." I told Steve that Ed constantly hounded me about buying one of his Porsches and Steve replied, "Man, you can't buy anything from that dude; his cars are all hot cars."

A couple of weeks went by at the shop, and one day both T and Steve were telling me how they spent the past weekend dirt bike riding. Both had extensive riding ability from several years of dirt bike riding together. Steve and T grew up together in the Daly City area and rode with each other as far back as when they were young teenagers.

T asked me if I wanted to go dirt bike riding with them that coming weekend when Charlie walked out of the office to see how things were progressing in the work station area. Charlie overheard the three of us talking about dirt bike riding and said he and Dave Bostrom and Dave's kids were all going to the Dick Mann Vintage Motocross Race at Sand Hill Ranch in the eastern San Francisco bay area. Charlie said Dick Mann himself was coming into the shop to discuss some of the details with him of the event that weekend. I asked Charlie if he knew Dick Mann personally and he answered, "Naturally. I've know Bugsy Mann for years." I was surprised because he never brought him up before, and it just seemed to add to the list of famous motorcycle personalities Charlie knew well. I asked Charlie if T, Steve and I could come along to the Dick Mann weekend, and he said it would be okay.

The next day on Friday, we prepared the bikes for the weekend. The only complete running dirt bike in the shop that I could find to ride was an old Suzuki TS185. With a little work it was soon ready to race up and down the street to test out. Charlie said the motorcycles must be earlier than a certain year to qualify for the event. T drove up in his Chevy El Camino with a very exotic looking motorcycle in the back and I rode over to him as he was unloading the bike. He said his bike was a Yamaha XS650, equipped with a Champion dirt track frame. The frame was nickel-plated and had special forks and wheels. T said this bike was his flat tracker and he was riding it at the Dick Mann event. I felt outclassed because his bike was extreme, and I knew he also had the talent to ride it fast.

We rolled our bikes in the shop together while Charlie was hanging up the telephone. Charlie said he spoke to his friends Mikey and Petey and they were also attending the event Sunday with him and Dave. Charlie then told us that Dick Mann would be visiting the shop later.

True to form, later in the afternoon, Charlie met an older-looking gentleman at the counter. Charlie looked in the back and yelled to us, "Hey, Dick Mann is here and we'll be in the office for a while so answer the phones if they ring and take care of the customers while I'm busy."

After some time passed, Dick came out of the office and left while Charlie walked to the back. He told us he was helping to sponsor the vintage motocross event Dick Mann was putting on. They thought vintage motocross was growing in popularity with older riders who still wanted to race and have fun. Charlie said he was going to the races with his friends and T, Steve and I would have to make arrangements to get there ourselves.

Late that afternoon, Dave Bostrom came into the shop again to see Charlie. Dave's visits to the shop became more frequent and many times when Dave came in during the week he would have his three sons with him. I began to wonder why the boys were always at the shop on the weekdays and not in school. On this particular trip Dave made to the shop the boys were not with him and instead, he had an Asian woman accompanying him. I was surprised because she didn't look like she could be the boys' mother and looked a bit younger than Dave.

Charlie said her name was Tami and she was Dave's girlfriend who lived with him. Charlie told me Tami and my younger sister knew each other and got along really well. I wondered, since Dave was twenty years older than me, how young Tami must have been if she was hanging out with my younger sister. While I was kicking all this around, I was still wondering who the three Bostrom boys' mother must be if not Tami.

Dave and Charlie talked for a while at the counter, and then Tami and Dave left. Charlie asked me to come up to the counter and help him put some tire inner tubes away on the shelf. While I was stacking the tubes and Charlie was checking them off the sales invoice from the distributor, I asked him about the Bostrom boy's mom.

He said, "Tami is Dave's girlfriend now, and Dave isn't together with the boys' mother anymore." I asked Charlie, "Is Dave and the boys' mother divorced?" Charlie told me Dave and the boys' mother, were never married.

Charlie had many friends like Dave who were in the Viet Nam war, when they came back they developed a free style of living and didn't marry. Charlie said many of his friends from Viet Nam were bad-asses and you really needed to watch out around them because of all the things they went through in the war. Charlie always pointed out his Viet Nam veteran friends to me when they would ride in and say hello to him and buy parts for their bikes.

I pressed Charlie further and said to him I didn't know Dave was in the Viet Nam War. Charlie said Dave was indeed in the war and Dave was a tank mechanic and an expert in welding and hydraulics. I remembered Pin Head told me he was also in the Viet Nam War. When I told this to Charlie, he started laughing uncontrollably and said Pin Head was in the military but he was never sent to Viet Nam. He said when Pin Head was in the Army he was trained to be a battlefield medic.

Pin Head washed out of the U.S. Army and never made it to Viet Nam because he developed a habit of getting hooked on the drugs in the bag that were supposed to be given to the injured soldiers. When Charlie stopped laughing, I asked him, "If Tami isn't the Bostrom boys' mother then who is?"

Charlie looked at me and said with a cocky expression, "Verna, naturally."

I never heard Charlie say the name Verna before and wondered who she was. Charlie said, "She's the owner of Oakland Honda in the east bay." I thought it was rather strange when he told me this because I wasn't familiar with a woman owning and running her own motorcycle dealership. Charlie said Verna did things the right way and he wished he could do things like Verna and run a tight ship without a lot of fucking around. He went on to brag that Verna had tons of motorcycles and put away new models for storing because she knew the motorcycles would be worth much more money in the future. He boasted about how she was smart by taking some of every motorcycle model made and putting them away in the country.

I wanted to press Charlie further about the lady and her mysterious fleet of motorcycles in the country, but before I could muster another question about it, he said to me, "I have to go over to the east bay and check out a Honda and Kawasaki dealership in Alameda that is closing down. Charlie said he would bring in a few loads of parts from this dealership. He wanted me to keep an eye on things because he was leaving for a while, meeting with the dealership owner and making the deal for the parts and maybe a few bikes.

When Charlie left, I went into the office and sat down at my desk. While I ate lunch, I noticed I left my racing program from the last Champion Spark Plug 200 Race held at Laguna Seca Raceway sitting on the top of some papers. I flipped it open and started to read it, eating my sandwich. This was the program from the 1983 race, which featured the famous Kenny Roberts retirement from racing announcement. Everyone thought racing in the international scene would never be the same again after Kenny retired. About midway through the program there was a full-page advertisement about a grand opening for a new Yamaha dealership in San Jose, about forty miles south of our shop.

The dealership was owned by Kenny Roberts after his retirement from racing and was called Kenny Roberts Yamaha Country. The advertisement featured a smiling Kenny Roberts, with a promise Kenny would meet or beat any price on any new 1983 Yamaha motorcycle. The ad also said Kenny was dealing and to check his prices before you bought anywhere else. I thought to myself as I looked at the page, why are so many dealerships closing because of slow business, but Kenny Roberts opened a brand new dealership in an area that already had slow bike sales?

In the evening after we closed, Charlie was talking to me about the shop and said, "I think it's a good idea that we put more trust in T around the shop and give him more responsibilities helping run the business as well as the mechanic." I already knew Charlie thought T had both riding and mechanical skills that were far beyond my talent, even though he was four years younger than me. I answered Charlie and said I thought it was a good idea to move T up if it was in the best interest of the shop. He said he will give T his own set of keys to open the shop in the mornings because that way things could get done smoothly in the beginning of the work day, just in case he needed to send me out on pickups or errands.

Sunday morning turned out to be a sunny day for the Dick Mann race. I waited at my place for T to come pick me up since both of our bikes were loaded in his El Camino the night before. T was late, and I stood outside watching for him. I knew Charlie left earlier with his friends, and I was certain he was there at the races already. T arrived thirty minutes later and said he overslept because he was partying the night before with his girlfriend. He also said Steve wasn't going so I opened the door and climbed into his car with my riding gear, and we left for the east bay.

About an hour later, we made it to the track at Sand Hill Ranch. There were vintage motorcycles all over the place and some of the races already started. T and I parked the car and unloaded our bikes then signed up for the classes we were racing. We walked over to the track and noticed Charlie and some friends watching the race. Charlie's good friends Mikey and Petey were racing and running in positions one and two. They were riding vintage dirt bikes and rode them very well. Petey led Mikey around the challenging and difficult race course. Charlie was almost rabid and foaming at the mouth while he cheered for his protégés as they took the checkered flag winning first and second place. T said Charlie's friends rode well but he thought he could do much better on his XS650 flat tracker.

Since we were late getting to the track we had no time for practice, therefore we didn't know the layout of the track. After Mikey and Petey finished their race, there was a short lunch break so the track was quiet. T said he wanted to ride a couple of practice laps on the track before his race so he climbed on his bike, fired the motor up and dropped it in gear. He took off at full throttle and drove up the hill on the track to the steepest part to look it over. T was up on the top of the hill for a minute when I could see an old man riding up the hill in his direction.

When this old man rode to where T was, I could see the man using hand gestures and waving his arms erratically. After that, T came riding down the hill slowly and rode back over to where I was standing. He parked his bike, took off his helmet and with an angry look on his face said, "Wow! That friend of your dad is a real dick.

Maybe that's why they call him Dick Mann." I asked T what the problem was and he told me Dick Mann yelled at him saying, "Hey, you! Idle that son of a bitch down the hill right now and back to the pits, or I'll have your ass thrown out of here and you won't get to race." I was taken aback by what Dick said to T and I knew T was pissed off about it, but we decided not to say anything to Charlie because we were just there to race.

Charlie was pitted with the Bostroms and hanging with Mikey and Petey for most of the day. We didn't see him much because he was popular with many of his friends at the races. Charlie walked over to T and me in the afternoon and said proudly with a grin on his tan unshaven face, "Davey's kids, Ben and Eric won trophies today because they're riding so well against the competition. I want you guys to be at work on time next week because I expect the place busy from of all the exposure Ben and Eric brought my shop sponsoring them in their racing." Charlie said he wanted to talk to Dave about Ed Woo and ran off to find him.

My Suzuki qualified me to ride in only one race. I put the bike on the starting grid with about 40 other riders. When the race started, I had a good start up the hill, but with a low powered bike and no practice I was soon swallowed up by the pack. Over all it was a good day, with long-lasting memories of the Dick Mann Vintage Race.

1985

Charlie's shop was open for almost two years, and the place was getting popular. Many riders from San Francisco made the drive down the Peninsula to his shop because parts were getting harder to find in the city and dealerships continued to go out of business.

Dave Bostrom's visits with his three sons had grown in frequency, and the three boys were becoming quite a fixture around the shop. Charlie and Dave met often in the office, and by now the boys felt comfortable hanging around the Salvage Squad. Before Dave and Charlie would go into the office, Charlie would yell out loud to us in the back, "Hey, I want you useless idiots to keep an eye on the boys and I don't want to see anything except assholes and elbows working while I'm in the office with Dave." The Bostrom boys always enjoyed a good laugh watching their Uncle Charlie order his employees to get to work in that fashion.

The oldest Bostrom boy was named Torsten, after a famous dirt bike rider. They called him Tory for short. He was about thirteen years old and was the tallest of the brothers and also the most reserved. The middle boy was Benjamin, but they called him Ben. He was about eleven and on the other hand was quite the mischievous one. Ben would sneak around behind us and play little prankster tricks while we worked on bikes and then run back to the office for safety when we would chase after him. The youngest of the gang was Eric. He would try to copy his older brother's actions around the shop given he was only 9 years old. The three boys would run around the entire shop and play games while Dave and Charlie met in the office with their secret paperwork deals.

By now Charlie made many junk parts deals with dealerships in the bay area that went out of business. The shop was filling up so much with old parts racing in the building was harder for us to do. We took the racing out on the street, drag racing and mini road racing alike. When some customers bought their parts, they would talk about how well their bikes ran and were willing to roll them in the street to prove it with drag races in front of the shop. The posted speed limit in front of the shop was 25 MPH, but most drag races reached 100 MPH by the time we made it to the end of the street.

On occasion when Dave and the boys were at the shop, Dave would act as the starter of the different races, which involved anything from a KZ1000 all the way down to 50cc scooters. The Bostrom boys and customers would stand outside and watched as we raced by. Once in a while, Dave would feel lucky and pick up a bike out of the shop and join us on our track around the building.

On the days we would race with Dave, Charlie would be happy and not his usual grouchy self about no work getting done. Charlie said we had to watch out for Dave because he was a professional racer and the smoothest rider Charlie ever saw on a dirt tracker. However, the legendary skills didn't shine so well most of the time on our track; we were able to stick it to Dave on the pavement sections as well as the dirt sections of our track. Most of the time, the Bostrom boys couldn't believe their dad would be defeated by the Salvage Squad, made up of a bunch of young punks on weed.

One afternoon during the week, Dave and Tami came in the shop to see Charlie on some paperwork. It was the standard visit; they went into the office and closed the door behind them.

Without knocking on the door I walked in the office to grab a work order receipt on my desk and saw Charlie and Dave going over some DMV paperwork forms on his desk. They were talking with Tami about my sister at the same time they were working on the paperwork. Dave was saying to Charlie he thought it was a great idea if he could hire my sister as a babysitter for his three sons. Charlie thought my sister would fit the position well. He said it would work out great since my sister and Tami were friends already. I wondered how my younger sister met Tami since I never saw her before and I also thought it was strange they knew each other at all since Tami appeared to be about five years older than me and my sister was three years younger than me.

Dave and Tami packed up the paperwork and told Charlie my sister should go to Dave's house in Brisbane that weekend for the babysitting job.

They left the shop while I was stayed in the office with Charlie and I noticed Charlie had some of Dave's papers on the desk. I asked him what it was, and he said Dave and him were doing paperwork on motorcycles Dave owned. I said, "I thought Dave had his own dealership; why doesn't he do his own paperwork?" Charlie snapped back, "Hey, we're in business to make money. Dave is paying our shop to provide a service for him, so why don't you just shut the fuck up and get back to work!"

I thought we were supposed to be selling parts off of bikes, not doing paperwork for other people's dealerships without the motorcycles even coming through our business.

Charlie interrupted my thought process and said firmly, "You should keep your attention on the customers and repair work and not worry about what me and my friends are doing behind the scenes." Charlie fumbled around with Dave's papers and some books which he was always recording VIN numbers, while I left the office angry and went to the back of the shop.

I could see T and Steve talking with some of their friends by the back door. They weren't smoking any marijuana, but T was exchanging money with some guys for some small bags of weed. Since T had a large network of friends, his weed sales were increasing and he was making good money doing it out of the shop. Charlie didn't seem to mind the selling as much as he did the smoking. Besides, he seemed to be okay with many things as long as he had his side deal going with Dave in the office.

I walked up to Steve and told him my younger sister was the new babysitter at Dave Bostrom's house. Steve looked at me surprised and said, "Dude, that's crazy. You mean his house in Brisbane?"

I answered, "Does he have more than one?" Steve said he didn't know how many houses Dave owned, but it was a few. He said the one in Brisbane, a large house on the top of a hill, was known as a coke palace and many people go there to party until the early hours. He said, "That Dave Bostrom is a snake, you don't even know, dude."

Charlie saw us standing at the back door and told us to get back to work and said T's friends should leave. While Steve and T settled in on some repair jobs, I was in front when Charlie said to me, "Hey, don't talk too much to the other guys about me and Dave with my paperwork deals and things like that. Dave and I go a long way back and what's our business needs to remain our business and doesn't need to be heard by anyone else."

Charlie told me he knew Dave since Mikey, Petey and Davey were little boys. He said Dave also had a brother named Paul. He reminisced about flat track racing with the Bostrom brothers in the 1960's and 70's as Charlie told me one story: A long time ago he had a Greeves motorcycle he loaned to Paul Bostrom on which Paul crashed in a dirt track race. One of Paul's thumbs was amputated by Charlie's bikes chain.

While he told me the story, he pulled out his keys and showed me a masterlink he had on his key chain that he carried for years. Charlie said, "This is the masterlink that was on the chain the night Paul chopped his thumb off while riding my bike. I've kept it all these years as a lucky charm."

I said to Charlie I didn't know Dave has a brother and asked Charlie what Paul did for a living. He said Paul has a job fixing up old houses and then selling them for more money and making a profit. I asked Charlie if Paul was a carpenter or a plumber and he replied as he took off his cap and scratched his partially bald head thinking, "No, the only thing Paul does is painting; that's about it."

I already heard Charlie say Dave was smart by putting houses in his children's names so he could avoid things like taxes and the government. Now Charlie was telling me a story about another Bostrom, who was also in the house juggling business. Charlie said smirking, "We know how to do things right, and we've been doing it for years. We know how to play the 'Name Game,' and we play it well."

During most afternoons at the shop many of T and Steve's friends/ weed clients came by after four o'clock. Some had jobs working for different types of companies in the area. Every time someone would come in and get a bag of marijuana from T, the friend would ask T if he wanted to smoke a joint out of his sack of weed. Soon T would be on smoke break every half-hour because a different friend would stop by.

Eventually there would be up to a half dozen people hanging out at the back door. Many of these guys were in their early teens to late twenties and knew T and Steve from their past, way before Charlie opened his motorcycle shop. When I would go talk to T and his friends and smoke with them, I tried to catch as many names as I could.

One of the older guys that visited T to get a quick sack of weed would ride up on his new 1984 Yamaha FJ1100. His name was Joe. He was my age and was largely built and tall with a confident and cocky attitude. He would always brag about how good of a sport bike rider he was and how he had no fear when it came to riding fast. He came by more often than the other clients because he was hanging out with T on the weekends as well. They were doing some very fast street bike riding up in the hills of the peninsula. Joe had recently purchased his Yamaha FJ1100 at Daly City Yamaha from Dave Bostrom. He said he did his homework before he bought the street bike of his dreams and his Yamaha FJ was the fastest thing around and handled great too. Joe bragged he just came off Highway 280 and was riding 145 MPH on his way to the shop.

Joe said he made many new friends at Dave Bostrom's motorcycle shop since he purchased his brand new Yamaha FJ1100 there. He said he knew a few of the mechanics in the back of Dave's dealership that worked on his FJ and other customers' bikes. While T was giving Joe his bag of weed, T also pulled out one of his own personal joints he rolled earlier, and fired it up.

As we passed the joint around, Joe reached in the zippered pocket of his black leather jacket and pulled out a small brown glass vile. He asked if we wanted a blow for our noses. We said no on the offer while Joe smiled and unscrewed the lid from the vial and took the black cap off. When he held the cap in his hand I could see there was a small spoon about one inch long mounted to the inside of the cap. Joe tilted the brown vial to the side and loaded up the little spoon with white powder. He carefully raised the spoon to one nostril and quickly inhaled. After he scooped into the vial a second time, he raised the spoon to his other nostril and inhaled again. He lifted one of his dark brown eyebrows and with a big smile said, "Hee hee... More cocaine for me."

Joe said weed was good to get high, but if you wanted to go fast, a little sniff of cocaine was what really got you going. He said he was new to the cocaine game, but everyone was doing it and it was his way to get high and ride. He said when he met one of the mechanics in the service department at Dave's dealership in Daly City this mechanic turned him on to cocaine. Joe said he could get cocaine anytime, and if any of us wanted to score some, we should let him know because he was in tight with what he called Dave's lieutenants.

After the partying stopped, all the guys left because Charlie returned in his pickup truck from doing some errands. This was the normal ritual because Charlie wasn't aware of how many people were now coming by to smoke as well as purchase weed from T. The numbers increased dramatically.

T felt since he was able to fix bikes very quickly, it didn't really matter if there was weed smoking and whether or not he was high on weed. T also thought it shouldn't be a problem that his entourage of friends and weed clients could watch in amazement as he wrenched bikes together or dismantled them quickly. After all, Charlie was happy when T was working quickly.

T would sit on the floor wrenching on a bike and joke, "I can fix anything in only one second, honestly."

A few days later, I arrived at the shop, and since I was the first one at the warehouse, I opened the doors and waited for the phone to ring and customers to arrive. T was late, and Steve was scheduled to be off that day. The first customer that morning was a woman. I asked if I could help her with something, and she said she was there to see the owner. She was carrying a large clipboard with papers on it and wore a badge on her waist belt that looked like a policeman's badge.

After talking with her for a moment, I looked behind her and could see other people dressed similarly. They were getting out of parked cars in front of the shop and filing in. The others all had badges too. The woman said she was from the Department of Motor Vehicles and was there at the shop for an investigation with the owner. She asked me if I could tell her where the owner was.

I knew they were all DMV officers and thought Charlie was in some kind of trouble because they appeared as if they meant business so early in the morning. I answered her question by saying the owner's name was Charlie and he didn't arrive for work yet. She said sternly that she had the right to search the place.

She told me she would wait until Charlie came in to speak to him while several of the plainclothes officers walked around the counter and proceeded to walk in the back to spread out with clipboards in their hands. The men read as many frame VIN numbers and engine numbers as they could and wrote them down. No one told me what they were looking for or what was going on.

The same DMV woman who appeared to be in charge of all the officers asked me if I knew where the books were kept on the premises. I didn't know what books she was talking about and told her she would have to wait to talk to Charlie about any kind of books or paperwork concerning the business.

A few minutes after the officers arrived, T rode in to work. He took off his helmet and noticed immediately things were out of the ordinary and asked what all the people were doing there so early in the morning. I told him I thought they were DMV cops and were here to see Charlie about running the business. T flipped out completely when he heard that police were in the shop; he was worried he might get into trouble because he carried weed on him. I tried to calm him down by saying we were not in any trouble and they only wanted to talk to Charlie about his books. T said he watched police TV shows and during any kind of raid the cops always put everybody in handcuffs until the police sorted everything out. I told him it was nothing like the police on the TV and they were only the DMV police asking about motorcycle business.

While I discussed this matter with T, Charlie walked in and wondered why we were standing in the front talking and not working. I told Charlie a lady police officer from the DMV was in the shop taking numbers off of bikes and writing them down, and she was asking about a set of books she said were supposed to be kept on the premises. While I was telling this to Charlie, the woman walked up and asked Charlie if he was the owner. After he answered yes, she introduced herself to him as an investigator with the DMV. Charlie looked very surprised and asked her what she wanted.

The short well dressed woman said firmly to Charlie, "I need to see your books you keep with the VIN numbers of all the motorcycles that come into this business." Charlie asked her why, and she answered that she needed to check his records because his record-keeping appeared sloppy and he was making errors on the documents he was submitting to the California DMV. Charlie seemed puzzled, but he said he kept the books in the office and was willing to show her what she needed to see. The investigator went with Charlie in the office and closed the door. T looked at me with his panicked eyes wide open and said, "Dude, I'm out of here. I'm taking the rest of the day off."

After T left, Charlie came out of the office, and I told him T left because he was worried about the cops and thought he was going to get in trouble. Charlie said, "He doesn't know his ass from a hole in the ground. They're not even here to see him. They're only here to check my books."

He said they were looking at his record books which list all the VIN numbers of motorcycles that supposedly came into the shop to be dismantled for parts. Charlie explained in order to run a shop and sell used parts from junk bikes, you had to be registered and licensed as a dismantler in the state of California. He told me he needed to follow rules concerning filling out paperwork and notifying the DMV of all the motorcycles that come through the business. The rules stated the dismantler must have the motorcycle owner's name and address and ownership papers of the motorcycle that was intended to be dismantled for parts. Charlie said "She's only checking my records."

While Charlie was explaining this to me, the woman came out of the office and said she was seizing Charlie's books to further her investigation. She said there were inconsistencies in the paperwork submitted to the DMV by Charlie. She also said he was not following the rules concerning storage of the motorcycles in a certain area while the paperwork processed at the DMV for the bikes to be cleared before dismantling. Charlie was completely livid when he heard her say she was seizing the books and putting him on probation. He waved his arms in the air and yelled angrily to her with saliva flying out of his mouth, "Why the fuck don't you guys just put me out of business if that's all you assholes want?"

She gave him a stern look and told her officers to finish their business collecting numbers. She said to Charlie firmly, "You can only sell parts right now and you can't do any more dismantling or paperwork processing until you hear back from me on your case." She filed out the door with the other officers.

By now Charlie and I were the only ones in the shop, and he was really showing his frustration. He said loudly, "That broad's just a dumb fucking cunt, and she doesn't even know what the fuck she's talking about." Since I had absolutely no experience with the paperwork end of the business, I didn't know how to address things further with Charlie. He broke the silence saying, "I was filling out the paperwork correctly, and that bitch is just picking on me because she's just a cunt with too much power. That fucking cunt better watch out because my friends and me don't get mad, we get even!"

Charlie said while he and the woman were in the office she complained because the handwriting in his record books was so bad she couldn't read the names or addresses of any of the people that Charlie said sold him bikes.

Charlie seemed a bit worried since she took his books and said she would check the names and addresses, to see if the people Charlie said sold him bikes were indeed people who were living at the addresses supplied with the information in his books. I thought about what he said, and since we were only getting in old broken-down parts bikes from dealerships that went out of business, I didn't think there would be any problem. Maybe it had something to do with Charlie and Dave's deal.

Since the opening of the shop Charlie always took care of the DMV paperwork. I, on the other hand, was in charge of dismantling the bikes and stocking the parts away on the shelves. Charlie would tell me which bikes were ready to be dismantled and which ones had to sit around until the DMV paperwork cleared. I decided since Charlie was pretty mad because the officers showed up and put a big dent in things I would try to stay out of the way of his anger for the rest of the day. I went in the back while Charlie stayed in the office, still complaining and mumbling about the woman.

As I settled down to work, I thought about how easy it was for Charlie to become enraged at a woman of authority who was questioning him. I figured the woman must be an expert in the paperwork process since she had the job and the badge to go with it. I remembered Charlie had other problems with female authority figures in the not-so-distant past, since he married my mother.

Around the time Charlie married my mother in 1977, he was still having issues with his ex-wife and his divorce. His ex-wife was constantly forcing Charlie back to court to increase the amount of child support he was paying her for his four children from their marriage. Charlie was always complaining because he had to pay a lawyer every time he went back to court at his ex-wife's request.

I didn't really give it too much thought when my mom married Charlie, but I guess I could see why his ex-wife wanted money to raise his children. It seemed in Charlie's first marriage, riding his motorcycles with all his friends down in Baja and Cabo San Lucas, Mexico was more important than being responsible and raising his family. Many of Charlie's racer and dirt track buddies had similar situations going on with their wives and girlfriends too.

Charlie's first wife must have had enough of his antics, because by the time my mother met him, he was living in the garage of his very elderly parents' home in the Daly City area. Charlie was single again and living an easygoing life with his friends when he decided to marry my mom who had her own four kids from a previous marriage. He and my mother thought it was wonderful because she had four kids and he had four kids, like the Brady Bunch on steroids. Charlie's kids, however, lived full-time with their mother who was not too happy about Charlie's new family, while my three siblings and I lived in the house Charlie and my mother purchased by liquidating two houses my mother received in her divorce.

Near the end of a few years of court wrangling, Charlie was back in court to finish up business with his ex-wife. It just so happened that the judge in the case was a woman, and while Charlie was listening to her rule on his case, he wasn't very happy to hear what the judge had to say. The judge stated Charlie must make increased payments to his ex-wife until his young children reached the age of 18. Charlie went ballistic in the courtroom after hearing the ruling against him saying out loud to the judge, "Hey, this has been going on too long and I'm paying too much already. I'm paying for a lady I'm not even married to anymore and I have to pay all these lawyers too...This is bullshit!"

The judge instructed Charlie he couldn't use that type of language in the courtroom and he would have to watch himself or else. This only fueled the flames of anger, and Charlie told the judge he was leaving and said, "This whole deal with this entire court procedure is bullshit! I'm out of here!"

Charlie proceeded to storm out of the court room as the judge told the sheriff to restrain him. The judge then ordered Charlie to be held in the upstairs prison for three days and fined him for contempt of court.

I remember visiting Charlie in jail and getting checked through and proceeding to a room with glass walls and telephones. Charlie appeared angry, but he looked funny at the same time and couldn't wait to get out. He had an orange jumpsuit on and little paper slippers and was in a room with about 25 other men. A disheveled Charlie said hello on the telephone and said he wanted to get out of jail because it was hard living conditions in one room with 25 men and only one toilet. He said, "I can't stand it in here with all these druggies, gang bangers and niggers."

He also said, in an angry tone before he hung up the phone, "I wouldn't even be in here if it wasn't for that fucking scum bucket ex-wife of mine. Did you hear me? That's what I want everyone to call my ex-wife from now on. That's her new name, Scum Bucket."

After I left the jail, I thought about my visit with Charlie and what he said. Before my mother met Charlie I went to school and interacted with many White, Asian, Hispanic and Black friends who were my own age. People were always people to me, and skin color wasn't an issue in the neighborhood I grew up in before my mom met and married Charlie.

Once my mom moved our family in with Charlie to a new neighborhood, it was a primarily all-white community. Charlie is a guy who always blurted out his negative comments about different races, even though he thought it really didn't do any harm. When we would say something to him about his racism, he always gave the same answer. Charlie would say arrogantly, "Hey, I'm James Duck, and I don't give a fuck."

I thought about one of the more recent times Charlie was James Duck in the face of female authority. Charlie would usually ride his motorcycle to work on sunny days. In the afternoon, he would go to his local bank down the street from his house to make business deposits. He knew the woman working at the bank and always acted like a VIP when he was there.

During one afternoon trip to the bank Charlie parked his motorcycle outside and went into the building to do business. When he came out of the bank, he saw a three-wheeled motorcycle policewoman writing a ticket on his BMW motorcycle. She said it was parked illegally in front of the bank. Charlie went crazy and said the motorcycle was not parked illegally. He started to get on his bike before the policewoman finished writing the ticket and said to her, "I'm not parked wrong, and you can take your ticket and shove it up your ass."

The large police woman ordered Charlie to stop until she was done writing his ticket. Instead of listening to her, Charlie fired up his bike and attempted to ride off. She ordered him to stop dropping her ticket book and pen in the street while throwing her leg over and across Charlie's front wheel facing him straddling the front end between her legs. Charlie yelled, "Get the fuck off of my bike, you stupid fucking cunt." The woman hastily called for backup while Charlie was attempting to ride away.

A few backup police cars arrived quickly and all of the officers that arrived were men, so Charlie was able to communicate better with them. He said to them he was a local bay area fireman with many years of experience. Charlie knew he could easily talk his way out of things concerning police matters because of his fireman status.

A couple of weeks passed since the raid, and Charlie didn't hear from the DMV about his case yet. One afternoon during work, the woman from the DMV who was part of the original raid came back to talk to Charlie. She went over his books with him and asked questions concerning who was selling him the bikes that were listed in his books. She already went to the addresses listed in Charlie's book to see if the people were indeed living at those addresses Charlie wrote down. She said when she checked the addresses in the book the people Charlie said sold him a motorcycle did not ever live there.

She wanted to know why all the names came back wrong and if the motorcycles were purchased by Charlie's business or not. She said if Charlie did buy the bikes and if the names and addresses were wrong, he was going to be fined for each vehicle because the procedure wasn't done correctly.

Charlie started to become pretty angry when he heard the investigation was getting more involved and that he had to pay fines. She said to Charlie she also had a problem that he wrote in his books he was finding many motorcycles as abandoned vehicles. She asked, "How many of these abandoned bikes are really out there in the public?"

She then asked Charlie about him selling bikes to himself that were recorded in his books that way. She said, "How are you supposed to sell a motorcycle to yourself or a business that is owned by you from yourself?" She wanted to know where the bikes came from and how he sold them to himself without having an ownership title for each bike.

She attempted to question Charlie further when he abruptly interrupted: "Hey, if all you guys want to do is put me out of business, then fine. Consider the place closed right now. I'll just take the fucking license off the wall and tear it up in a million pieces, and I guess that will make all you assholes down at the DMV happy!"

Shocked, the woman told Charlie she wasn't there to put him out of business but only make sure he was obeying the rules. She ordered him to keep better records and do a more accurate job with the names and addresses in his books. She also said she fined him based on how many vehicles were improperly done. She placed Charlie on probation for six months and told him he could resume business.

After she left, Charlie threw a shit fit, yelling, "You assholes have to keep all the motorcycles to be dismantled over in the corner in a certain area until the paperwork clears, or that cunt will have my ass again." Charlie's mood quickly changed when he noticed Dave Bostrom walked in the shop to say hello with his boys. Charlie looked at me and said, "You lob cocks get working because I'll be meeting with Dave for a while." Charlie walked off toward the front of the shop, while the three young Bostrom boys played around the bikes and junk. Dave and Charlie went into the office as usual and closed the door.

The Bostrom boys gathered around the back because we had a couple of newer small bikes for our shop racing track. We figured since Charlie and Dave were in the office doing their usual hideout show and there were no customers, we could put down a few hot laps on our track. T didn't have to ride an old bike anymore because he saved his money and purchased a brand new Suzuki GSXR50 and was the first guy around to have one. The Bostrom boys were drawn to T with his new bike, especially Ben because T and Ben already knew each other well since T worked for Ben's dad at Dave's Honda dealership in the past.

After ten minutes of racing around the track, Charlie and Dave came out of the office and Dave collected the kids and left. Charlie smirked and said to me, "That cunt from the DMV won't be sticking her nose in my business anymore. Now we have this new deal called the 'Couples Name Game.'" He added laughing, "We got your sister and Eric Bostrom married now."

I said back to him, "Eric Bostrom is only 9 years old. What do you mean by that?" He replied, "Eric and your sister aren't really married. They're only married on paper." Charlie put his books under his arm and rushed out of the shop and left.

T and Steve were busy with mechanics in the back of the shop and while I was alone in the front I wondered what Charlie said about my sister being married to Eric Bostrom. My sister was only the babysitter up at Dave's house, I didn't know why it would make any difference if they were married on paper or not. A marriage didn't make any sense because my sister was twenty years old and Eric was only 9. I found it humorous Charlie said Eric was marrying the babysitter. Besides, I wondered why it would be important for Dave's youngest son, Eric, to be married when Dave was never married himself.

Early that evening, around closing time, T's eighteen year-old cousin Bob came into the shop to see him. T and his cousin were doing some street bike riding of their own since his cousin rode a Kawasaki KZ 550. They were both close in age and grew up together and were close as brothers. They also enjoyed riding fast around the streets of San Francisco and went off to do that for the evening.

As the weeks passed, T was opening and closing the shop more often. This involved unlocking the front gate and door and getting a few things set up for customers. Charlie recently purchased more used motorcycles from Dave's dealership and we stored them in the front of the shop as well as the back because we had too many junk bikes and problems finding space for everything. On one particular Saturday evening at closing time, we had trouble fitting all the bikes in the shop but finally managed to do so by squeezing them into the front space. We closed the door and snapped the lock shut for a well-deserved two-day weekend.

The next day on Sunday, it was very quiet around my house because Charlie was working at the firehouse that weekend. Monday started out just as quiet as Sunday. I was in the garage tinkering with my Yamaha R5's carburetors when the phone rang several times. When I answered, I was surprised to hear it was T on the other end and I thought it was unusual for him to call me at home because he had a life of his own on the weekends and we mostly saw each other at work. He was talking with a cracked voice and sounded distraught as he told me something very bad happened. I never heard him act like this before, so I was concerned.

T told me he was at a local hospital only ten minutes away from my house. I found it strange he was in that area because it wasn't near his house. While he choked back the tears he told me his cousin and their friend and him were involved in a very serious motorcycle accident out by the coast. He said the accident was bad and his cousin was helicopter-lifted from the accident scene to the hospital. T said he was okay and he didn't crash but his cousin Bob was badly injured and the doctors were working on him, T wanted me to come to the hospital. He said he didn't know what to do or whom to call.

I was worried as I hung up the phone, and I was thinking the worst because of the way T was acting. I jumped in my truck and took off to the hospital. When I arrived, T was waiting outside the emergency room doors. He was crying and said it was already too late, his cousin Bob died. T gave me a big hug and tried his best to tell me what happened. He was still in a state of shock as he told me of their adventure out to the coast and how it began and ended.

T said in the morning he went down to Charlie's shop and unlocked the door and snuck out two running motorcycles to go riding with Bob and one other friend. Since Bob had his own KZ 550, T and his other friend rode the two bikes he took out of the shop. I didn't know what bikes he was talking about, but I thought maybe they were the bikes Charlie recently purchased from Dave Bostrom. T always knew he wasn't supposed to remove anything from the shop to use for himself, and he was very sorry and ashamed for what he did.

We sat down on the curb outside the hospital, and he told me the three of them were riding along a straight stretch of road by the coast when a small animal came out from the bushes and crossed the road in front of them. Since they were riding close together in a pack around 90MPH, they tried to avoid the animal all at once. T said his motorcycle made contact with his cousin's and this caused his cousin to lose control of his bike and leave the road. Bob hit the only tree standing next to the road and he never woke up from the crash. T said his other friend rode to a farmhouse and used their telephone to call the sheriff for help. The doctors did everything they could at the hospital, but because of the impact with the tree Bob suffered serious chest injuries and died, even though he was wearing a helmet.

T was never quite the same again. After taking a few days off from work, T called up one day and said he wanted to come back. He said coming back to work would be the best thing for him to get through these tough times.

After he came back to work, Dave Bostrom came in one day while Charlie was at the firehouse. Dave walked into the back to talk to T for a few minutes and then left. T came up front and said "Dude, Dave just asked me if I was still happy working here and if I wasn't he would be okay with me coming back to work for him up at his Honda dealership as a mechanic. He even offered to send me to Honda school for free."

I was worried because I thought we were about to lose our only mechanic to Dave and I was mad because I felt Dave was trying to hire T away from our shop. T smiled as he pulled out a joint and fired it up saying, "Don't worry I don't want to work for Dave anymore, I'm happier working here."

I still felt Dave was a snake for doing what he did shortly after T's cousin was killed. Dave had plenty of mechanics at his dealership who liked to party and we only had T which we depended on for mechanics. I did not trust Dave's motives.

1986

The New Year began with Charlie deciding since things were running well at the shop he was ready to purchase a new pickup truck. He wanted to use it as a tow truck for junk motorcycles. He said it was also beneficial because it would be a tax write-off against his business.

One afternoon, Charlie pulled in front of the shop in a brand new 1986 Ford F150 pickup truck. He just finished purchasing it for $9,000 at the Ford dealership where Mikey worked. The truck was equipped with a six-cylinder engine and a four-speed manual transmission. Charlie said it was good on gas and would be a tow truck for bikes.

About the same time I was checking out Charlie and his new truck, I noticed Ed Woo pulled up in front of the shop, but he was driving a different color Porsche than the black one I saw him in previously. The car Ed was driving on this trip was a bright red Porsche with very wide wheels. The car also had wide fenders in the rear, as well as an aero wing mounted on the back. Ed said to me, "I just finished getting this one put together, and it's ready to sell. Are you ready to buy one from me yet?"

I told him I didn't have any money to buy a car from him. Ed laughed as he threw his arm around Charlie, and they proceeded into the shop with Ed carrying his duffle bag again. Charlie yelled out as they went into the office, "I have some things I have to discuss with Ed so you lobos get to work, and I don't want to hear any fucking around!"

After working in the back for a while, I needed to get a tool out of the office so I walked in. Charlie and Ed were both seated and were laughing about something while I proceeded over to the file cabinet where the good tools were located and dug around to find the one I was looking for. Charlie said to me, "Ed and I are leaving for lunch and I want you to run things while I'm gone."

Charlie said Ed was taking him for a ride in his new red Porsche. After the two of them left the office, I could hear the sound of the Porsche firing up and the engine screaming while the tires burned out as they zoomed down the street.

Sitting on Charlie's desk was that familiar duffle bag Ed carried around. It appeared as if he either forgot it or left it sitting on the desk, because he was returning with Charlie. I wondered what the bag contained so I reached for the zipper, slid it open and looked inside. It was filled with different types of tools I never saw before. There also was a small wooden box about the size of the palm of a man's hand. I reached again in the bag and pulled out a tool that looked like a slide hammer. It had a special screw on the end of it, and it appeared as if it was used for pulling out auto ignitions. I found a key in the bag that seemed to be a master or skeleton key that could be used to fit ignitions.

I stood there in amazement, guessing these must be the tools of Ed's Porsche stealing trade. I returned the items to the bag but still wondered about the little wooden box. I grabbed it and removed the small square top. Inside the box was something strange: 9 small number punches that were made of very hard quality steel. Each stamp had a digit on the end of it, ranging from one to 9. I thought to myself that this must be the way Ed Woo changes the numbers on the Porsches he builds.

I put the box back in the bag, zipped it closed and went back to work. An hour later Charlie and Ed returned and went into the office. When Ed came out with his bag, he yelled to me as he was leaving, "Hey, kid, I'll see you later. Keep saving your money because I have another Porsche I'm building that will be coming up for sale soon."

A week later, after opening the shop one morning, Charlie told me T and Steve were running the shop for the day. Charlie said he wanted me to go on a long drive with him in his new truck to Sacramento, an eight mile drive north east out of the bay area. He said we would be away for most of the day and return to the shop to close. We headed north east to Sacramento.

Forty miles out of San Francisco, Charlie said he was making another deal with a friend in the East Bay with another motorcycle shop that was going out of business. Charlie also said he thought it might be a good idea to open a second cycle shop in the Sacramento area, because there was a huge amount of stock coming in. He had friends in the motorcycle business who told him Sacramento was a very good market for selling used motorcycle parts. I told Charlie

I thought a second shop would result in much higher bills and the need for more employees. He replied, "I think it may be a really good opportunity for us in a new market."

I told him a second shop in Sacramento was too far from the first shop in the bay area and also said, "Charlie, no one is coming in buying the old used parts in the shop we already have." He didn't pay much attention to what I said and it seemed as if he already had a location in mind, even though he said he was still only floating the idea.

We continued along the interstate for another hour as Charlie told me about the owner of the motorcycle dealership in the east bay he was making his next parts deal with. He said the shop was called Oakland Honda and the owner's name was Verna. I asked Charlie if he was talking about the same Verna who was Ben Bostrom's mother.

He said, "Yes, naturally. Verna owned the Honda dealership for years in Oakland and she is going out of business soon because many bay area dealerships are hurting and having a hard time selling the motorcycles. Verna has a place in the country, and she wants to live the good life, retiring on her ranch."

A short time later, we arrived in Sacramento and Charlie turned onto a street called Antelope drive in an industrial area of the city. I saw some auto wrecking yards and we pulled up in front of a run down building. I reached for the door handle, but Charlie said, "Hey, you wait here while I see the landlord about renting a space in this building."

Charlie jumped out of the truck and disappeared into the building, a real dump. It was in far worse shape than any place I saw before, and I knew it would not make a good place for selling used motorcycle parts. There were junk cars everywhere, and the driveways were not paved.

Fifteen minutes later, Charlie emerged from the office with another man. They walked toward the back of the property where the rental units were located and Charlie signaled me to come along to take a look at the units available. They were run down and small, some had dirt floors. The metal building was hot inside, with no air conditioning. Charlie said to the guy, "I'll give you a call later after I think about it some more."

As we drove back to San Francisco, I said, "I think that place was a little dumpy, and I don't think we should rent it." He agreed, and

Charlie never mentioned Antelope drive in Sacramento again. Little did I know, Charlie had other plans in mind.

The next few days around the shop were very hectic because Charlie was getting ready for the new load of bikes and parts he was buying from Verna. Because Verna owned a very large dealership in Oakland, it would take a big effort to get all of the merchandise moved over to Charlie's shop. The pickup trucks were not useful because they were unable to carry enough parts so Charlie said he would rent a large moving van in order to load the many bikes and parts.

Charlie arrived early one morning with a moving van about thirty feet long. While he was outside with the engine running, he yelled, "I'm going over to Verna's to get the first load of stuff. I'll be back soon." I asked him if he needed any help, but he told me to wait at the shop until he came back.

Charlie took off in the truck, and I went inside. I walked in the back to talk to the guys, who were working on a couple of repair jobs. T said, "Dude, I hope your dad isn't bringing back a whole bunch of junk for us to unload and dismantle again. Charlie always brings in old bikes and junk parts that we can't sell." I told him I thought this trip would be different because Charlie said he bought good bikes and parts this time.

A few hours passed and when Charlie returned, he backed the large truck to the front door and we couldn't wait to see what was in the first load. Charlie unlocked the handle on the roll-up door and pulled up as hard as he could. After the door opened fully, we all stood there in amazement. The truck was stacked with complete and semi-complete junk motorcycles, piled all the way from the floor to the ceiling. The motorcycles were very old and looked as if they were sitting around a long time.

The guys and I were a little angry because it wasn't a load of good selling parts and bikes, just a repeat of the same old Charlie junk-juggling. We knew we were in store for a large dismantle project because Charlie was already saying he wanted this bunch of parts and bikes unloaded quickly so he could get back to Oakland to get the next load from Verna. The truck was equipped with a pull-out ramp, so once we unloaded most of the junk on top of the bikes we could sit on and coast the whole bikes that were missing their engines down the ramp and into the shop.

Once inside we threw everything onto a giant pile of junk so Charlie could get underway to get the next load. I just finished throwing a motorcycle with no engine on the junk pile when T came coasting fast on another bike with no engine. He yelled out, "Dude, get the fuck out of the way while I crash my Verna-mobile into the junk pile." I quickly stepped aside as T came sliding into the pile sideways on the bike he was coasting on. While laughing, he jumped off the bike and ran back to the truck to get another one.

In about an hour the entire truck was unloaded and sitting in the middle of the shop. Charlie yelled out, "Hey you lob cocks, get to work on dismantling the stuff that's no good so you can make more room for me to come back with the next load."

I said to Charlie, "The next load? What the fuck? We're already up to our elbows in this crap. When will you bring back any good bikes?" He barked at me, "Hey, Verna has a ton of stuff over there to go through. I'll bring back what she gives me, so just shut the fuck up and get back to work."

As soon as he drove away in the truck, I turned around and saw T staring at me with a comical look on his face. He also had a large joint in his mouth and said, "Dude, its way past smoke time, so let's have one or two before Charlie gets back with more crappy Verna-mobiles." I laughed at the new name T gave the junk bikes.

I said it was a good idea because I knew we had hours of dismantling because Charlie would probably bring back another un-sellable load like the one he just left. While we were smoking, T asked, "If Charlie's just buying all the junk from Verna then what do you think Verna's doing with all the good bikes from her closing dealership?"

I thought about answering him, but Steve interrupted. "I heard Charlie bragging that Verna has a place in the country with large barns. That's a good place to store whole motorcycles." I started to laugh and said, "I think you guys are right. Verna will probably give us all the garbage she doesn't want, and she'll keep all the good bikes for herself." I wondered how many motorcycles did Verna need to store in the country, and where was the place located that she was storing them?

With Charlie returning soon we figured we'd better get some dismantling done. The three of us broke down as many incomplete, wrecked junk bikes as we could. In a few hours we sorted many of the parts out. Unusable parts were thrown away in a large scrap metal pile while only a very small number of good parts were put on the shelves.

When Charlie returned with the second load in the late afternoon, Dave and his three sons drove up behind him. Charlie backed up the truck and yelled out, "Hey, I'm back with the next load, so I want you lob cocks to get out here and start unloading these parts and bikes." When the three of us looked in the truck, we saw a second load of junk just like the first, so we again removed the top row of crap then pulled out the ramp and started to coast the newly named Verna-mobiles in the shop to crash them into the pile.

The Bostrom boys watched laughing as we raced their mom's Verna-mobiles in the shop, while Dave and Charlie went into the office and closed the door. When we were finished unloading the truck, Steve said angrily, "These fucking Verna-mobiles are making me sick. This is way too much work."

T looked over at Ben and Eric and asked, "Verna's your mom, right? What did you say her last name was?"

Young Ben answered back, "Ober." Then T laughed hard while saying out loud, "What's that mean? Verna Ober...Gets the fuck over?"

Ben appeared mad and before he could answer, Dave and Charlie emerged from the office, and Dave yelled for his boys to leave. They scrambled into Dave's truck and drove off. Charlie told us he was leaving to Oakland to get the last load out of Verna's dealership. Since it was late afternoon, he said once the truck was loaded in Oakland, he would leave it parked overnight in front of his shop so we could unload all the parts and junk bikes first thing in the morning.

After Charlie left, I talked to T about the Bostrom boys and asked him, "What did that kid Ben say his last name was? Did he say Ober? I thought his last name was Bostrom."

T answered, "I guess his mom's last name is Ober, like Ben said, and she's not a Bostrom because she was never married to Dave." I said to T that I thought it was strange Verna was closing her dealership so fast and Charlie was running his ass off to get as much crap as he could. T said he thought there were probably much stranger things happening over at the dealership in Oakland and out at their secret hideout in the country.

20 minutes later, I went outside to check on things in front of the shop. I noticed a Porsche in the driveway, as Ed Woo jumped enthusiastically out of the driver's seat. He said with a sly smile, "Where's Charlie?"

I answered, "He is on another run to Verna's dealership to get more parts." Ed seemed worried because he was supposed to meet Charlie before he left to Verna's dealership. I told him Charlie said he wasn't returning before the end of the day.

Ed raised his left wrist and pulled back his sleeve to see what time it was. He wore a very large black wristwatch which read Porsche design on the face. Ed noticed I was looking at his watch and said boasting, "Hey kid, check this out, this thing's a Swiss-made genuine Porsche wristwatch. It's very hard to find and very expensive to buy. It's just the thing you need when you're driving these cars and hanging with the big boys."

I asked Ed about his latest car. This Porsche wasn't one I saw him drive previously. The color was a deep rich purple with black trim and the interior was light tan, plush leather. I said, "Is that thing a turbo?"

Ed smiled and winked, "Twin turbo, kid." He said he recently finished putting the car together and was testing it on the way to Charlie's shop. He bragged he took it up to 140 MPH on Highway 280 and the car handled great and had a strong motor. I was relieved he didn't ask me if I wanted to buy it as he checked his watch again and said while leaving. "I'll probably just see Charlie at Dave Bostrom's house tonight."

A couple of weeks later, after a long, hard day of dismantling Verna-mobiles and listening to Charlie complain, T and Steve asked me if I wanted to ride out for a few beers in San Francisco with them at closing time. Steve said their friend Joe with the Yamaha FJ1100 would be there with a friend. I thought it would be fun, and since I recently purchased a used Honda Interceptor 750 I could race around the city and keep up with their more powerful sport bikes.

After we closed we headed out to the city. T recently purchased a Suzuki GS700ES, which he learned to wheelie very well. Steve rode an older GS750 Suzuki, but it had performance upgrades added. The two of them said we would meet the other guys in San Francisco at a motorcycle bar.

We rode north on highway 101 for about ten minutes to reach San Francisco. Once in the city we went on a quick ride through the middle of town and arrived at a small bar. We parked our bikes outside along a line of other motorcycles, took off our gear and went in the crowded bar filled with many sport riders. We found Joe sitting at a table with another guy in the corner so we joined them and ordered a few beers with some food.

Everyone talked about motorcycles and sport bike riding. Joe's friend was a factory-trained Honda mechanic and worked at Dave Bostrom's Honda-Yamaha dealership in Daly City. I wondered as I took a drink from my beer, could this guy be one of the so-called lieutenants that worked for Dave Bostrom?

As the evening rolled on, we drank beers and enjoyed a good time. After a while, T said he was leaving to see his girlfriend, so he was the first to go. Joe and his friend were not tired and said they wanted to ride around more, so the rest of us left the bar and took off riding through the city. We rode fast in the foggy wet night, racing around riding dangerous and daring wheelies down the steep hills of San Francisco. After an hour, we stopped in a parking lot to take a little break and nobody knew where we should go next, so Joe said, "Let's go up to Dave Bostrom's house." Steve agreed to go as well, and I just planned to follow along. I was never invited to Dave's house, so I was curious to see what the place was like.

From the parking lot Joe and his friend took off at a high rate of speed through the city and in about five minutes the pack of us reached the freeway. It was dark and very hard to keep Joe and his friend in sight as they pulled away, riding quickly down the freeway. They passed in between traffic, using all four lanes, at over 100 MPH while I tried to keep up through the bends of the road.

About five miles south of San Francisco, Joe and his friend pulled off the freeway in the town of Brisbane and started racing through narrow streets lined with houses, climbing up into the hills. When they reached the top of a hill near the end of the street called Harold Drive, they veered into the driveway of a large house. The garage door was open, and there was a black Porsche sitting in the garage. The lights were on and I could see there were pieces of shop equipment for working on motorcycles but no bikes.

Joe and his friend walked up to the front door, and the friend walked in without ringing the doorbell, as if he lived there. Steve and I followed along behind Joe. The place was large, with a sunken living room. We sat down in the room with wall-to-wall carpet, a large white leather sofa and chairs with a glass-top coffee table in the center.

Dave wasn't home, but Joe and his friend seemed very comfortable in the house. It appeared this wasn't the first time they partied at Dave's place. Joe's friend reached into his pocket and pulled out a small white piece of paper and unfolded it on the glass coffee table. He opened it fully and turned it over to deposit its contents onto the glass. He pulled out a small razor blade from his wallet and proceeded to chop up the powder on the table into two huge lines. After rolling a $20 bill into a small tube shaped like a straw, he snorted one line up one nostril and then blasted the second line up his other nostril. He leaned back on the sofa holding his nose and blurted out, "Yeah... That's good." Joe eagerly produced a small packet himself and started to chop up lines of cocaine similar to the ones his friend just snorted. He lifted his eyebrow, smiled and offered some to Steve and me but we passed and said no.

Joe finished making two big lines of cocaine for himself when young Ben Bostrom came out of his bedroom to see what all the commotion was about. While Joe snorted his first line of coke, Joe's friend said out loud to Ben, who was watching by now, "Hey, we're just hanging out here until your dad gets back." Ben looked at me and then stood there staring at everyone. Joe proceeded to snort the second line of cocaine off the table and looked to his friend saying, "This is really high quality stuff we have these days." The friend looked at Joe and boasted, "Yeah, we only get the best coke around."

The front door opened a few minutes later, and Dave and Tami walked in. Dave seemed okay that his mechanic and Joe were sitting on his couch, but he wasn't very happy to see me in his house. He glared at me with his steely eyes and without saying anything walked into his kitchen with Tami.

In what seemed to be only five minutes later, the doorbell rang and Dave answered it. The guys and I were surprised to see it was Charlie at the door. Charlie came over to us and said firmly that it was time for the party to end because Dave and Tami were tired. We grabbed our riding gear and left out the front door.

Outside as we climbed on our motorcycles and fired them up, Charlie pulled me aside and said quietly, "Hey, you can't be up here hanging around at Dave's house." He acted as if there were things at Dave's house he didn't want me to see. Charlie then said something that was shocking and started to put things in perspective. With a nervous voice, he said whispering, "Ed Woo was recently arrested because he sold some cocaine to an undercover cop. Ed's in trouble and he's all fucked up with the police and I don't want you to come up here to Dave's house again." Charlie stayed behind talking to Dave as the group of riders, including myself, rode down the hill from Dave's. We split up at the bottom of the street and called it a night.

As I rode the freeway home I thought to myself wondering how much cocaine Ed sold to a cop, and whose cocaine was he selling in the first place? I wondered if it was the big boys Ed always bragged about or maybe even Dave Bostrom himself. It appeared Dave was in a bad mood about something and wasn't wearing the usual cocky care-free smile he wore around Charlie's shop. I knew it was worse than Charlie made it out to be. I would come to see later I was right.

1987

A long time passed since Charlie completed his Verna deal. All the parts were sorted through and the junk bikes dismantled. The task was hard on Steve, T and I, working constantly through the rainy, cold days. There weren't many customers during the rainy season, so Charlie had us in the back working full-time dismantling Verna-mobiles.

Steve was working in the shop since nearly the beginning and took enough of Charlie's complaining and difficult working conditions. One day Steve told me he found another job and was moving on from Charlie's shop. He felt since he had such a unique look with his long hair and rock star personality along with extensive guitar playing skills, he believed he could get a job in a band or something of the sort. He said he took a position working at a strip club on Broadway in San Francisco as the door man so he could become more involved in the entertainment industry.

I came to rely on Steve helping me around the shop quite a bit, especially since Charlie spent the last few years loading the shop with junk parts from dealerships that went out of business. I was worried because I thought it would be difficult for us to find another good employee with a motorcycle background. I tried to talk Steve into staying, but he said, "Dude, I can't work here any more because your dad brings in too much crap and treats us like shit. The only thing we ever do around here is dismantle junk motorcycles then we wind up throwing away ninety percent of everything."

I couldn't argue with this statement. Charlie did have the place completely full of junk. He promised to buy good bikes from Verna's shop and Steve was upset that Charlie never followed through. Steve said he would still come back and hang out to party with us, but he had enough of working for Charlie. After Steve left, T and I were the only ones working in the shop.

On one busy Saturday afternoon, a couple of black riders on Kawasaki motorcycles pulled up and walked in. They said they rode down from the Hunters Point area of San Francisco to look around and buy some parts. One of the guys rode a shiny red and black Ninja 900 and the other rider had a nice KZ1000. The rider of the KZ1000 needed a used rear tire for his bike because his was so worn out that the cords were showing through the tread. Pointing at the tire, he said, "My tire's that way because I've been doing burnouts against the brothers up and down the street in my hood." I recognized the rider of the 900 Ninja from the auction at the Kawasaki dealership in the city a few years ago.

I told the two riders I could sell them a good used tire for the bike and install it as well, so they rolled the KZ1000 in the shop to get the work done. When the tire was off, the two of them talked about how hard it was to find any shops in the city where they could have their bikes worked on.

The guys said the shop they used to go to on Geary, a very big dealership, recently closed down. I believed the dealership was one of the shops Charlie took me to on his cash register repair errands, and I wondered if it could possibly be one of the shops owned by the Bostrom clan. After all, it was located about 10 miles from Dave's Honda dealership in Daly City. The owners of both shops always had a warm welcome for Charlie when he arrived to fix their cash registers. Sometimes Charlie and I would actually pay a visit to both dealerships on the same day.

After the tire was installed, the rider told me he wanted to test it out to feel if the tire was good. He rode the bike outside, dumped the clutch and shot down the street with the motorcycle weaving from side to side in a controlled tank slapper. His friend said smiling while looking at me, "That's the way us brothers all ride in the hood. We drag race up and down Third Street; it's all about gettin' out da hole."

The guy returned in a matter of minutes and said the tire felt good. He told me he didn't have much money because he was recently laid off from his job and wanted to know if he could give me $40 for the tire installed. His friend added they knew many black riders in the city who needed to get parts for their bikes because there weren't too many dealerships left in the city. They told me if I gave them a good deal, they would tell their friends to come down and spend their money at our shop. The rider of the Ninja 900 stuck his hand out to me and said with a friendly smile and a firm hand shake, "They call me Dark Ninja, and my friend here is named Bernard." I said it's a deal. Bernard smiled and reached into his pocket and handed me two $20 bills, shook my hand, and they both took off ridding back to the city.

Over the course of the next few weeks, Dark Ninja and Bernard made good on their promise. More black riders from the Hunters Point and Sunnydale areas of San Francisco came in for service on their bikes. The black riders seemed to be in favor of riding Kawasaki's and T was excellent at keeping their bikes tuned and running fast. Frequently Dark Ninja and Bernard would escort their friends down to Charlie's shop from San Francisco and they would visit on Fridays and Saturdays.

One Saturday afternoon, a group of eight black riders came in, including Dark Ninja and Bernard. Some of their friends wanted to get tires installed and a couple others wanted to order some Kerker aftermarket exhaust pipes for their bikes. The pipes were loud and were all the rage at the time. T started to know Bernard pretty good, and some of Bernard's friends were already purchasing small bags of marijuana from T. When we were finished working on their bikes, they would roll them outside for test riding.

Charlie was outside talking to Dave Bostrom because Dave pulled up with his three sons in his motor home. Dave was taking his sons to race at Lodi Cycle Bowl for the weekend. The black riders did burnouts down the street together as Charlie looked over at me while I checked out the riders taking off. He said arrogantly lifting both his hands in the air, "That isn't how you learn to be a racer." He added, as he patted Dave on the back, "You have to learn how to ride like I taught Dave in order to be a good racer."

As the three Bostrom boys looked on, Charlie continued, "You have to learn how to pitch it to the locks, just like Davey does."

Confused, I said, "Pitch it to the locks, what's that?"

Young Ben Bostrom was smiling as Charlie answered back, "You have to pitch the motorcycle sideways so the steering goes all the way to the steering stop."

I asked Charlie, "How are you supposed to pitch a motorcycle sideways to the steering locks riding on the street?"

While smiling at Dave he said, "Dave doesn't ride street. Right, Davey?" Dave lifted his eyebrow and smiled back. Since Charlie didn't talk about it anymore, I just figured it was some kind of Bostrom family racing secret.

Charlie said it was time for Dave and the kids to leave because they needed to get to the races in Lodi by the evening. Dave was now spending a good amount of time taking his three sons to Lodi and racing them in the dirt track races. The Bostrom bunch just finished piling into the motor home when Charlie remembered something in the shop and told Dave not to leave yet. Charlie ran into the shop and quickly returned with his arms full carrying bottles of oil and cans of chain lubricant while he walked to the motor home. He handed everything to Dave, smiled proudly and said to me, "Remember. We sponsor the Bostrom boys and their racing at Lodi Cycle Bowl." Dave and the boys took off in the motor home.

While Charlie and I walked back to the entrance of the shop I asked him, "Charlie, what do you mean by Dave doesn't ride street?"

He answered back, "Hey, Davey isn't like all these idiots you know who come in here riding these crazy street bikes. Davey only rides on the dirt." Charlie said he and Dave rode all over the dirt hills of San Francisco for years, back in the days when most of the houses on the Peninsula were not even built yet. Charlie said it would take a person an entire lifetime to learn how to be as smooth as Dave was on a motocross bike or a dirt tracker. He said Dave could conquer any hill climb even today with his riding skills. He boasted proudly, "Hey, Davey can climb up any hill. Dave goes right up."

I thought about what Charlie said. There weren't many hills to climb in the bay area because most dirt bike parks were gone by now. Charlie was always complaining that riding areas were closing because of the EPA rules concerning the environment. He used to always complain saying, "Hey, fuck ecology."

Throughout Charlie's early life he and Dave and the rest of his gang were free to ride wherever they wanted: the deserts of California or up and down the white sand beaches of Mexico. Times changed since then and most of the open spaces for dirt bike riding were locked up by the government, and Charlie and his friends were very angry about it.

I started to wonder where Dave and his family did their dirt riding. If they were racing at Lodi they must be practicing somewhere, because Charlie was describing Dave riding up giant hills. Maybe the Bostroms trained at Verna's secret place in the country.

As the weeks progressed, it became increasingly harder to keep things running with just T and myself. Charlie was still spending half the work week at his job as a fireman. This made the shop short-handed during busy times when Charlie was away.

One day while Charlie was working a shift at the firehouse, it was busy and some customers were waiting to buy junk. The phone was ringing constantly with customer requests. Bernard was hanging around the shop more often and had developed a good friendship with us. He came in to see T and noticed all the customers and said he would help us out at the front counter. I had him look at the customer's old part and he was able to match it up with a used part from our stock. It worked out well because he was friendly and interacted well with the customers. Sometimes we needed to help four or five customers at once, and trying to keep everyone happy was a hard task. Bernard made things easier around the shop with his up beat disposition.

Around closing time, T asked if Bernard and I wanted to close out the day by smoking a few joints. While smoking, Bernard said he enjoyed hanging around the shop and wanted to know if he could pick up a job working for Charlie. I knew the shop was short-handed and thought Bernard would work well with us so I told Bernard I would talk to Charlie about the shop picking up another employee.

The next morning, I gave Charlie the money from the previous day's receipts. Charlie was always accurate at counting the money from the register and he wanted the money to match the sales recorded in the cash register. This is how Charlie would make sure all the sales were being rung up. He wanted the money and the register receipt tape placed in a white envelope and sealed up. As I handed him the envelope he grabbed for it quickly, tore it open and spread the money out all over the desk. I told him we had a good day but we were short-handed.

While he recounted the money I already counted, I told him we had some extra help to get the sales and service done the day before. I suggested a new employee was available to start right away saying, "The guy has good motorcycle experience and talks well with the customers." Charlie said, "I don't want to spend too much more money on employees because I'm already spending a ton of money on you lob cocks and trying to pay the rent around here at the same time." I told Charlie we needed the extra help.

He said, "Who's the guy you're talking about?" I told him it was Bernard from San Francisco, the guy who came down with all the black riders who were spending money at his shop. Charlie finally said it was okay to bring Bernard in working full-time if his friends continued to come in and spend money.

During the course of the next few weeks Bernard worked out well. We stayed busy with the customers while we also dismantled and worked on junk motorcycles because Charlie continued to bring piles of crap in the shop through a network of dealership friends. One afternoon when Charlie pulled up, he had a load of bikes on his pickup truck.

He backed his truck up to the rear door and yelled while leaning out the window, "Hey, you useless idiots get out here and get this load off my truck real quick-like." T was doing some mechanics in the back, so Bernard and I went outside to unload Charlie's truck. Once we unloaded, we stood back and took a good look at the stuff. The load consisted of five Japanese bikes, including two smaller bikes. The first small one was an XL175cc Honda four stroke single cylinder. The second was a bit of a surprise. It was a fairly decent condition 1986 Yamaha YSR50 mini road racer.

The three large street bikes didn't run, but the two smaller bikes were complete and able to start as soon as they came off the truck. Bernard sat on the 175 Honda, and I sat on the YSR50 as I said, "Dude, Charlie is in the office doing something, so why don't you follow me around and I'll show you how our racetrack works."

We fired up the two bikes and raced down the street. I turned the YSR50 into the yard and took off with Bernard behind me. The YSR50 was smooth running and I couldn't believe how well it handled. After one lap I turned around and Bernard was nowhere in sight. I went around the track a second time and found that Bernard crashed the 175 Honda in the yard. He was okay and said laughing while he brushed the dirt off his pants, "Damn. I couldn't even keep up with you."

The clutch lever broke on the 175 Honda, so Bernard rolled the bike back to the shop. He asked me while I was walking beside him, "How do you ride the bike so fast?"

I told him it was just a matter of practice and I've been riding the track for quite sometime. I said, "You can get just as good as me on the track in time; all you need to do is practice. The biggest thing we need to worry about is staying out of the way of Charlie chewing our asses off about riding his bikes."

As expected, when Bernard and I arrived back at the shop with the bikes, Charlie was waiting outside. He looked angrily at us and said with his clenched fists on his hips, "Didn't I tell you assholes not to ride my bikes around because you're going to break my shit? Get back to work and stop fucking around with my stuff."

Charlie was always bitching about his personal property ever since the day I met him. He was a very selfish man who always gave the same answer for anyone who asked him to share: "Hey, buy your own." He had the nick name of Cheap Charlie; he was greedy and not ashamed of it. He was so tight with his money he was known to never leave a tip at a restaurant.

A few weeks went by, and it was business as usual around the shop. When times were slow during the days that Charlie was at the firehouse, we would get some track time in. Using a variety of motorcycles on the track, Bernard now became quite a different rider. He was riding well and was a good addition to the Salvage Squad. He already taken his share of tumbles and had a few bruises and bumps to show for it. However, with enough practice he became smooth and fast on almost any small bike we had in the shop.

One Saturday afternoon, I was working in the shop when I heard that old familiar sound again: a screeching locked rear wheel is something I didn't hear for some time. It turned out to be the person I thought it was. It was a while since Pin Head came to the shop. He arrived with all his usual bells and whistles to say hello to Charlie and the gang. Pin Head walked in the back to talk to us. He was excited because he said he was hiding out for about a week and proceeded to tell us the story of what happened to him.

He said he was on the Sunday morning ride the past weekend and needed to ditch the cops. While leading the pack of riders, he went over a rise in the road and the wind helped lift his bike in the air. He said he cranked the bike up on the rear wheel at 100 MPH. He bragged as he simulated riding a bike with his hands, "I was just playing with it, kid. I was on the rear blowing everybody away on the ride."

He told us while riding the wheelie far ahead of the rest of the pack, a California Highway Patrol car approached from the opposite direction. Pin Head shot past the police car on the rear wheel and opened the throttle wide once his front wheel touched back down to the pavement. The police car hit its brakes and spun around in the middle of the road to chase after him. Pin Head boasted he knew the road like the back of his hand because he rode the Sunday morning ride since its beginning and because he was riding 100 MPH he had a good lead on the patrol car. He said he still had no driver's license and would most likely be taken to jail if he was caught, so he needed to run and said it was all under control because he knew the right spot to ditch the cops.

He bragged arrogantly, saying, "I was heading northbound on Highway 1, looking for my favorite spot to lose the cops. I always know precisely where to get ready to pull off the road; you have to look for the place where you see old boats in the water. It's like a ghost fleet of small fishing boats right in the town of Marshall. Right after you see all the boats, there's a small road on the right you can zoom up that's on a blind turn. You can get up the hill before the cops can see that you took off on the side road. Just in case that isn't enough, there's a small red church you can hide behind and watch and laugh as the cops go driving by looking for you." Pin Head seemed happy he eluded the police and bragged he was an escape artist.

When Pin Head finished his story, he noticed the shop's YSR50 sitting in the back and said to me pointing, "Hey, kid, where did you get one of those bikes?" I told him Charlie brought it in and the bike was fun to ride. Pin Head wanted to try out the YSR50 on the track, but I told him Charlie would get mad because he wasn't in a good mood. Pin Head said confidently, "Let me go talk to Charlie, I'll cheer him up with my story about smoking the cops."

As Pin Head walked up to see Charlie in the office, Dave arrived with his three sons, also to meet with Charlie. The visit from Dave must have altered Charlie's mood because it was only a few minutes before Pin Head came in the back and told us Charlie said it was okay for him to try out the YSR50. He jumped on the bike kick started the motor and rode it out the door. After a few minutes, he came back in the shop, and I was happy to see the YSR50 still in one piece.

By now it was near closing time, and Charlie said since Dave and the kids were around it was okay to stop working and start racing. We each grabbed a small bike and lined them up on the street. Pin Head grabbed the Honda 175 and I rode the Yamaha YSR50. T rode his Suzuki GSXR50, and Bernard rode a Yamaha 125cc that T recently finished putting together. We took off down our track and threw down five hot laps without stopping. Charlie and Dave and the kids watched in front of the shop as we came by lap after lap. They were accompanied by some customers who were also having fun watching the racing. When we finished the first heat, we sat in front of the shop when Charlie said to us, "Hey, you lob cocks should go around your track with Davey and let him show you guys the fast line around." The Bostrom boys were happy with Charlie's idea because they were hoping to see their father blow off the Salvage Squad.

Within minutes we lined up the bikes on the street with the Bostrom boys acting as their father's pit crew. Charlie gave Dave one of his bikes from inside the shop, one he didn't want any of us touching that he kept parked in the corner for special occasions. The bike was a Honda XL250 from the mid-1970's. Charlie acted as the starter for the race while Ben, Eric and Tory stood on the curb in front of the shop with some customers and waited for the action to begin.

Once Charlie dropped his hands to start the race, the five of us shot down the street and attempted to make the hard right turn into the yard at the same time. I managed to tuck in behind Pin Head as he laid the 175 Honda all the way over on its side with a shower of sparks flying out from the foot pegs dragging on the pavement. Pin Head slid the bike through the first turn and took off across the yard. He was riding very fast, and I did my best to stay behind him by spinning the YSR engine all the way to the red line. I didn't have any time to see who was behind me or if everyone made it through the first turn.

Pin Head rode around the building and drove his motorcycle into the street for the second part of the track, racing back to the shop while I was 20 feet behind him. We shot past the entrance to the shop close to where the Bostrom boys were standing as I stayed close behind Pin Head for the beginning of the second lap. The yard was the part of the track that was a dirt surface, and this is where Dave Bostrom was expected to distinguish himself. The YSR50 I was on slid around quite a bit on the dirt surface, so I needed to keep my foot out in the turns to keep it from falling over or going out of control. I had no time to think about where Dave was, but since he was riding a 250cc I expected he might pass by any second because Charlie said we were supposed to watch out for Dave's killer flat track riding technique.

While Pin Head was completing the second lap, he tried to stay ahead of me because I started to close the gap slightly. When he turned around and saw me closing, he flew his bike off the curb and into the street, narrowly missing an oncoming car. I copied his move and tried to stay on his rear wheel as best as I could. Pin Head rode dangerously and paid no attention to automobile traffic as he whizzed by startled drivers causing them to panic in an attempt to avoid a collision with him. When we rode around the track again, after completing another lap, we could see T was parked in front of the shop. He was unable to keep up with the pace; his bike overheated and he stopped before he damaged the engine.

I stayed behind Pin Head while the two of us blasted past the front of the shop where the Bostrom boys and Charlie stood with T. Pin Head continued around the track with only one lap left to go. He rode the 175 Honda fast, displaying all of his Lodi Cycle Bowl talent he took most of his lifetime to perfect. He slid the bike everywhere, all over the track.

As the race continued, we had one straightaway left until the final right turn. While on the last straight, I quickly turned my head to look behind me because I wanted to see if Dave would pull a last turn pass on me.

I was shocked to see it wasn't Dave Bostrom who was almost getting ready to pass me instead it was Bernard on the Yamaha. Immediately I lost my focus because I couldn't believe that Dave was running nearly 100 feet behind Bernard although he was riding a much more powerful bike. I quickly turned my attention forward and buried the YSR50 into the last turn and upon the exit I let the bike drift out so I didn't lose speed coming off the turn. This tactic was enough to hold off Bernard so I could take a second place behind the wild and dangerous Pin Head.

Pin Head made some daring moves, tearing through cars on the street and dicing between slow moving semi-trucks in the yard in an attempt to shake me off. The salvage squad was a dangerous bunch of riders who rode hard and never wore helmets.

On the cool-down lap I slowed through the yard, even though Pin Head took off. He always rode fast, even on the cool-down lap. Bernard pulled alongside me as we motored slowly through the yard heading back to the shop. He motioned me to pull over with him and stop. He was laughing and having a great time and wore a smile on his face that went from ear to ear while he said he wanted me to take a look at his foot. Since the entire track was all right turns, Bernard had his right foot out while trying to control the bike and keep up with Pin Head and me. We started laughing when I noticed Bernard burned most of his right shoe away. The shoe had a big hole, and we could see his sock and toe showing through.

I looked at Bernard and said, "Dude, you don't even know what you just did." He looked back at me with a puzzled look while I added, "You just smoked Dave Bostrom."

Bernard smiled and said, "What's so special about smoking Dave Bostrom?" I told Bernard that Dave was Charlie's professional dirt track racer friend. "That dude's an AMA Pro racer, and you just beat him on our Salvage Squad track. Charlie told me Dave was around motorcycles his entire life, and he's supposedly the best racer around. His sons are racers too and Charlie said all three of Dave's boys race at Lodi Cycle Bowl dirt track racing and are on their way to being pros too. The Bostroms are racing at the Cow Palace arena in San Francisco where there's a motorcycle show happening along with a racing program coming up in a week."

I told Bernard Dave owned a Honda Dealership in Daly City and Charlie said Dave's young boys Ben and Eric both race motocross and dirt track. As we continued back to the shop, Bernard looked over to me, lifted his eyebrows, and said smiling, "Damn. Back home in my hood, they'd be calling that Ben kid 'the Honda prince.'" We both laughed.

Bernard and I arrived back at the shop on the bikes. Pin Head was inside, and he was his usual self, bragging to the Bostrom boys about how he won the race. Pin Head was busy describing his riding techniques to a young Ben Bostrom and his two brothers. Dave was also in the shop, talking with Charlie about other things besides the race. They were discussing the fact that Charlie's shop was sponsoring the Bostrom boys at their upcoming Cow Palace race.

Charlie said there will be a public address system that will announce a racer's sponsors for the indoor audience to hear. Charlie thought it was good advertising for his shop to be involved in racing so potential customers in the audience would come down to his shop. Bernard and I rolled our bikes past the gang and put them in the back of the shop while Charlie said, "Okay, that's enough fucking around for today, it's about time we get things closed up. Davey said he was just taking it easy on you guys this time, and he'll be back to beat you lob cocks next week."

As the next few weeks passed, Dave made good on his promise to return and compete against the Salvage Squad. The only problem was now there were quite a few more riders for Dave to try and beat. T still had his friend Joe with the FJ1100 coming around to buy sacks of marijuana, and Joe recently purchased a brand new YSR50 himself from Dave Bostrom's dealership and was racing with us.

Joe was now coming around more often and hanging out with his new friend John. Joe raced his YSR50 and since John didn't have a small bike to race he would grab the latest bike from the shop T repaired to running condition. Dave had his hands full at this point because the grid was now full of up to eight other riders looking to win. Pin Head wasn't always around to set the pace so there were new leaders in our races to show Dave the fast line around the track. Joe and John both had street bikes they rode fast up in the mountains everyday to hone their riding skills. John, who was a few years younger than Joe, had a 1984 Kawasaki GPZ750 he learned to ride well by chasing Joe around the fast and dangerous tight mountain roads on his Yamaha FJ1100.

Joe was able to ride his YSR50 quickly on our shop racetrack and he was always near the front. On most occasions when Dave would compete with us, he never led a heat race or could ever defeat the Salvage Squad.

As the races progressed, the lap times on the track only seemed to go lower. Dave, during most races, was usually well in the back of the pack regardless of the amount of cheering from his sons and Charlie watching on the sidelines as the bikes whizzed by. On most weekends Dave and his three sons had to leave the shop early because Friday and Saturday were race nights at the Lodi Cycle Bowl.

One evening after the Bostrom gang took off in their motor home to the Lodi races, I asked Charlie about Dave. I was thinking Dave had lots of time on his hands to go racing with his sons and didn't have to work like everyone else. I said to Charlie, "How does Dave manage to pay all the bills and keep his sons racing with their new bikes and equipment costs?"

Charlie said, "Hey, Dave's been in the game a very long time and you should pay attention and try to be more like Dave. He has many investments in real estate, and so he's able to take time off to go racing with his kids. Dave knows how to save money and do things the right way because he's smart. You should learn to keep your eyes open and your mouth shut and don't ask any dumb questions, then maybe you'll have what Dave has in the future when you get older."

1988

Charlie's shop was going strong for five years. As dealerships continued to go out of business in the bay area, Charlie's shop was known as the place to go and hang out.

Dave Bostrom's visits to the shop were also on the rise as he and Charlie met in the office frequently. Dave still brought his sons for visits and he squeezed in a few races with the Salvage Squad while picking up his sponsorship supplies, before heading off with the boys to race at Lodi Cycle Bowl.

Charlie also had other friends who came by the shop to visit him. Many of the men I never saw before. Charlie knew these guys for a long time since they were his flat tracking buddies from the old days. Charlie didn't always introduce me to his friends because they would be busy talking about the old times while sitting in the office with the door closed. Some of Charlie's buddies who were into racing were also involved in the motorcycle dealership business after they retired from racing.

One sunny morning while opening the shop, I was surprised to see Bernard arrive to work on a new motorcycle. He was riding a near new condition Kawasaki Ninja 900 he purchased from a newspaper advertisement with money he saved from working at Charlie's shop.

Later while working in the shop I noticed Dave arrived for a visit with Charlie. This visit didn't seem out of the ordinary except Charlie's mood quickly changed for the worse after Dave left. Charlie started ranting and yelling he couldn't find his favorite pen and somebody took one of his special small tools and lost it.

I could tell there was something else on his mind and I asked him in the office, "Charlie, what's up? Is there something wrong with Dave?"

Charlie said, as he removed his cap and angrily threw it down on his desk, "No, it's not Dave; it's that fucking stupid shit head Ed Woo that's the problem."

I asked Charlie what Ed was up to lately because it was some time since I seen Ed and his Porsche juggling act.

With a pissed off look on his face he answered, "That dumb fucking gook has gone and fucked things all up by getting his ass thrown in prison. He was sentenced to go away for selling cocaine to a cop." Charlie said with a stern voice as he stared at me, "Now before you go shooting your fucking mouth off with the guys in the back, you'd better keep this information to yourself."

Charlie was momentarily lost in thought, then said as he turned his back to me, "I shouldn't even be telling you this so why don't you get the fuck back to work and shut the fuck up and don't talk about Ed Woo anymore?" I left the office with Charlie saying, "You know, that stupid shit head will ruin everything for all of us; that Ed is a fuck up." While I returned to the back I wondered what "us" he was talking about. I didn't even know Ed.

The following Saturday, at the end of the day, we were sitting around waiting to close when Charlie said, "Hey, just because there's no customers doesn't mean that you assholes can't be doing some work. It's not six o'clock yet." Charlie ordered Bernard, T and me to go in the back and dismantle and clean out some old Honda brake calipers until closing time.

While Bernard and I were washing and cleaning out some old corroded calipers, we noticed Dark Ninja pulled into the shop to say hello. Bernard and Dark Ninja were meeting up to have a few drinks and ride around San Francisco on their Ninjas that evening. Dark Ninja took off his helmet and sat down on a stool where Bernard and I were working.

A few minutes later we heard Charlie's voice in the front of the shop: "Hey, it's the Bostrom gang." Charlie happily welcomed the Bostrom group and said they were racing at Lodi Cycle Bowl that Saturday evening. Dave and Charlie went in the office closing the door and the boys did their usual hanging around.

Ben Bostrom wandered in the back and saw what Bernard and I were doing. Ben was about fourteen years old now and had developed a more arrogant attitude. He looked at the corroded brakes we were working on and said to us smiling, "My dad only gets new brakes."

He then said with a proud look on his face, "My dad doesn't have time to beat you guys tonight on your shop track because we're racing at Lodi Cycle Bowl for trophies."

It was soon closing time, and Charlie went through his normal ritual of grabbing oil and other products off the shelves. He told Ben and Eric as he handed them the products, "I want you boys to blow everybody away tonight and bring home more of those trophies you're winning all the time now." Dave gathered them up and took off.

Dark Ninja and Bernard was suiting up to leave and asked T and me if we wanted to join them in the city that evening. T said he had to go home to his girlfriend and would not come. I had my Honda Interceptor 750 outside and said to Dark Ninja and Bernard that I would go along so we fired up our bikes and headed north to San Francisco. I was riding behind Dark Ninja, who was following Bernard when I noticed Dark Ninja changed out his rear turn signals on his 900 Ninja. He replaced the stock units with ones that resembled chrome chandeliers which glowed blue at night.

The three of us approached the freeway on-ramp for the trip to San Francisco. Bernard was in the lead, and as he rounded the turn and began to accelerate onto the freeway, he pulled his 900 Ninja onto the rear wheel and while shifting through the gears, rode a wheelie on the bike up to 60 MPH. I rode next to Dark Ninja, watching Bernard wheelie, and noticed Bernard was now a very skilled rider since he was working at Charlie's shop and training with the Salvage Squad.

After a short trip to San Francisco, we arrived at a bar Dark Ninja frequented. We parked our bikes, went in and pulled off our helmets and took seats at the bar. Dark Ninja said to the bartender, "I'll have the usual and get my two friends here anything they want." Bernard and I each ordered a beer. The bartender served two beers and gave Dark Ninja a cognac glass that appeared to be half full. "I always drink Hennessey," he said while taking a slow sip. "That's how you wanna do it, nice and smooth."

Dark Ninja had a very smooth way about him in all aspects. He was a few years older than Bernard and I and loved the music and the mellow sounds of the Motown era. He was tall and slender with a powerful build which could intimidate anyone who didn't know him well.

Dark Ninja said he was employed at an automatic transmission shop and told Bernard and me about his work week. He was just paid and had quite a few dollars he was looking to spend because it was Saturday night.

As we sat around talking, Bernard and I told Dark Ninja funny stories about strange people who came in the shop with weird requests for bike parts during the week.

Bernard busted out laughing and said while sipping his beer, "How 'bout that crazy lady who came in today?"

We told Dark Ninja a burly woman came in looking for a tire change. She had short clipped blue hair and many tattoos and piercings. When I started to write up her work order, I asked for her name and she answered back, "Trash." I looked up at her and then over to Bernard standing next to me, who was finding it hard not to laugh. She glared and said firmly while pointing her finger at us, "The name's Lady Trash to you guys."

Dark Ninja was having a good laugh as he ordered himself a second drink and another round of beers for Bernard and me. When the drinks arrived, he said, "Damn...For years you crazy-ass white folks didn't like to be called white trash, and now ya'll are calling yourselves trash." We all laughed.

After we finished a couple more rounds, Bernard said he was leaving to go home and Dark Ninja said to me as he lifted his glass, "If you don't have anywhere else to go tonight, why don't you stay here and have a few more rounds with a lonely old black man?"

I said, "Okay, I'll have another beer." Bernard threw his leather jacket on and while leaving he shook my hand and said to me smiling, "I'll see you next week. Try not to get in too much trouble with the Dark Ninja."

Once Bernard left, Dark Ninja continued to ask me about life around Charlie's shop. I told him a few more funny stories about customers when Dark Ninja asked, "What's up with that kid at your shop today talking about his dad and racing. Who's he?"

I answered, "That's Ben Ober or Ben Bostrom. I really don't know what the kid's name is."

Dark Ninja inquired, "Why was he talking about his dad having new brakes? What's Lodi Cycle Bowl?"

I told Dark Ninja that Lodi Cycle Bowl was a place far from San Francisco, I said, "The place is located in a city called Lodi, which is close to Stockton out on Highway 99. It's a dirt track racing venue and Ben and his brothers are both motorcycle racers there." Dark Ninja looked at me surprised and said, "Motorcycle racers? That kid ain't even old enough to have a driver's license."

I told him Charlie said the Bostrom boys come from an elite dirt tracking world where a kid is put on a dirt track racing motorcycle by the time he is six or seven years old. Dark Ninja shook his head from side to side laughing and said, "Man. Here in the hood you can't ride until you can afford your own ride. After that, the only fast riding you do is when the cops are chasing after your ass or if you're drag racing on the street."

I told him the Bostrom boys' mother and father both owned motorcycle dealerships. He said, "I guess you don't have to be paying for no bike shit when your parents own the dealership. Those boys must get all their racing bikes and equipment for free then."

I laughed and said, "The name Ben has around the shop is 'the Honda prince' but he doesn't know it. Charlie said his mother's dealership went out of business a couple of years ago. Where do you think Charlie got all that junk in his shop? Ben's mother dumped a ton of junk motorcycles on Charlie a while back when she tanked her dealership called Oakland Honda."

Dark Ninja was surprised. He lifted his eyebrow and said while holding his glass, "Oakland Honda? All my riding friends in Oakland must have gone there for business. You say it ain't there no more?"

I finished off the last of my beer and as I sat the empty mug on the bar I said, "Yep, tanked out. Charlie told me motorcycle sales in the bay area are slow and that's the reason for a bunch of dealerships going out of business."

He gestured as he pointing with his thumb and asked, "That Kawasaki dealership down the street from here also closed down a while back, and I remember the owner's name was Dave. Was that shop owned by the Bostrom family too?"

I answered, "The guy who owned that Kawasaki shop was named Dave but not Dave Bostrom. When it closed down a few years ago, they had a big auction."

Dark Ninja said, "I was there when they had that auction, and they didn't sell any new bikes in the place. What the hell happened to all those new Kawasaki motorcycles they didn't sell?"

I replied, "Charlie said they couldn't sell all the motorcycles because they had bank loans against them." I told him Charlie was supposed to get a few good running bikes from that Kawasaki shop, but all he got was a load of old junky bikes and parts.

Since it was late, I told Dark Ninja I thought it would be a good time for me to take off because I had a 20-mile ride home and he only had a short ride a few blocks away. We shook hands and said good night for the evening.

T's friend Joe came by the shop almost every day with his friend John. They partied hard and were always carrying cocaine and marijuana when they came around. They both were married, and Joe had a very young daughter. However, the lure of fast motorcycles and easily obtained cocaine coupled with loose girls looking to party quickly put both of their marriages in jeopardy.

Joe would come by the shop in the afternoon when he was off work and party with T and his friends, instead of going home to his wife and daughter. John was having problems with his own marriage because he was also indulging in cocaine-fueled sex on the side with a much younger neighbor girl. John said if his wife ever found out she would kill him for sure.

T started to frequent San Francisco with Joe and John at night looking for hookers down in the seedy part of town. The three of them talked openly around the shop about their exploits in the city chasing loose women and running from cops on their motorcycles high on cocaine. Many visits from Joe and John were filled with explicit stories, bragging of their extramarital and drug infused wild affairs. They boasted their wives would never find out. The arrogant attitude they portrayed seemed to be backed up by their young good looks. They knew it and would always brag they could get any girl in their saddle because of it.

In the afternoon one day during the work week, Joe and John pulled in the shop. They just returned from a fast street bike riding session on the winding roads through the San Mateo county coastal mountains at speeds around 100 MPH, racing with many strangers they would encounter during the ride.

Joe was excited as he pulled off his helmet and said to John, "We blew those dudes away up there, didn't we?" John agreed as they met up with T in the back of the shop to buy a couple of bags of marijuana. Joe bragged of their fast riding and said they blasted up a couple of fat lines of cocaine in order to get the blood pumping. Joe said the two of them were heading back up to the mountains later in the week for another ride and asked if any of us at the shop wanted to go street racing with them.

Charlie could hear the loud commotion they were making telling everyone about their street racing day while he was helping a customer with a part deal. When the telephone rang, he yelled out, "Hey, I'm busy up here, so why don't one of you idiots get off your asses and answer the telephone around here?"

I walked up front and answered the phone. When I was finished with the call, Charlie said with a quiet voice, "I want you to watch out if you go riding with those two guys."

I replied, "I know Joe and John ride fast and dangerous, but I know I could keep up with them. They can't ride any faster than Pin Head."

Charlie said, "I wasn't talking about the riding, I was talking about the drugs they're using and carrying when they're riding fast. Joe's doing a bunch of cocaine and hanging around at Dave Bostrom's house. He's too cocky and he drives fast without thinking while he carries drugs on him." He then said angrily, "Ed already got himself thrown in jail for that cocaine shit, and I don't need for that to happen to you because you're racing around with those idiots. Be smart. Don't draw attention to yourself. Besides, you won't have a lot of time to go riding with those guys anyway."

I asked Charlie what he meant and he replied, "I'll need you and the guys to work extra hard in the next few weeks because we're moving the shop."

Alarmed, I asked him, "What? Why are we moving the shop?"

Charlie explained the landlord told him he wanted Charlie to move the shop to another location inside the same complex. The yard in front of his shop became too messy with junk motorcycles, and the landlord wanted to get it cleaned up. He said customers were jumping over the barbed wire chain link fence on the weekends to get free parts off of junk motorcycles when the shop was closed. The new location was completely inside the warehouse, with no junk yard outdoors. The landlord told Charlie he could have a spot around the corner which was a busier street frontage, so customers driving by could see the place more easily.

I said, "We have tons of parts and junk to move. Won't that take an army of men to get this done?"

He appeared agitated at my question and said, "Well I don't care! I want you guys to do all the work by yourselves because I don't want to spend any money to pay for more help. I'll still run the shop while we're moving, because I need the money to pay the rent."

Surprised, I asked him, "How long do you think it will take to get this job done?"

Charlie yelled as he turned his back to me and walked in the office, "Hey, you guys have thirty days to get the whole thing done because I'm not paying the fucking rent on two units, so let the others know that I want the three of you ass-holes to start boxing things up and get my fucking shop moved real quick-like!" He slammed the office door.

The next few weeks consisted of moving everything from the old shop to the new shop around the corner. At the same time this was being done, Charlie had his construction friend build an upstairs loft in the new shop. The loft was 10 feet high and measured 1,500 square feet to form an upstairs space for racks to store wheels and rims. The ceiling rafters of the building were now reachable from the new loft and used to hang motorcycle exhaust pipes.

With all the hurry in moving the shop, Charlie's construction friend also built the new office. The construction went quickly while the guys and I moved the parts and set up the shelves on the lower level to hold the parts. The front counter was moved to the new shop and set up in the front by the office, with Charlie's same old familiar cash register sitting on the right end of the counter.

Joe and John came by in the afternoons to help move. Charlie said he didn't want to hire any new help, so the guys were happy to lend a hand and hang out and smoke weed.

Thirty days passed, and the new shop was open. By the time we settled into the new location the motorcycle riding season was slowing down. Charlie was now complaining more around the shop about money because of the expense of moving. To make matters worse, the new shop was slightly larger than the old shop, so the rent went up from $1,500 a month to $2,000 a month with yearly increases written in the lease.

Charlie complained all the time that more money was going out than was coming in. As was customary, the bills piled up on his desk during the month, and he waited until the end of the month to pay them, then he would bitch out loud, "Okay, now that the rent and the other bills are paid I'm fucking broke."

We've heard that song and dance from Charlie since 1983.

One morning Charlie came to work and said, "Since the motorcycle riding season is winding down soon, I don't think I need Bernard around here anymore. I still have to figure out how to save more money monthly. I have to pay each of you assholes $1,200 a month, and I just can't afford to pay the three of you lob cocks that kind of money anymore so Bernard has to go."

I told Charlie Bernard worked out well at the shop and we grew accustom to him being around. Charlie said, "Well, I can't afford to pay him anymore, but Dave Bostrom has a friend who's opening a motorcycle tire store down the Peninsula and I'll help Bernard get a job there."

Around Charlie's new shop we saw much more of Joe and John. Recently John purchased a used 1986 Yamaha FJ 1200 to keep up with Joe. One afternoon while the two of them were in the shop visiting, Joe told us how much faster his bike was running because he recently acquired a stolen Yamaha FJ 1200 engine and just finished installing it in his FJ 1100. Joe was laughing and said, "Now that my new motor is in I'm blowing everybody away, and I'm getting laid more by fine young bitches."

John looked back at Joe, started to laugh and said, "Dude, it's not the bikes that's getting us laid; it's our cocaine the chicks all want us for."

Apparently John was right about the wild life and cocaine use. Joe and John had become inseparable when it came to partying hard and speeding around. Joe was happy because he recently dumped his wife and young daughter and would brag he was free. John continued with his wild lifestyle with other young women behind his wife's back. Joe and John were out of control with the fast riding, loose chicks and cocaine.

On August 6, 1988, a Saturday morning, the phone rang. It was T's girlfriend crying hysterically, saying John was found by his father the night before in the back of their house hanging with a rope around his neck. John killed himself. She said despite John's fathers best efforts after cutting him down John could not be revived.

It was a mystery as to why John took his own life. No note was found and his family members were never able to understand why he killed himself so suddenly.

1989

It was several months since John's funeral, and we didn't see Joe around the shop that much. Most of the time it was business as usual until one evening when I was rolling some junk motorcycles in the shop around closing time. While I was outside grabbing a bike, I noticed Joe pulled up in a car in front of the shop. He walked around the car and opened the passenger door and a female stepped out. Joe introduced me to her saying, "This is my new girlfriend, and we're going out to dinner tonight."

I asked Joe where he was going to dinner because the two of them were dressed up in nice clothes for an evening out on the town. Joe smiled and said, "I'm going to dinner at Dave Bostrom's tonight. I just wanted to stop by and show off my newest girlfriend to you guys."

Since Joe dumped his wife and young daughter it appeared he was well on his way to a new life. I watched them drive away north toward Dave's hilltop home. As I watched the car taillights disappear down the street, I thought Joe now had what he always wanted: an exciting new life with Dave Bostrom and loose, wild cocaine-tooting chicks.

As I closed the shop door and snapped the padlock shut, I wondered if Joe made it to a lieutenant's status with Dave. Maybe since Ed Woo was out of the mix, an opening was created that needed to be filled by Joe.

Charlie came into work a few days later and said he was driving to San Francisco to pick up some junk motorcycles from a Honda dealership on Van Ness Avenue. Charlie knew the owners because this was one of the dealerships he would visit on his service route in his old cash register days. When he went into this dealership to work on the registers, Charlie would walk in the place like he owned it and say hello to everyone. Everyone in the place would yell back, "Hey, it's Cash Register Charlie."

Charlie returned in the early afternoon with his load of parts and junk bikes. The new shop had a side door similar to the old one so Charlie backed his truck to the side door and jumped out saying, "Hey, I want you guys to make yourselves useful and get this stuff unloaded and put away in the shop." As usual, it was the same load of un-sellable crap.

I told Charlie I was worried because we were only getting in old junk parts and bikes and not any current motorcycles and parts customers were always asking for.

Charlie snapped back, "Why don't you just let me worry about what the fuck comes in and out of this shop and you worry about the tire changes! Get my truck unloaded and stop complaining!" He stormed off into the office.

One afternoon T was working on a customer's repair job, he said he needed to get a new gasket to ensure a tight seal on the engine. On occasions when we did order new parts around the shop, I was the person to make the call to the dealership to see if they had them in stock. The closest dealership was Dave's Honda dealership in Daly City, so that was the one I called most of the time. I developed a phone relationship with a counterman named Jeff who worked at Dave's dealership.

I needed to get that gasket for T so I called Dave's dealership and asked to speak to the parts department. After a moment of being placed on hold, an unfamiliar voice came on the line and said, "Can I help you? What do you need?"

I said I needed to talk to Jeff to get something ordered. The voice on the phone replied, "Jeff's on tour...Flock of Seagulls."

I answered the unfamiliar voice: "On tour? What's that?"

The kid on the phone asked, "What part do you need?" I told him I needed to order an engine gasket for a motorcycle, and I wanted it right away so I would pick it up if they had it in stock. The kid said he would check stock and returned to the phone in a few minutes. He said I was in luck because they had one left in stock and I should come and get it now.

It was a fog-shrouded trip of about 15 minutes in my truck up to Dave's dealership. After I parked my out front, I went into the dealership and was amazed at what I saw. It appeared the entire dealership was on tour because there were hardly any motorcycles for sale in the place and there were vast amounts of cardboard boxes lying around the floor and showroom. I waded through the mess to the back of the shop, where the parts counter was located. There was a guy who was a few years younger than me behind the counter who said he was the one on the phone and introduced himself to me as Arty. He handed me the gasket as I asked him, "What's going on with the dealership, how come you guys don't have any motorcycles for sale? Where is everybody?"

Arty didn't say what was going on with the dealership but he did tell me the saleswoman who worked for Dave many years became disillusioned with motorcycles and she quit. He said she claimed she would rather get a job rounding up shopping carts in the parking lot for the grocery store next door than work for Dave's dealership anymore. He smiled with an attitude and said, "I don't know why she quit but now I'm the new salesman and parts man."

I paid him for the gasket and walked outside to my truck. As I drove past the grocery store, I turned my head and saw exactly what Arty said. There was Dave Bostrom's ex-saleswoman in the lot next door, rounding up shopping carts people left around the grocery store parking lot.

After I returned to the shop, I gave the gasket to T so he could get his repair job finished and the rest of the afternoon was business as usual for us. Around closing time, after we finished rolling the junk bikes in, Charlie said to me, "I want you to come in the office, so we can talk turkey for a while." Charlie sometimes would get into moods where he talked about the advancement of his shop and various ways of doing it. Some of the time he discussed things in the office over a few beers after the shop closed for the day.

On this particular evening, T left to go home and Charlie and I sat down to have a talk in the office. Charlie told me about his new deal. He said he wanted to buy more motorcycles and parts in a deal between Dave Bostrom and himself. Charlie said, "I want you to figure out a way to get this shop cleaned up so I will have more room around here for a big load of stuff from Dave."

I reached down to change my boots and said, "When I was up at Dave's dealership today I noticed the shop is almost entirely empty, with not a lot of business happening."

He said, "Hey, Dave's having a really hard time trying to keep that dealership open these days. He has a bunch of motorcycles and parts in all types of conditions stored in the private back room of his dealership, and I made a deal with him to buy some of the stuff because he's planning to close down his dealership."

Surprised, I looked up and said. "Wow! Close his dealership? That's a big deal, what's up?"

Charlie answered, "Dave's already spending close to $1,000 a week to keep his three boys racing and he feels that keeping his dealership open is just too expensive when bike sales are slow."

Since we always had to worry about paying the rent at Charlie's shop, I asked him how much rent Dave Bostrom paid at his dealership. He said, "Well, Dave doesn't pay rent. He owns the building his dealership is located in. Dave happens to own the building next door to his dealership too; it's occupied by the thrift store that also pays him rent every month."

Charlie seemed a bit frustrated at my question and quickly snapped at me, saying, "We're not talking about what Dave does and doesn't own. We're talking about buying his motorcycles and helping him out. Hey...Dave's really hurting."

Charlie felt we spoke enough about business and said he was going to his usual Thursday night ritual pizza get-together with his motorcycle friends like Mikey and Petey and some other guys in the motorcycle and automobile industry.

I left the office while Charlie picked up his things and the receipts from the day. He rushed out to his pizza dinner and I closed the door and locked it. As I headed out to my truck I thought a little about what Charlie was saying about Dave Bostrom hurting in business. Charlie's main complaint around the shop was he had to pay the rent. He would say the rent was priority one and it was the hardest and most expensive part of running the business. He also complained about the other bills, like insurance and paying taxes and paying his employees, but his ranting about the rent was his number one complaint. I wondered as I drove off, if Dave Bostrom owns the building his dealership is operating in I guess he pays no rent.

A few days later, Charlie said in the morning, "I'm ready to make my deal with Dave; he started closing down his dealership in Daly City, and you guys should get ready to work hard because I'm buying lots of parts and parts bikes from him.

After Charlie left T said to me with a worried look on his face, "Oh, shit, dude. I wonder what kind of stuff he'll bring back here."

I answered, "I hope he's not planning on loading us up with tons of crap because we'll have to work our asses off to get this place cleaned up after that."

Charlie returned in a couple of hours and backed his truck up to the side door as T and I went to see the load. Much to our dismay the entire truck was loaded with old parts, consisting mostly of motorcycle luggage racks, old gas tanks and other useless parts. Charlie seemed very happy with the load and said he made a great deal with Dave.

He yelled out to the two of us, "I want you guys to get this stuff unloaded real quick-like because I have to get right back up to Dave's dealership to pick up more loads."

While we unloaded the truck, T asked Charlie, "How many more loads of crap did you buy?"

Charlie answered, "Dave needs to get the place cleaned out quickly and he has a large amount of inventory in the back of his shop."

I asked, "Did you already get a price from Dave on all the stuff you're buying?"

Charlie said proudly, "Hey, Davey gave me a great deal on the parts and parts bikes. He said I could have all the junk in his place for only $6,000. Now, I don't want any fucking around on this deal because Dave's in a real hurry to get this done. So get this truck unloaded so I can get back up there to pick up another load."

In about 20 minutes, T and I had Charlie's truck unloaded and ready for his return trip to Dave's closing dealership. Charlie came out of the office and yelled out, "Hey, I'm heading back up to Dave's to get the next load."

He jumped into his truck and drove away. T talked to me about the first load of parts while he fired up a joint he had in his pocket. As he passed me the joint he said, "Dude, if this first load is any indication of all the stuff he's bringing back, I think Charlie got burned by Dave paying him $6,000 for all this crap."

It was nearly two hours before Charlie returned with the next load. He backed his truck up to the side door and honked the horn for us to help him unload. When we opened the door, Charlie was already throwing parts off his truck, including more old gas tanks and some old parts bikes. After we unloaded he left again and returned two hours later with more of the same crap parts from Dave's.

Charlie said as he climbed out of his truck he needed to go in the office to take care of some paperwork for Dave and didn't have time to go back to Dave's dealership to get the last load. He pointed at me while saying, "When you guys finish unloading, I need you to take my truck and get the last load of junk from Dave's place. I want you to make sure that when you get to Dave's you drive up to the rear door of his shop to get the last load."

He told me Dave and his friends would have a large truck in front of the dealership loading up whole bikes, so I should go to the back door to load the last of the junk. T heard Charlie talking to me and while he was swimming in a large pile of newly arrived junk parts he yelled out, "Wow, Charlie! I thought we were honestly getting whole running bikes from Dave's dealership for the $6,000 you paid him, not just a bunch of crap."

Charlie walked off quickly towards the office and shot back at the two of us, yelling, "I know what I'm doing with my deal with Dave, so why don't you useless idiots just worry about dismantling and stocking the parts, and I'll make the fucking decisions around here." We heard the office door slam shut.

T said to me, "Dude, try not to take so long up there at Dave's because your dad will drive me crazy while I'm stocking all this junk until you get back."

After unloading, I took off for the last load at Dave's. In about fifteen minutes I arrived at the dealership. It was a foggy and cold afternoon. I pulled up to the rear door of the shop just like Charlie told me to. After entering, I saw Dave and his three sons in the service area of his shop. Dave was busy telling his oldest son Tory and some other guys to finish loading a large truck parked out front with newer bikes. Eric, now about thirteen, was busy practicing skateboard spin tricks around the service area and fifteen year old Ben was standing next to his father.

Dave took me and Ben through another door into a back room. He showed me various piles of junk around different corners of the room and told me to take all the junk Charlie purchased because he was closing his dealership. Dave said he needed to help the guys up front load bikes so he looked over at Ben and said to him, "Now, Ben, while I'm working up front I want you to keep an eye on Charlie's kid here while he works cleaning up all this junk." Dave turned around and walked to the front of the shop.

I thought it was a bit strange because Dave wanted his fifteen year old son to keep an eye on me in a dealership that was in the process of closing down. I was now twenty six years old and not too happy having to be watched by a fifteen year old kid while picking up the last few pieces of garbage from his father's failing business.

I walked around the room and grabbed a few piles of old seats and gas tanks and loaded them on Charlie's truck. Ben kept a hawk's eye on me, while Eric continued to gleefully spin on his skateboard and do other various tricks. While I continued picking up the piles of junk motorcycle racks and loose exhaust pipes, I watched Eric on his skateboard, wondering why he and Ben were not in school. It was the middle of the week, and all other kids their age were in school.

The back room was now almost empty, and Charlie's truck was nearly filled to capacity with junk stacked as high as the roof of the cab. While loading the last remaining pile of old junk and rusty exhaust pipes, I was momentarily startled by Ben who had snuck up behind me, he said, "This stack you're taking isn't supposed to go."

Still loading I said, "I thought your dad said all of this garbage in this room is supposed to go to your Uncle Charlie's junk shop." I picked up another set of old rusty exhaust pipes off the floor and threw them on top of the load on Charlie's truck. Ben became upset and ran off, looking for his dad, and I drove off and headed back to Charlie's shop.

While I was on Geneva Street driving back to the shop, I looked out the right window and saw the Cow Palace, by now a mainstay in the Bostrom boys' racing scene. Charlie always attended the yearly cycle show and racing program that was held in the Cow Palace and Ben along with Eric Bostrom were now taking home trophies as tall as they stood and were big hits at the yearly event.

As I drove by the arena I couldn't help wondering how Ben and Eric would continue to get motorcycles to race if both of their parents' dealerships went out of business. In the racing scene it was very important to always have the next model motorcycle as soon as it hit the market because the best riders always have the best machines. According to Charlie, Ben and Eric were the best riders on the track and were well on their way to becoming something special in the racing scene.

A few minutes later, I arrived at the shop and went inside. I could see T was stocking parts while Charlie was in the office. T looked at me with a funny expression on his face and said, "Dude, your dad's been driving me crazy. Where the hell have you been? He doesn't just want to stock these parts; he wants to change the whole shop around in the process."

When we went outside to unload the truck T was surprised and said, "I can't believe this load of shit you have is the last load. Where the fuck, are the running bikes we were supposed to get from Dave?" I told T when I was up at Dave's place the whole shop was almost empty except for some newer bikes they were loading into a truck out front, but they only wanted me to stay in the back and load up the junk.

Charlie wanted all exhaust pipes hanging from the upstairs rafters so T and I walked the old stock exhaust pipes from the truck upstairs to hang. While we were finishing up T said to me, "Dude, these are stock pipes that people take off of their bikes because they want to upgrade to a newer exhaust. Nobody will come in and buy any of this rusty shit. If we don't get anything else from Dave, then it looks like Charlie was ripped off buying all this junk for $6,000."

T and I were in the loft hanging the last of the exhaust pipes and just as T was telling me how hard it was on him to work for Charlie, we heard Charlie yell out to me: "Hey! Dave and his kids are here, and Ben says you took a bunch of things that you weren't supposed to take."

Charlie and Dave walked up the stairs, and Charlie questioned me on which exhaust pipes I took. Charlie looked up in the rafters among the various types of stock motorcycle pipes that were hanging and said to me, "Alright, look. You've got Dave and me all pissed off about taking things you weren't supposed to take, so I want you to point out all the pipes you took from Dave."

At first, I was taken aback by what Charlie was saying. I thought the deal was Charlie paid Dave for his junk and Dave's shop was to be cleaned up by us. I couldn't imagine why the junk exhaust pipes were supposed to stay in Dave's building, because nobody was packing any of the junk pipes in the other truck in front of the dealership, where all the good stuff and bikes were loaded.

Since I didn't answer Charlie and Dave quickly enough about how many pipes I did or did not take, they decided themselves an entire pickup truck load of pipes returned to Dave's dealership was the only way to square the deal. Charlie angrily ordered T and me, with one fist sitting on his waist and the other hand pointed up to the pipes on the rafters, "I want you two assholes to empty out these two rafters completely of all those pipes and throw them down from the loft next to the side door. Dave, and me will load them onto his truck with the boys."

Dave and Charlie went downstairs, and T and I started to grab the exhaust pipes and walk them over to the edge of the loft, tossing them down to crash on the concrete floor below. I guess Dave felt the pipes becoming damaged from falling didn't matter, because he only wanted to get the pipes back. The number of pipes held by the two rafters was over fifty, enough to fill an entire pickup truck bed.

T was bothered by Charlie's odd request of returning the pipes and said to me while working, "Dude, if we just finished buying all Dave's crap for $6,000, then why are we giving him back a load of old exhaust pipes? Some are not even pipes that we bought from him in the first place."

I felt just as puzzled as T because we were tossing down old junk pipes Charlie owned for years, and they were loading them onto Dave's truck.

After about 30 minutes of T and me tossing pipes and the Bostrom gang and Charlie loading them in Dave's pickup truck, Charlie yelled out, "Okay. That's enough pipes. Don't throw down anymore."

I was standing at the top of the stairs wiping off the sweat, dust and grease from all the dirty pipes when Charlie looked up at me from the bottom of the stairs, with Ben standing next to him, and demanded, "Now, I want you to come down here and apologize to Ben for stealing his dad's things when he told you not to take them."

I stood there, all sweaty and greasy looking down the stairs at Charlie and Ben standing there, I became real pissed off. I thought to myself momentarily before answering and wondered why in the hell should I be apologizing to Dave's kid because his father is throwing away the keys to his Honda dealership. I also thought why was it necessary for me to go and retrieve the last load of Dave's junk while kept on a leash by Ben Bostrom, when Charlie was in charge of moving the other loads. Why didn't Charlie just get the last load of junk and pipes from Dave and Ben himself?

I answered back to them angrily, "I don't think I'm going to be able to do that, Charlie. I didn't steal any of his dad's crap. Besides, maybe Ben's dad is the one who should be apologizing to the Honda Motor Corporation."

Charlie snapped back at me and said, "Well, if you won't come down here and apologize to Ben, then why don't you find a fucking used tire to change?"

In an instant I yelled back with a deep roar, "Fuck You!!"

With a disgusted look on his face, Charlie turned around angrily and walked over to the side door with Ben, where his father and brothers were standing. I could hear the Bostroms getting into their truck and Charlie saying goodbye while T said, "Wow! That was a good line you said about the Honda Corporation. That's fucked up Charlie wants you to apologize to Dave's fifteen year old kid. Dave Bostrom was in the Honda business a long time, way back when I used to work for him. I can't believe with the amount of money and real estate Dave has, he doesn't have enough cash to keep his dealership open." I started to wonder the same thing myself.

At closing time T and I walked into the office where Charlie was sitting at his desk counting up the day's receipts. We changed our boots and T said to Charlie and me he would see us in the morning and took off. I could feel the tension in the air between Charlie and me as he spun around in his chair and barked at me, "Hey, you really pissed me off today with your fucking around with Dave and Ben's pipes. Dave needs a certain amount of pipes and parts remaining inside the dealership after he has the place closed down."

I was puzzled by Charlie's statement and said, "You've got to be kidding. I thought you paid him $6,000 to clean the place out, now you're telling me it's necessary to keep old parts in the dealership after it's closed. Why? I don't fucking get it."

Charlie fired back at me, yelling, "You're not supposed to get it. You're supposed to do what I tell you to do and shut the fuck up and mind your own business. If I can't even trust you to do what I tell you to do, how can Dave or any of my other friends ever trust you?"

Angered by what he said, I shot back to him, "Well, Charlie, if the Bostroms need somebody to trust I guess Dave will have to wait until Ed Woo gets out on parole, since Ed is Dave's trusted main man."

Just at that moment, the office door opened behind me and Charlie's mood quickly changed. He threw a big grin and said, "Hey, it's time for my haircut appointment now, so we don't need to talk about Dave or Ed anymore."

Charlie had grown quite accustom to his monthly haircuts he would receive in the office from Joe's ex-wife Bert. She would come by and give Charlie and his friend's haircuts. She even used to do John's haircuts in the office, before he hung himself a year earlier and she also cut Ed's hair before he went off to jail.

Bert was a quiet nice girl; we never could quite figure out why she was ever hooked up with a guy like Joe in the first place. Apparently they met after high school, and when they had a baby girl, she tried everything she could to make the marriage work until finally deciding she had enough of Joe's wild partying and womanizing. When they were married, she would call the shop looking for him and Charlie would tell her Joe was at the usual place, Dave's house. She used to come in with Joe at times and sit quietly on a bike waiting for him while he would hang out. Everyone at the shop enjoyed having her around and was happy to get their hair cut by her, especially Charlie and me. She continued to visit and cut hair even though her and Joe were over.

Bert cut hair in a downtown San Francisco salon during the day and would come by every month in the evenings to cut Charlie's hair and some of his friend's hair for extra money. She said she had a hard time getting by since the divorce from Joe. Bert said he wasn't paying her any child support or alimony at all and added that Joe didn't want anything to do with his young daughter or her anymore.

I knew Joe was having a high time with Dave and all his new friends but never talked to her about it. After all, the last time I saw Joe when he came by the shop, he did refer to himself as being a party animal after his divorce.

Charlie moved his desk chair to the middle of the office, and Bert whipped out a black cape and snapped it around his neck. She produced a pair of precision shears from her leather case and proceeded to give Charlie his trimming. Her father recently passed away and Charlie asked her, "How are you doing since your dad died? Your dad was a good guy, I knew him for years from my old cash register days when I visited where he worked on service calls."

She answered Charlie back that she missed her dad very much and was sad that he died. It was just her and her daughter now and she was having a tough time getting by.

Charlie formerly serviced cash registers on a route consisting of various Italian restaurants and bars. Combined with the motorcycle shop routes for cash register service this would keep him busy during his days off from the firehouse in the past. Bert's Italian father ran a large Italian club a few miles down the street from Dave's closing Honda dealership. If you had an Italian daughter getting married in the area, Bert's dad was most likely the manager and host of the ceremony. The entire area where he worked on Mission Street was known as Little Italy.

Once Bert was done with Charlie's haircut, he pulled off the cape and said he had to leave right away. He was meeting up with all of his motorcycle friends for their other weekly ritual, a Tuesday night get-together for dinner. Charlie said to me, "Since I have to get going why don't you make yourself useful and sweep up the hair?" He walked out quickly and left the building.

Bert picked up the broom and dust pan and swept up the hair she cut. When finished, we walked outside and I locked up the shop and we decided to go and get a bite to eat together. Bert suggested we go to a local Italian restaurant she and her father would eat at many times in the past.

By now Bert and I were dating and seeing each other frequently. She was a year younger than me and was half Asian and Italian. She was good looking, kind and pleasant to be around; we got along very well. I still couldn't understand what reason Joe had for abandoning his beautiful wife and his precious young daughter except that he wanted to party with Dave and his gang on cocaine. Charlie didn't express any feelings about me and Bert getting serious, but I knew he still saw Joe on a regular basis through the Dave Bostrom network Joe was now a part of.

Bert was afraid if Joe found out we were dating he may become enraged and hurt her like he did in the past because he was a personality that insisted on having his cake and eating it too. I told Bert not to worry about that, if Joe tried to do anything to her or her daughter I would break his fucking head off with a Dave Bostrom exhaust pipe.

The next day, when Bert walked out of her apartment she was horrified to see all 4 tires on her car were slashed by a bandit in the middle of the night. She knew it was Joe and his creepy friends. She recalled when Joe did the same thing to his own mother when his mom and dad divorced and it was his trademark of evil in the past.

1990

"The English are coming!! The English are coming!!" Charlie exclaimed as he walked in the shop one cold winter morning. When T and I looked at Charlie, he repeated, "Hey, I'm Paul Revere and I'm telling you guys the English are coming."

I quickly referred back to my seventh grade history class and said, "I think the phrase that Paul Revere made was the British were coming."

Charlie answered, "Well, I don't give a rat's ass if they're called the British or the English. All I know is they're coming here in a few months, and buying a bunch of old parts and bikes we have lying around here. These are two guys from England coming to fill a shipping container full of bikes and parts to ship back to England to sell over there." Charlie walked into the office to make some phone calls and do some paperwork.

T whipped out some tools and started to work saying, "Dude, it will be nice to see your dad get rid of some of the crap around this place."

T was right—Charlie's shop became so full of old, non-running bikes and junk parts that it was difficult to move around inside the place anymore. Junk motorcycles needed to be rolled outside every morning just to make enough room for the customers to walk around and for work to be done. We had shelves around the shop that were overflowing with old junk parts and engine and wheel piles which measured up to six feet in height. We stacked and dismantled so many junk motorcycles for years the shop was filled to capacity with all sorts of unwanted cycle parts.

As I was loading a motorcycle onto one of the lift tables I noticed Steve came to the shop to pay T a visit. It was quite some time since we saw him around the shop. Steve was surprised at the way the shop looked and said, "Man, what the hell happened in here? Where did you guys get all this junk from?"

T told him that Charlie made a big deal with Dave Bostrom because Dave's dealership went out of business a few months back. Steve was puzzled. "Do you guys mean Dave closed down his Yamaha shop?"

I said, "It was his Honda dealership on Mission Street."

Steve thought for a moment and then said, "Oh, wait a minute. A Yamaha dealership was located across the street from Dave's Honda shop and I remember Dave bought out that Yamaha shop a few years ago and combined the Honda and Yamaha dealerships in his one building."

I laughed and said, "Yamaha or Honda. It really doesn't matter because all we got was a ton of this crap. Charlie paid Dave Bostrom a bunch of money for the loads."

Steve asked T if he had any weed for sale because he wanted to smoke a joint. T was still slinging weed on the side and produced a small sack to sell to Steve. While they were doing the transaction T said, "Charlie thinks he will get a bunch of money for all these crap parts because some guys from England are coming to buy a container full of parts to take back to their country."

Steve busted out laughing and said, "Nobody will want to buy any this shit in here. Charlie's tripping out. He's crazy."

During times, Charlie had different friends who came in the shop to do paperwork deals with him. Dave was still coming by on a regular basis too. Charlie met with Dave and other old flat tracking buddies in the office and joked around about the past. Lately Dave would bring Eric with him, but we didn't see much of Tory or Ben around the shop anymore.

I wasn't familiar with what Charlie did in the office with the paperwork, but he was now carrying around a new book for entering the vehicle identification numbers for DMV processing. He had been entering the VIN numbers in the old black book for years, but now he started a new blue book for the process.

The phone rang one day, I picked it up and heard a strange recording but couldn't clearly hear because the shop was located directly under the flight path of the departing planes leaving out of San Francisco International Airport.

Once the plane flew over the building, I heard the end of the recording. The recorded message asked me about a collect call from the San Mateo County Prison. The recording said, "If you are willing to accept the charges from an inmate from this prison, please press one." I knew Charlie had a son who was six years younger than me from his first marriage who was always in and out of jail. He would call the shop collect from the jail on occasions to say hello to his dad and ask us to send him cigarette money. I thought it was him so I pressed one to accept the telephone charges.

I was surprised to hear the person wasn't Charlie's son. It was Pin Head saying, "Hey Kid, I'm in jail. I got arrested for drunk driving." Pin Head laughed and added, "Oh, I mean drunk riding. I was arrested on my bike so let Charlie know that I'm in jail and I'll be getting out soon. I was busted leaving a bar, and they impounded my bike so I'll be looking for another bike when I get out."

I asked Pin Head how long he was in jail for, and he said because he was broke he couldn't pay the fines so he was paying with time instead of money. He said it could be a few months before he gets out.

Charlie came in and I told him about Pin Head. He laughed and then pointed out one of our cheap motorcycles for sale in the front of the shop. He said, "I can't worry about Pin Head because I have this bike sold to a customer for 350 bucks, I want you or T to make sure it has fresh gas and new spark plugs because he will pick it up in an hour."

A little while later after the bike was ready to go, a small skinny guy who was about my age came in the shop and talked to Charlie about the deal. The customer immediately started to complain about the condition of the motorcycle and tried to coax a new battery for the bike out of Charlie. He said, "My name's Dick, and if you guys give me a good deal on this bike, I'll come back and buy more bikes and parts. I run a side business selling used bikes out of my house a few blocks down the street from your shop." He convinced Charlie to lower the price with his promise.

Dick smiled while Charlie said he would write up the paperwork that Dick needed at the DMV to get the motorcycle registered.

Charlie said to him with some papers on the desk, "Okay, here's how the paperwork needs to be done." Charlie handed Dick a shop sales receipt that showed the purchase for $300. With a second document Charlie said, "Here's another form you need; it's the brake and light certificate to inform the DMV that all the brakes and lights are in working condition. You also need to take the bike to the DMV and have them look at the frame and engine numbers to verify the digits are correct when the bike is registered. The bike will be a salvage title vehicle when you get it registered, not a clean title."

Dick was fine with the instructions and as he was leaving, Charlie said happily, "The next time you buy a bike from me you can skirt the process of taking it to the DMV to get it verified, because I've applied and paid the DMV to become a licensed vehicle verifier myself. I'll be able to make out the verification form for you here." When I heard that, I found it suspicious Charlie wanted to become a vehicle verifier and pay the large amount of money to do so when we didn't sell many running motorcycles, only junk parts.

Rolling the vast number of junk motorcycles outside in the mornings and back in the building at night would often take thirty to forty minutes. T had one of his weed customers come by in the mornings and evenings to help us with the motorcycle rolling procedure. His name was Norm, and he would roll the bikes for free as long as T would smoke him out with marijuana and send him home with a few extra joints in his pocket.

A few weeks later, T told me Norm wasn't around to help us with the bikes anymore because he was arrested while hanging out with a friend who was burglarizing a house, and they were caught in the act. While T and I finished moving the junk bikes outside, Dave and Eric walked up. They needed T to help them look around in Charlie's shop for a special set of front forks for the new flat tracker Dave was building for Eric for the upcoming dirt track season.

Charlie was late arriving to work this particular morning because he went to the DMV to turn in his paperwork. After arriving, Charlie asked me how things were and I told him T was up in the loft with Dave and Eric looking for some forks. Charlie seemed very happy and said, "I just came from the DMV and found out some good news about that pain in the ass lady investigator who used to hassle me all the time. She moved on to another department, so I don't have to worry about that cunt messing around with me ever again."

While Charlie walked upstairs to say hello to Dave and Eric he turned and said to me, "I also picked up my vehicle verifier's license this morning, so now I can verify whatever I want and nobody can do or say anything about it."

I wondered about Charlie's new verifier deal. We didn't sell many running motorcycles out of Charlie's shop, maybe only one or two bikes a month if we were lucky. I couldn't see the reasoning behind him becoming a vehicle verifier because it was a large expense without much return on his investment and time. Charlie still complained about keeping costs down around the shop.

Many years later I would come to find the criminal reasons why Charlie really wanted to be a vehicle verifier. One particular vehicle that would be verified on his license would turn out to be one of the greatest motorcycles in the world involved in a controversy that could shake the entire sport of motorcycling to its core.

I saw Charlie talking to Dave and he was happy and telling him about his new vehicle verifying license. Dave appeared to hear the news with a big smile, and they shook hands with a sense of accomplishment.

Charlie was glad the Bostroms found the forks they were looking for. He told Dave they would do the usual on the deal, which was Dave and his kids paid for nothing in Charlie's shop because of the continuing sponsorship program. Charlie looked at Eric and said, "All I want you to do is go out there and get wins so you'll bring my shop exposure at the track. Customers will come here and spend money because they want to be a winner like you."

Charlie then said to Dave, "I think Ben and Eric are going fast now because they just don't have any fear." Dave smiled and agreed, as Charlie said to Eric, "Now, good luck this weekend. I want you to go out there and do it just the way we told you to."

Charlie said with pride as he patted Eric on the shoulder, "Eric's my little Speedo. Right, Eric?" Eric smiled and agreed that he would go and smoke them this weekend for another Bostrom victory. The Bostroms and Charlie walked up to the front of the shop, where Charlie performed his usual ritual of handing free bottles of oil and cans of chain lube to Eric.

The following morning, after T and I rolled the junk motorcycles outside, Charlie said, "The English guys will be here in a few minutes, so I want you two idiots to help them out and show them around the shop. Let them pick out things they want to buy. Now, I don't want you to say anything to them about money. Let me worry about making the deal with them because I don't want you guys fucking up my deal."

In twenty minutes, a small yellow rental truck pulled up to the side door and parked. In walked two middle-aged men who said with a thick English accent that they were here to meet Charlie about a load of motorcycles. I said hello to the men and directed them to the office. T started laughing and said, "Dude, those guys only have a small truck and can't haul enough crap out of here to make a difference at all. They won't even put a small dent in this place."

Charlie came in the back, followed by the Englishmen, and told T and me to show them around. I directed them to engine piles of various Japanese motorcycles we dismantled over the last few years. The two Englishmen were amazed at the size and immensity of Charlie's salvage operation. However, they stated they were mostly interested in small Hondas from the 1970's.

They told me they were in the restoration business in England and it was popular for people to buy the vintage Hondas as well as the modern sport bikes. The two men said they were interested in finding clean old Hondas that were in excellent running condition.

The men decided they would only buy two old bikes from Charlie's shop. They continued to look around the shop for a few hours before telling Charlie they had selected the small amount of parts they would buy. Charlie told the Englishmen they could have their load for $1,000. After they loaded their truck, they paid Charlie and said they would return next year around the same time.

They gave Charlie cash, so he was very happy and said, "Now that these guys gave me all this money I can pay the rent around here."

T was mad and wondered why they didn't buy more stuff because they left with their truck only half full. T said angrily, "I thought those guys were taking all this crap out of here, honestly."

Charlie snapped back, "Until you two assholes come up with a better idea for paying the fucking rent around here why don't you just shut the fuck up! Hey, I don't pay you two idiots to think; I pay you guys to work!"

The next morning Charlie showed up after T and I opened the shop and rolled all the bikes out. Charlie said to me, while fumbling with his morning coffee, "I want you to drive up to San Francisco this morning and check out a police impound auction for some cheap bikes."

When I arrived at the auction, I was happy to see Dark Ninja there. We talked together until the auction was over and while walking back to the parking lot, Dark Ninja said, "How's my man T and the rest of the gang down at the shop? I saw T downtown the other night riding his bike around. I guess T likes to frequent the same ladies of the night that I do downtown. You take care, and we'll talk again soon." He rode off back to work on his Ninja.

After the drive back to the shop, I parked my truck and walked in through the side door. T was in the back working on some stuff that Charlie told him to do. He said, "Wow, dude. Your dad's pissing me because he's telling me to move this crap here and that crap there and we should get this place cleaned up. When I'm working underneath the loft on these junk parts I can hear the wood creaking above me, like the whole loft is going to fall down on my head if we have another earthquake."

I knew T was right. Charlie told us to pile heavy metal parts upstairs by the ton and now, since the big San Francisco earthquake last year, the loft beams sagged dramatically. T said he was happy I was back because his girlfriend Murr was coming by to take him out to lunch and he needed a well deserved Charlie break. T went on to say, "Working here with Charlie is getting harder on a one-on-one basis. The only time things run smoothly and I'm happy around this place is when Charlie's at the firehouse and not working here with us. Dude, I look forward to the days he's at the firehouse because he can't bitch at us all the time and we can take a few smoke breaks while I sell some bags of weed to my friends."

Charlie walked in the back and said, "Good, you're back. How did it go at the auction? You didn't spend too much of my money, did you?" I told Charlie the bikes at the auction sold too high and I didn't buy anything.

Charlie had other news T wasn't prepared to hear. He said, "Hey, I have good news for you two. I'm retiring from the fire department, and now I'll be here working with you guys every day we're open." At that moment, T's girlfriend Murr arrived and she along with an angry T left for lunch together.

Throughout the rest of the year it was pretty much business as usual around Charlie's shop. Charlie retired and made good on his promise because he was at the shop every day it was open. As a result, T was constantly complaining about having to work with Charlie and his bossy, controlling ways.

T was always happy to see Charlie leave on errands because it was the only way he could get in a marijuana break these days. One day while Charlie was gone, T finished a repair job and rode the motorcycle from the back to the front of the shop and told me the job was ready. He parked the bike and asked me if I wanted to smoke one with him. At the same time we were surprised to see Bernard walk through the front doors to say hello. It was some time since we saw him, and he was ready to smoke a joint too.

We went out the side door to light one up. Bernard asked us how we were doing and how Charlie was. I told him Charlie retired from the firehouse and was here every day. He laughed and said, "I bet he gets on your nerves all day long." Bernard was wearing a blue uniform and told us that Dave Bostrom's friend, who owned the tire store in the South Bay where he was working, closed his shop down. Bernard said he had a new job with a major tire manufacturer, working on trucks in a shop close by. He said he loved his new job since it paid good money and offered health benefits. He told T his employer was looking for other qualified mechanics to work on trucks and they could use a guy like T. After we finished smoking, Bernard told us he needed to get back to work and said, "I'll see you two guys around soon." He shook my hand and said to me, "Tell Bert I said hello. I know you and her are hanging tight these days."

Charlie came walking through the side door a short time later and said, "Hey, it smells like fucking dope in here." He added, as he glared at T, "Are you and your fucking friends smoking dope in here?"

T was in the process of answering when Charlie stormed off into the office. T said to me "Wow, I don't want to get your dad pissed off or anything but as far as working for him anymore, I can tell you that the $300 a week he pays me isn't even worth the bullshit. I can honestly make $300 in one day by just selling a few sacks of weed to my friends. I think I'll get a job over at Bernard's in the truck tire business so I guess today is my last day working here, dude." I didn't blame T at all because he worked for Charlie for years and Charlie treated us like shit. I recalled the few times I walked out on Charlie but I always returned because I was told it was in the best interest of the family business.

The next morning, I realized I had to push all the junk motorcycles outside myself and I started undertaking the job. Halfway through the job, I heard someone who was walking yell out to me, "Hey, kid, it's me, Pin Head. I was just released from jail, and I'm going to work here at the shop again for your dad in exchange for a used bike I can ride so I don't have to take the bus to get around."

I rolled my eyes and thought that Pin Head working at the shop would be the same old song and dance it was in the past. I realized I had no choice because I needed someone to help me roll all the junk bikes in and out every day.

I knew things were going to be different around the shop.

1991

Pin Head working at the shop turned out to be the same old crap as in the past. He was always late in the mornings to push out the motorcycles, and I did most of the work by myself. When he did arrive, he would still do his usual tire screeching slide to a stop in front of the customers to dazzle them.

Charlie was very happy with the way things were turning out with Pin Head as the mechanic because he didn't have to pay him in cash. Pin Head was back to his old ways of impressing the customers with his expertise and was very astute at assembling junk motorcycles to sell. However, Pin Head's performance was hindered by the fact that he was still a full-blown intravenous drug addict, using both heroin and speed. Pin Head lied to Charlie about his drug use and said he was prescribed methadone by the doctors of the state of California. He bragged no drugs affected his work or riding ability.

I arrived at work one morning and rolled the junk motorcycles outside because Pin Head wasn't there yet. Charlie pulled up in his truck a few minutes later and said, "You guys are supposed to have this place open already, where's Pin Head?"

I said, "Pin Head's late again, and I opened late because he's not here to help me."

Charlie said, "Well, hurry up and finish getting the bikes out, and I'll answer the phones in the office until you're done."

I finished rolling the bikes out and was in the back of the shop turning on the work station lights and the air compressors when Charlie came back after hanging up the telephone saying, "Well, that's just great. That was Pin Head on the phone, and he's back in fucking jail again."

I said, "You've got to be kidding. What happened?"

Charlie was angry and said, "That stupid Pin Head was arrested on the motorcycle I gave him because he was riding it around too fast and still doesn't have a driver's license or a registration on the bike."

Charlie gave Pin Head one of the shop's Verna-mobiles even though I told him not to give the motorcycle to Pin Head until he was finished paying for it. The bike was now impounded and not likely to be returned. Pin Head would be in jail for a while and the tow charges would soon amount to more than the value of the motorcycle. I knew we would have to find someone to replace Pin Head as the mechanic.

One evening as I was rolling the bikes in, I noticed one of T's old friends had pulled up in front of the shop in his car. He walked over said, "I came by to pick up a sack of weed from T, is he around?"

I remembered him because when T was working this guy would visit to buy weed. His name was Mac and he was a short burly guy with a large protruding belly who was my age. He was always greasy from working on cars all the time. I told Mac T moved on after years of working for Charlie and was employed in the truck business, not too far from the shop. Mac asked me if I was working by myself and inquired if we needed help around the shop. He said he was an unemployed car mechanic who knew how to work on motorcycles as well as cars.

Charlie walked out of the office and noticed Mac and I talking. I said to Charlie, "This is Mac. He's T's friend, and he's looking for work."

Charlie said to him, "If you can work on bikes and get your ass here on time in the mornings and you don't mind being paid in cash, then you can have a job here." Mac shook hands with Charlie and said he would see us in the morning to start work.

As the months progressed into summer, Mac worked as the mechanic in the back of the shop installing tires and doing minor tune-ups on customer's bikes. Charlie and I were now running the front counter together.

None of Charlie's prior employees had been perfect, and Mac was no exception. He had wrench-throwing tirades when things didn't go right with his mechanical work that reached panic levels of anger. He would take off from the shop for long periods of time to blow off steam before returning to finish his projects. Mac complained Charlie was demanding too much work from him since repair work piled up and junk bikes needed dismantling. Charlie didn't realize at times when Mac took off from the shop to blow off steam he was around the back of the building taking his much-needed marijuana smoke break too.

One afternoon after Mac returned from one of his temper tantrums, Charlie told him that he needed to find someone to help him with the dismantling in the back because the work load had grown beyond his capabilities. Mac told Charlie that the ideal person would be someone who would listen to everything Mac told him to do. Mac said he had a friend in the auto repair business that would make a good motorcycle dismantler and listen to Mac without any arguing back.

The next morning an old beat up black van was sitting out in front of the shop when I arrived. A man, who was a few years older than Mac that appeared to be living in the van, opened the rear doors and said, "Hi, I'm Willy." He was sweaty and dirty and wore wrinkled clothes that were not washed in days. He was a small man with glasses and short messy hair. His face needed a shave, and he definitely needed a bath. His hands and arms were covered in mechanic grease and the smell of grease and gasoline permeated from his body. He said to me with a cigarette in his mouth, "I'm Mac's friend who's working here now." Willy jumped out of the van, closed the door behind him and said, "I'm leaving this van here because this is where I live."

Charlie drove up in his truck and parked next to the black van. I told him the new employee was ready to work and Willy needed to park his van at the shop because he was living in it. Mac pulled up in his car about the same time, and Charlie told all of us to get the shop open and the bikes rolled out. He told Willy to park his beat-up van on the side of the shop instead of the front if he was parking it overnight.

Since Charlie's retirement from the firehouse, there were more frequent visits from his buddies. His usual friends Dave, Mikey and Petey were visiting more often, along with Charlie's flat tracking buddies from his old days. Most mornings and afternoons, Charlie was heard laughing and joking around in the office with his friends, talking about the good old days of riding in the Bay Area.

Outside the office it was a completely different world. Mac was working hard at repair jobs and Willy was busy dismantling and finding parts Mac needed for repairs. With the back of the shop taken care of, it left the counter and phones for me to look after.

It was about noon one day while I was working on the counter when I noticed a Kawasaki 900 Ninja pull into the shop. The rider pulled off his helmet and I saw it was Bernard, who stopped by on his lunch break. At the same time he arrived, Charlie and a few of his buddies walked out of the office and said they were going out to lunch. Charlie said hello to Bernard as he and his friends filed out the door.

I asked Bernard how he was and he said, "I need to get a front tire for my Ninja mounted up, and I thought I would come by and smoke a joint with you on my lunch break." Mac was gone for lunch, and Bernard and I rolled his bike into the back of the shop. We walked out the side door when Willy said, "Hey, where are you guys going?"

I told him Bernard and I were smoking a joint, and Willy asked if he could come along and join us, since there were no customers in the shop.

Bernard pulled out some marijuana but quickly realized he had no rolling papers so Willy said he had an extra pack of rolling papers in his van. The three of us walked out to the van, and Willy banged his fist on the rear door. When the door opened, we could see the extremely messy interior of the van with soiled clothes thrown everywhere, along with a very large, heavy-set woman who appeared to be living in the van with him. Willy asked her for some rolling papers, and she handed him a pack. We walked away from the van as the woman closed the door and we retreated to the very back of the shop, which housed a small secret smoke room where T used to hide out from Charlie.

While Bernard was rolling a joint, I asked Willy who the woman in the van was. He said, "Oh, do you mean the Big Block? She's my girlfriend."

Bernard laughed hard while he fired up his joint and said, "Damn, she's mighty big. She must be payin' like she's weighin', that's for sure."

Willy smiled and said proudly as Bernard passed him the joint, "You're right. She pays for all my drugs and food, and she even holds my arm steady while I shoot my drugs. Living in the van with her outside has been okay, except the cops show up every now and then and harass me about us living in the van next to the shop."

Willy handed me the joint and told us because the cops busted him a few weeks back taking a piss outside the van, he developed a toilet system in the van by cutting a round hole in the floor so anyone could urinate through the hole without leaving the van at night. Willy then said to us laughing, "The good thing is that I have the Big Block to keep me warm at night."

After we finished smoking the joint, Bernard and I installed a front tire on his Ninja, and he told me he had to get back to work. I asked him how T was doing and he said, "My man T is having a good time working with me. It's a good job."

As Bernard rode his Ninja out the front door a familiar face walked in the shop looking for Charlie. He was the son of the friend of Dave Bostrom who opened the tire store where Bernard worked previously. His name was Phil, and he was looking for his father, who was one of the guys that went out to lunch with Charlie earlier.

Phil said, "Hey, how's it going? Was that Bernard who just left on that Ninja?" I said it was. Phil told me that working with Bernard went well at his father's tire shop, but they had to let him go when his dad closed down his shop. Bernard never told me why the tire store closed so I asked Phil, "Why did you guys have to close down?"

Phil said with a frustrated look, "My dad's mom, my grandmother, was financing my dad to run his tire shop because she has loads of money. My dad chose to not operate his business correctly because he would rather be in bed with Dave Bostrom snorting cocaine than running the tire shop."

Taken aback at what he told me, I thought to myself, when Phil's dad ran his tire shop, Charlie sent me down to the shop a few times. The place was nothing like Charlie's salvage operation. His shop was located in a brand new building, and they spared no expense filling the business up with hundreds of brand new tires and the best equipment for mounting and balancing the tires for customers.

Phil said he could no longer road race because his dad wouldn't sponsor him anymore, now that the tire shop was closed. He complained he was now unemployed, and his dad kept himself busy managing his grandmother's properties.

Running the shop with Mac and Willy was a different scenario than it was with T. Willy had his share of drug problems, and Mac still needed to go on marijuana breaks whenever he and Charlie had disagreements about repair jobs. Mac was always angry because Charlie was telling him what to do and when to do it. Charlie didn't seem to mind running the shop with these incompetent employees, because most of the time he was still in the office doing paperwork deals with his friend Dave Bostrom.

Dave still came around the shop weekly to see Charlie with Eric. On most visits Dave and Eric would go into the office and visit privately with Charlie, and then they would spend some time kicking around the shop, always looking for that special bolt or part that was hard to find but was needed to build whatever race bike Dave was currently working on. Eric Bostrom was now 15 years old and no child anymore. He stood taller than his father. Charlie said Ben and Eric were dirt tracking professionals who both now held Pro Racing licenses.

One Saturday afternoon, a 1986 Suzuki GSXR-750 pulled up to the shop and parked outside. I was very surprised to see it was Chris Crew who came by to purchase some parts and say hello. It was some time since I saw him in the shop, and he hadn't changed at all. Still tall and thin with light brown hair and eager about motorcycle riding. He possessed an unquenchable thirst for riding and racing along with good times.

Chris told me his motorcycle courier business took off like a bolt of lightning. Many people needed important documents delivered quickly, all over San Francisco. His motorcycle couriers could deliver documents in half the time it would take for the bicycle couriers to get it done.

Chris said he took up road racing with a local race club and most of the races were held on Sundays at Sears Point Raceway in Sonoma. Chris was leading the points chase in his class and was scoring wins and podium finishes. He was enthusiastic about his fast riding and told me about a new race he put together.

Chris said proudly, "Me and some of my fast friends from the Sunday Morning Ride in Marin County have started a high speed motorcycle race from the border of California to the tip of the Baja Peninsula in Mexico. It's a wide open race we call the Cabo 1000; the first guy who gets to the end of the Baja Peninsula is declared the winner."

I said, "Wow that sounds pretty wild."

Chris replied, "Yeah, it's exciting and scary too, with all those beat-up roads they have down in Mexico, the ride's a real blast."

Chris told me how he recently was able to fulfill a dream of his to race at the Isle of Man over in the British Isles. He said with his business running smoothly he was able to take time off and pursue his passion, which was road racing. When Chris was leaving, he said, "Every Tuesday night my fast friends and I have a get-together we like to call Simpson night. We get together and smoke a few joints and watch *The Simpsons* on TV and talk about fast riding and racing. You should come by Tuesday and check us out." I told Chris I would ride up to the city to see him and his friends.

That Tuesday, I arrived at the house Chris told me about. There were a few sport bikes outside, so I parked my bike in the row and walked up to the house and knocked at the door. A guy I wasn't familiar with answered, and I told him I was there to see Chris. The guy directed me in the back of the house to the TV room where Chris was with some friends. As I entered the room I saw Chris seated in the corner while his friends passed a few joints around. Chris motioned for me to sit next to him because the show was about to start and everyone was taking their seats.

It seemed Chris wanted to talk to me about riding fast and racing more than he wanted to watch *The Simpsons*.

Chris asked, "I heard you bought a new bike. How come I don't see you on the Sunday morning ride?"

I told him that recently one of Charlie's friends came into the shop and sold me his bike. The guy had a 1989 Kawasaki ZX10 Ninja 1000 he purchased new but he was afraid of the power and wanted to sell the bike. I said, "Last year I decided to move out of the bay area to Fairfield to buy an affordable house with my girlfriend, Bert. The ride is a 120-mile round trip commute and since I ride so much during the week, I prefer to stay off the bike on the weekends." Chris said, "Wow! That's a long distance to go every day. How's it going?"

I told him that commuting on the ZX10 was exciting and a fast ride. I said, "The bike is so fast and handles so well, that on some days I could turn a one-hour commute into a 40-minute thrill ride. I'm taking the ZX10 on a long distance ride this weekend. Charlie and me are riding to Nevada and will speed through tight winding mountain back roads to get there. Charlie recently acquired a '89 Suzuki 1100 Katana. He showed up with the bike in his truck one day and said he bought it from a guy who was in an accident on the thing."

Chris said while he passed me the joint, "That's a good bike Charlie bought. Was there anything wrong with it from the accident?"

I answered as I took a hit, "The bike only had some fairing damage, Charlie is home gluing the fairings back together in order to repair it. He said he's looking forward to take the Katana on this high speed run to Nevada to see what the thing will do."

The Simpsons was now over and people started to leave on their bikes and Chris said he was going home too. After saying goodbye to him, I grabbed my helmet and jacket and walked outside into the cold, foggy night. It was dark, and I fired my ZX10 up for a fast trip home to Fairfield, where I knew Bert was waiting for me in a warm house with a delicious dinner. These days, my home life with Bert gave me more pleasure than life around Charlie's hectic shop. We would try and spend all the free time we had together and that wasn't much with our schedules.

A few days later on Saturday, Mac and Charlie were working together on something in the back while I was up front working the counter. I could hear that familiar sound of them having one of their ritualistic arguments. Soon thereafter, I heard Mac yelling and walking out the side door, firing up his hot rod car and taking off.

After Mac stormed out, Charlie came over to me and said, "I'm really getting tired of that fucking Mac's bullshit, and the next time he does his temper tantrum walkout show, it's going to be the last time he pulls that shit. I'll fire his ass if he doesn't stop being such a hot head."

Charlie said as he picked up his keys, "I'm having trouble collecting the rents over at my building in San Bruno, so I have to go over there and tell those bums I have as tenants to give me my fucking money."

As he was leaving he said to me, "I'll be at your house in Fairfield at eight o'clock in the morning tomorrow for our ride together, so make sure Bert has some coffee ready for me."

I told Charlie that I would be the one making the coffee because Bert was flying to Chicago on hair business for her boss that weekend. Charlie left to check on his building in San Bruno.

This one-story building had 5 units and was purchased by Charlie and my mother at the time they were married. Charlie's accountant told him that having a building where tenants pay you rent was a good investment and also an excellent tax write-off. It was working so well for Charlie that one of his dirt track buddies had purchased the building right across the street, so he too could have the same tax advantages that Charlie enjoyed.

Charlie always had problems with the renters at his building. There were a couple of low income characters living there, and Charlie was constantly trying to get them to pay the rent on time.

All the way back when Charlie first bought his building the tenants who lived there were problematic. Most of them already lived in the units when Charlie purchased the place. Charlie didn't mind even though most of them were drug addicts and some assembled motorcycles in the apartments on the carpeted floor.

Charlie always complained about the tenants saying, "They're just a bunch of bums who won't pay me my rent and the bitch that is living in number two is nothing but the local pin cushion for all the losers in the area."

One of the units in the back of the building was set aside and not rented so my younger brother Garg could live in the unit rent free and act as a maintenance guy for Charlie. This left plenty of time for Garg to enjoy a life of leisure. He could surf all day long and only had to work when something needed to be addressed at the building, which wasn't very often because Charlie never wanted to spend any money for expenses on his building either.

Willy walked outside and I told him, "Charlie took off for the rest of the day, so it's just you and me to work the phones and customers until closing time."

As the afternoon progressed, Willy and I were both surprised to see Mac didn't return. Each time Mac had a fight with Charlie, he took longer to come back. It was quite frustrating because with Saturday afternoon busy and Charlie and Mac not at the shop, Willy and I had a difficult time running things smoothly.

When evening finally came, I was dismayed because Mac never returned. Willy and I realized that both of us alone would have to roll in all the junk motorcycles. As I walked outside to grab my first junk bike to roll in, I saw a guy walking up to me. It was Norm, the friend of T who helped us roll the motorcycles into the shop at closing time in the past.

Norm said, as he grabbed a bike to roll, "I just got out of jail, and I came by to see you and T. Where's he hiding out?"

I told Norm it was a while since T moved on to a new job. He was surprised to hear that and said he would help us roll in the rest of the bikes while he told me why he went to jail.

Norm said, "I was with my friend who sells drugs, and he went to a guy's house to collect money that was owed to him. My friend broke into the dude's house and took a TV for the money. A neighbor called the cops, and when they showed up, I was arrested too because I had an outstanding warrant and the police thought I was robbing the house with my friend. When I went to court, the judge said because of my prior convictions he was giving me a year in state prison instead of sending me to county jail."

I said surprised, "That sounds like a bad deal you were given."

Norm said, "Yeah, it was a very rough year. They sent me to San Quentin, the toughest prison around."

After the bikes were rolled in and the doors closed and locked, Norm said he brought along a little marijuana and asked if Willy and I wanted to smoke a quick one with him before we took off. We went into the office and each took a seat. Norm whipped out a joint and lit it up then passed it to me I took a puff and passed it to Willy.

Once Norm exhaled, he said, "Man, it's good to be out of San Quentin and smoking again. All I did when I was in the place was work out with weights. That's the only good thing I got out of it."

Norm flexed his arms and showed us his enlarged biceps. He appeared to be in far better shape physically than he was before he went into San Quentin. After pushing all the motorcycles in the shop, Norm was hardly out of breath at all.

His personality seemed to have more of a hard edge than the Norm I remembered in the past. Before, he was a joke cracking prankster, and now he appeared to have a more serious disposition about him.

Knowing a little about San Quentin from reading about its notorious past, I said to Norm, "There were a bunch of famous criminals at San Quentin. I think they kept Sirhan Sirhan there, the guy who killed Senator Robert Kennedy."

As the joint continued to circle between the three of us, Willy said, "San Quentin is where they held Charles Manson, that hippie cult leader."

Norm took another big hit off the joint and said, "Yeah. They've had many crazy dudes there over the years. It's a hardcore prison and I saw a lot of wild guys. Guess who else I saw in jail when I was in San Quentin?"

I asked who and he replied, "Ed Woo...He was one of the toughest dudes in there when I was there, and no one wanted to fuck with him or they would get their asses kicked."

Shocked, I said, "No fucking way, what's Ed doing in San Quentin? I heard he went away for drugs, but I can't believe he was put in that prison."

Norm smiled and said, "I don't want to talk about what Ed was in for, but I know I saw him there and I know I was not mistaken."

At eight o'clock the next morning, there was a heavy knock on my front door. It was Charlie with his helmet and riding gear on. He said looking at me through his helmet, "Hey, like we say at the firehouse when the alarm rings, 'Drop your cocks and grab your socks and let's hit the road.'" Charlie said he already had his morning coffee before he left his house. He was chomping at the bit to get going, so I grabbed my gear and rolled the ZX10 out of my garage. We took off across the Sacramento River delta, taking country back roads to get to the Sierra foothills. Charlie didn't like to ride on the freeways and since he knew all the back roads he already planned out the route.

Charlie rode fast on the back roads and always knew when to slow down in the small towns to avoid local sheriffs and highway patrols. Charlie carved up the twisty roads on his Katana and hit around 130 MPH on the straight back roads. I stayed behind Charlie most of the way, but he pulled away from me in the fast sweeping turns at 80 MPH, with the undercarriage of his Katana scraping in the turns, shooting out sparks from the foot pegs grinding on the road surface.

After a few hours of high speed riding, we were on the eastern side of the Sierra Nevada mountain range. North of Truckee, California, Charlie pulled into a small town called Blairsden-Graeagle. He jumped off his bike and said, "I'm land speculating up here for my real estate association. My new angle is, since your younger brother Garg isn't working these days we might use his name in our association on a piece of property here and maybe in Reno too." After a while we fired up our bikes and Charlie cruised slowly around, looking at some empty lots while I followed behind. Charlie yelled out, "We have to get to my next stop before it gets too late."

We left Blairsden-Graeagle and quickly rode about an hour down to Reno, Nevada. We made one more stop while Charlie was land speculating. We drove down a street called Riley with many dilapidated houses and a run-down apartment building. Charlie looked at the building for a few minutes thinking, then after a long day of riding, Charlie and I headed back home.

As I rode home behind Charlie I wondered what he meant about using my brother Garg in his association or what his association even was. I was the only motorcycle rider in the family of the eight children and Charlie and I worked at the shop together while the other siblings had nothing to do with motorcycles. Since my younger brother never had a steady job in years I wondered what type of real estate investments Charlie had him involved in with his mysterious association.

During the holiday season Charlie would sometimes close the shop for the week between Christmas and the New Year holiday so he could snow ski with his own kids and enjoy other recreational things he did with them.

On the morning of December 21, 1991, a motorcycle messenger rode up to the shop, took off his helmet and said to me, "Did you hear the news? Chris Crew died of a heroin drug overdose the other night. He was found by a close friend at his place near Twin Peaks."

I was shocked because I wasn't aware Chris had a heroin drug habit. I knew it would be a blow to the San Francisco motorcycle community because his delivery business became a magnet for young riders to work at who moved to San Francisco to become active in the city riding scene.

Chris was also known internationally because he became one of the first riders from the San Francisco area to participate in the annual races over at the Isle of Man. Other racers soon followed his path to compete from the bay area motorcycle scene, racing the Isle of Man.

1992

Not long after the New Year, Charlie appeared happy one morning and said, "I have great news to tell you. Daly City Honda opened up again at 6232 Mission Street. That's Dave Bostrom's old place, remember? The shop isn't a Honda dealership like it was before, because Honda won't let Dave have a dealership again so it's a used motorcycle sales center and shop, owned by three partners. One owner is running the service department and the other one is running the parts department, the third owner is a silent partner because he's the one with all the money on the deal. You should remember the silent partner. He's the guy who ran the Kawasaki dealership up in San Rafael that closed. We used to go and repair his cash registers way back in 1977. The good thing is that Dave still owns the building the shop is located in."

I recalled the dealership building Dave owned sat quiet the past few years, with no tenants occupying the space. It seemed strange the next business that would occupy the space would also be a shop selling motorcycles when Dave's first one went out of business because of slow bike sales. I wondered what the new shop was selling for inventory if it wasn't a dealership selling new bikes.

Charlie leaned back in his chair and said, "My back is killing me. I just came back from a Sunday ride with Mikey and Petey, and we rode 400 miles in one day." He added as he winced in pain, "I've got to get to my chiropractor today so I can get my back fixed because I want to go riding again this coming weekend."

I asked Charlie, "Where are they getting all their bikes to sell? Is the new shop still called Daly City Honda?"

Charlie answered, "The place can't be called Honda because it's not a Honda dealership anymore, so now they're calling it Mission Motorcycles because Dave's building is located on Mission Street."

I was ready to ask Charlie why he thought the new shop would have more success than Dave had as a Honda dealership in the same location, when Charlie interrupted my thoughts and said, "Hey, I don't want to spend a lot of time talking about the new shop anymore when we need to concentrate on working and paying the rent around here."

Charlie stood up and while hunched over he said, "Mac is out as of right now. I'm tired of him coming and going when he wants and I'm sick of his temper tantrums. I'm through with his bullshit."

Charlie still had a few other friends on the Peninsula that were in the process of closing down their motorcycle dealerships. This included three dealerships in the city of San Mateo, one was a Kawasaki dealership another was a Yamaha dealership. The third one was a Honda dealership located across the street from a fish and chips pub, where Charlie met his motorcycle buddies weekly. With these dealerships going out of business the owners always had Charlie come down to buy their junk and funnel their garbage.

One afternoon, a customer asked me if we had any cheap motorcycles for sale. I directed his attention to an old Honda bike we had in the corner. The customer proceeded to tell me why he was looking for a used bike and what happened to his previous bike. He said, "I had my bike in the dealership on Van Ness Avenue in San Francisco for repairs, but when I went back to pick it up, the dealership closed down and the place was empty. I found out they moved a few blocks away. When I arrived at the new location to get my bike, they told me that the new dealership wasn't the same owners as the old dealership on Van Ness even though it was the same name. They said they didn't know what happened to my bike. The manager told me, 'Sorry, dude, it's not our problem.'"

I gave the customer a good price on the Honda we had for sale and told him, "Charlie will write up your paperwork, and he will verify the frame number on the bike."

The next week I was helping a customer outside on the street and as I crawled under the guy's bike to see what was wrong with it, the customer quickly yelled out, "What the fuck! Watch out, dude! Here comes a crazy guy riding fast on a wheelie."

I sat up in time to see a Yamaha FZR1000 pass by like a rocket with the rider executing a well-balanced standup wheelie. I figured his speed must have been 80 MPH as he disappeared all the way down the street on the rear wheel.

The customer said, "Who the hell was that guy?" I didn't know, but I thought the only rider who could ride the rear wheel like that was Pin Head. Then I thought to myself it couldn't be Pin Head because he didn't have that kind of money to afford a Yamaha FZR1000, and the last I heard he was still in jail working off his fines.

In less than a minute, we could see the FZR returning with the rider on the rear wheel again. Charlie and some other customers came outside to see what all the commotion was about. The rider dropped the front wheel to the pavement and abruptly brought his Yamaha to a screeching stop in front of the shop. He leaped off the FZR1000 and walked over to Charlie standing in front of the shop and gave Charlie a big hug.

He pulled off his leather gloves and black leather jacket, then un-strapped and pulled off his helmet. I was almost knocked over with surprise when I saw the rider was Ed Woo.

It was a different Ed than the one I remembered seeing in the past. Ed appeared as if he worked out with weights while he was away. He wore a thin white T-shirt which defined his large arm and chest muscles. His hair had thinned, but it was the same smiling and cocky Ed I hadn't seen in several years.

Charlie said to me, "I'll be in the office with Ed catching up with him, and I need you to take care of the customers." Charlie and Ed walked into the shop while I stayed outside. I looked up and noticed some people standing around checking out Ed Woo's new Yamaha FZR1000. The riders were drawn to Ed's bike because it was the brand new 1992 model. Most customers at our shop rode old bikes, so it wasn't every day you would see a brand new high line sport bike parked outside.

Ten minutes later, Ed came out of the shop and said hello. I asked him while he shook my hand with a strong grip, "What's up? How have you been?"

Ed smiled and said, "Oh, I've been here and there and hanging with the big boys."

He asked me as he put on his jacket, "What do you think of my new fizzer, kid?"

"What's a fizzer?" I asked.

Ed replied, "FZR1000. Me and the big boys call it a fizzer. This is the new model with the great handling new generation delta box aluminum frame."

Ed jumped on his bike, strapped his helmet on and fired up the engine. As he revved it and backed out of the driveway, he said, "I'm building a new Porsche up, and when it's finished, I'll bring it by here for you to check out because I have to get some paperwork done for it by Charlie."

Ed pulled out of the parking lot and yanked the FZR1000 onto the rear wheel while he rode another fast wheelie down the street and out of sight.

On a warm summer evening, after all the junk bikes were rolled in, Charlie and Willy each went their separate ways for the night. I was alone in the shop getting ready to lock up when I heard a knock on the door. I walked over to open it and was surprised when I saw Bernard. He said smiling, "I came by to say hello."

I told him to come in the shop and sit in the office for a few minutes while I prepared to ride home. We sat down, and as I changed my work boots I noticed Bernard's mood seemed a bit low.

He pulled out a joint and fired it up and said, "I received your wedding invitation in the mail you and Bert sent to me. That's cool to hear you guys are getting married. I came by to let you know that I'll be there at your wedding for sure next month."

Bernard paused, he then took large puff off the lit joint, handed it to me and said, "I also have some very sad news from the hood."

Concerned, I asked Bernard what he was talking about. With a serious and down look on his face he said, "I know it's been some time since you've seen the Dark Ninja around. He got real sick a while back and died a few weeks ago, on May 29th. I didn't even know myself he was sick until his mother checked in with my mom. That's how I found out."

I knew Bernard and Dark Ninja were close friends. I stood up and walked over to the old refrigerator in the corner of the office and opened the door. I found two bottles of beer in the fridge, so I pulled them out and handed one to Bernard and said, "Why don't we have a drink and remember the good times we had with Dark Ninja."

We both cracked open our beers as we continued to pass the joint. I said quietly, "Remember when we went to that bar with Dark Ninja and had those beers a few years back? I can't believe he's gone. He will truly be missed."

Bernard smiled and agreed and told me what happened to Dark Ninja saying, "The Dark Ninja had a pretty hard life. His dad wasn't always around and neither was mine, so that's how we got to be close friends and ride motorcycles together. He was a few years older than us, and he did a whole lot of partying in his time. Over the years, the Dark Ninja developed a habit for more powerful drugs than just marijuana and cocaine. Sometimes he would inject the drugs, and I think he died of a blood disease or something like that. I sure am going to miss him."

I was blown away and saddened at the news because I had no idea that Dark Ninja got sick. He was a good guy, and I felt that I would miss him as much as Bernard did.

The hot summer months involved Charlie and his friends Mikey and Petey with the rest of their association members embarking on long sport bike riding trips around the bay area. When Charlie's back wasn't giving him problems, he could outride and out distance most riders half his age, and he was now 57 years old.

With my wedding to Bert coming up in two weeks and Charlie's riding friends out of town, Charlie asked me if I wanted to go with him on his Sunday morning ride. I was happy to accept because it was a rare occasion when Charlie would ask me to go riding with him. He would ask only once or twice a year because he usually spent all his riding time with his buddies. He told me to ask Willy if he wanted to come along as well. Norm was hanging around that day and said he wanted to go on the ride also. Charlie was used to riding with his friends in packs, and said it was a safe way to ride.

By now Norm had acquired a Yamaha 750cc street bike and Willy was riding a Yamaha 1100cc bike. Charlie was riding his Suzuki Katana 1100, and I still had my Kawasaki ZX10. Charlie said for us to meet him at his house in Millbrae at eight o'clock on Sunday morning.

The next day we started the ride in the hills of the Pacific coast. Charlie said that we would eat breakfast up on Highway 35, a fast-winding mountaintop road which ran through the San Mateo County coastal mountains. With Charlie leading the way and me following close behind, the four of us arrived at the restaurant in about 45 minutes. We sat in the corner and ate breakfast while Charlie told us he already planned out the day's ride. He knew all the good roads from years of riding in the area. Charlie took us on tight roads down through the woods, leading to the beach and back riding very fast.

The entire day went smoothly and during our last stop Charlie said, "Now I want you guys to just follow me home and take it easy the rest of the way." He felt the fast riding was done for the day and we should all cruise back home easily just to play it safe.

Charlie was leading the four of us down a tree lined road at about 60 MPH when suddenly a blue car came out of a side road and attempted to cross the road we were traveling on. The driver of the car quickly entered from the left side, and this caused Charlie to instantly steer his bike to the right to miss the car. I was directly behind Charlie, and saw the driver of the car panic and gas the car suddenly to cross the road quickly, to avoid the approaching motorcycles. By doing so the car re-entered Charlie's path again and a huge collision occurred.

The Katana made a loud bang and a large dent as it crushed into the side of the car while Charlie was launched into the air. The 1100cc Suzuki motorcycle bounced off the car and continued to ghost ride momentarily until smashing directly on top of Charlie, who already hit the ground very hard face down. It all happened in a split second as I screeched the ZX10 to a halt and dropped it without thinking while running to Charlie.

He was crushed beneath the 500-pound Katana so I quickly flipped his bike off Charlie's back and rolled him over. He could barely breathe and motioned for me to remove his helmet. He appeared to be suffering from a severe chest injury. There was a panicked look in his eyes and he had difficulty with every breath. Trying to talk he said he was in pain while Norm and Willy pulled over quickly to help. I knew we had to get to a phone because Charlie wasn't looking good and his condition appeared as if it could worsen as time quickly passed. Norm was able to find a resident to use their phone and soon an ambulance arrived on the scene.

As the paramedics worked on Charlie, they were worried because they were not sure of the extent of his internal chest injuries. He was quickly moved to the hospital in order to be checked out and stabilized. As Charlie was loaded in the ambulance he was able to mutter, "Since that asshole ran me over, I will need you to open the shop and run things with Willy." He added as he moaned from the pain, "You don't need to follow me to the hospital. I want you to stay behind and find a way to get my Katana back to the shop and I'll call you tonight at home. Don't let the cops tow my bike away."

After the ambulance left, Norm, Willy and I stood quietly in the woods and figured out how to tow Charlie's destroyed Katana back to the shop.

Late Sunday evening, after I finally arrived back in Fairfield, I told Bert what happened on the ride with Charlie. She was worried about him as I told her the story. She grew to love Charlie as her own father and was sad. While we were talking the phone rang and I was surprised to hear it was a drug-induced Charlie on the other end. He said in a groggy tone, "Hey, it's me. The doctors say I'm alright, but I have six broken ribs and some other internal bruising."

In slurred speech he continued, "The doctors said it was a good thing you picked up the Katana off of my back and threw it to the side when you did, because if it was on me any longer the bike would have pushed my broken ribs into my lung puncturing it, and I could have died." Bert and I were relieved to see that he was okay.

I told Charlie I would take care of things down at the shop, and I would let Dave Bostrom and his other buddies know he was hurt.

Charlie was in the hospital for one week. When he arrived home, he still needed a few days bed rest. The phone rang in the afternoon and it was Charlie checking up on things at the shop. He was impatient and wanted to return to work so he could visit with his friends and get back to his old routine. He said, "I won't be in to work for a few days, so I need you to run an errand for me up to the new Mission Motorcycles. Go see the salesman and pick up some parts from him so I can begin to fix my bike when I return back to work in a couple of days."

It was late in the afternoon and slow around the shop so I figured it would be a good time to make a fast trip up to Daly City to pick up Charlie's parts. I told Willy I would return before closing time and took off on my Ninja. After a 15-minute ride, I arrived and went inside. I wasn't in the building since I butted heads with a young Ben Bostrom over how his father cleaned out his Honda dealership years ago. When I walked in the shop, I was nearly knocked over by the number of used motorcycles for sale on the showroom floor. I was puzzled because most of the bikes appeared to be older models in like-new condition and I wondered where they got them all. The sales guy greeted me and handed me a bag of parts and said, "Give this to Charlie; tell him I said hello."

My wedding with Bert had passed a few weeks back, and Charlie returned to work after a fast recovery, things were running smoothly around the shop. Charlie was on counter duty because he still had mobility problems with his ribs, so he used Willy as his guy to help round up parts for the customers.

One busy Saturday afternoon, Charlie was on the front counter working on removing a screw from a headlight to sell the part to a customer. Another customer walked in, and Charlie told Willy to find a rear wheel for his bike. Willy walked to the back and across a large pile of wheels and tires in an attempt to find the wheel he was looking for. In an instant, Willy slipped and fell on the tires and landed on the sharp sprockets mounted to the rear wheels, impaling his greasy wrist on the sprocket teeth.

A shower of crimson blood poured from the wound as Willy nearly went unconscious so I jumped in the pile to help him. I reached down and pulled his grotesquely wounded wrist off the sprocket teeth and the bleeding intensified. As I grabbed a rag to wrap around the bleeding arm, I noticed four large holes in Willy's wrist that looked like bullet holes. I wrapped his wrist tightly, and tried to walk him up front to show Charlie he was injured.

Willy could barely stand and was about to pass out while Charlie, not caring about Willy's injury, said pointing to the customer, "Hey, when you guys finish fucking around back there, this guy needs his rear wheel."

Charlie continued to work on his headlight project without paying much attention to the fact that Willy was badly hurt. Charlie said, "Well, if he has a cut, why don't you just put a fucking band-aid on the thing and get back to work?" I told Charlie Willy was bleeding hard and we needed to get him to a hospital right away for treatment. Charlie became angry because a few customers piled up at the counter. He said, "Fine, then tell Willy to go to the damn doctor." The Big Block took Willy to the nearest hospital.

It was around closing time and Charlie was alone in the office counting up the day's receipts. I said, "Willy's back and was treated at the hospital, he needed surgery on his wrist and they gave him twenty stitches to close the wounds."

Charlie was mad and barked out, "That's just fucking great. He won't be able to work around here because of his fucked up hand and now he's useless." I told Charlie that Willy said he couldn't be around any dirty environment for weeks because of infection. Charlie was angry and said as he pointed his thumb, "As of right now he has nothing to worry about because he's just a liability around here. You can tell him that his ass is fired and to get his fucking van and that Big Block the hell out of here tonight."

I was running the shop alone with Charlie for two weeks when one morning Pin Head walked in and happily said, "Hey guys! I just got out of jail, and came by to see if I could work for Charlie again in exchange for another motorcycle to ride."

Charlie thought it was a great idea for Pin Head to have another go as the shop mechanic because Charlie didn't have to pay him in cash.

Charlie gave the motorcycle to Pin Head up front again, and Pin Head promised to stay out of trouble with the cops. When Pin Head finished paying off the bike with his labor and installing all the fancy horns and lights that were his signature style, he asked Charlie if he could be paid in cash. Since Charlie was happy with Pin Head's mechanics and customers' bikes were being fixed and he was making money, Charlie agreed to pay Pin Head weekly as the mechanic.

Pin Head came in the shop laughing one afternoon and said, "I just heard Willy was involved in a large drug bust down at a car shop he's working at about a half a mile away. Some people who worked there were selling drugs out of the place. The cops raided the shop, took everyone to jail and closed the place down. Willy was found on the toilet in a bathroom stall just about to shoot up some heroin when a cop kicked open the door of the stall with his gun drawn and told Willy to freeze. Willy looked at the cop and his gun and realized that if he was going to jail he wanted to be high, so he took his chances the cop wouldn't shoot him and he quickly slammed the syringe into his arm vein and depressed the plunger." Pin Head couldn't stop laughing.

With Pin Head and me running the shop, it now left more time for Charlie to socialize with his friends and race buddies. When Dave Bostrom came by, he occasionally brought Eric with him and they talked with Charlie's other dirt tracker friends in the office about the world of racing. One new guy, who was hanging out at the shop more, worked his way into Charlie's group of friends. His name was Pat.

I walked into the office where Charlie and Pat were talking and Charlie said to me as he sat at his desk, "My new friend Pat has some good ideas about how to run this place more efficiently. I think we can use a guy like him to run the front counter, and he can help us make more money around here to pay the rent.

Pat sat at my desk arrogantly smoking a Marlboro cigarette when Charlie spun back around in his chair shuffling some papers saying, "So that's the new deal then. Pin Head is the mechanic, and Pat will run the front counter. You can handle everything else that needs to be done around here, so I can take more time off and go to the races to watch the Bostroms win. Ben just finished sixth place in the AMA 600cc national championship dirt track series with us sponsoring him."

He said firmly, "Things will change now with Pat in the shop and I expect to run a tight ship around here. I want you to tell Pin Head the new deal with Pat."

I didn't like what Charlie told me about Pat since I thought he didn't seem to fit the role of running Charlie's shop too well. He was just about Charlie's age, and I began to wonder where he came from and what he was doing before he started to hang out and work his way into Charlie's group of friends.

He was an older large guy who looked like he knew how to throw his weight around, and he spoke about having lots of wisdom understanding and handling different types of people. He was unshaved with a thick grey untrimmed mustache, and his wild messy white hair was dirty and yellowed. He wore greasy clothes with holes in them and constantly chain smoked cigarettes. Pat was a confident man who was the first to out talk anyone in the room with his quick wit and humorous one liner jokes. He would always finish a person's sentence with his unsolicited advice on what ever subject he claimed to be an expert in.

Charlie fell for his impression of motorcycle knowledge because he felt Pat would be an improvement around the shop.

I, however, knew we were in for trouble.

1993

Pat had new ideas as to how the shop should run, and Charlie thought most of Pat's ideas were great. Pat told Charlie the shop was managed incorrectly. He said the shop would run better if customers didn't have to wait at the counter and were allowed to enter the entire building to pick through everything to find what they wanted. The customers could then pay for their parts at the counter, where Pat would sit all day and drink coffee while smoking Marlboro cigarettes.

The problem was when customers came in the back to find their parts they didn't know where to look, so I had a new purpose: locating parts as well as dismantling the junk bikes. Pin Head was working out okay as the mechanic but now became involved in a contest with Pat to see who could dazzle the customers more with their bullshit.

Over the years, Charlie's salvage operation became completely filled to capacity with engine and wheel piles. The junk parts covered nearly every square foot of floor space. When the motorcycles were dismantled, scrap frames and engines were piled up in large volumes next to the side door, awaiting removal by a series of different guys who made their living picking up scrap metal to turn in at a metal recycler for money. I began to know a few of these guys well, and I knew they wanted the more valuable aluminum to recycle rather than the cheap iron and steel.

One afternoon after the junk pile had crawled fairly high up the wall and needed to be moved, I heard the metal collectors pulling up on the side. The father of the team pulled the side door open and stuck his head in and said, "Hey, you guys got any metal that needs to go out?" I said that he and his son could take the entire pile that was located by the side door. The man said smiling, "That pile's mostly cheap steel that I can't get any money for. Don't you got any good aluminum for recycle so a black man can have steak for dinner tonight instead of hamburger?"

I had a small pile of aluminum engines nearby from the latest round of dismantling, so I told the man and his son they could have the engines if they remove the steel too.

They loaded the frames and heavy metal when suddenly a car pulled up to the side door and a guy stepped out.

I was surprised to see it was Arty, Dave Bostrom's old employee. He said to me, "Is your dad here?" I hadn't seen Arty since Dave Bostrom's Honda dealership closed. I asked him where he'd been, and he said, "Amsterdam, dude. They have the best killer marijuana there and guess what? It's all legal." He walked past me looking for Charlie.

After Arty visited with Charlie for about 30 minutes, he came in the back and said to me, "Dude, I have good quality marijuana for sale I'm carrying in my pack, if you know anyone who wants to score some call me anytime. This stuff is the best, and I have a little sample if you want to try it out. Charlie is busy in the office with that old guy you have working here. They have some maps out on the desk, and they're talking about where they want to go sport bike riding this weekend."

We retreated to the very back of the shop and up a small wooden ladder to the secret smoke room. Arty opened his pack and reached in between the small bags of weed for sale and pulled out a joint. He lit it up and inhaled deeply. Arty passed me the joint and then said, "I want to tell you about my new business venture that I'm getting into. I have this new deal going with a friend to send black market Japanese two stroke sport bikes into this country from Asia by container."

By now two stroke engine street bikes were banned for several years in the United States because of exhaust emissions and noise, especially in California. I asked Arty, "How do you get them in the country?"

He said, "I can get the bikes into this country by stating on the paperwork forms at customs that they're intended to be used as parts only." Arty passed me the joint again and said, "The bikes I'll bring in from Japan only have an eleven digit VIN numbers on the frame instead of the standard seventeen digit VIN number. Charlie says to get them registered I can state the motorcycles are pre-1980 models on the paperwork because motorcycles weren't made with seventeen digit VIN numbers before 1980."

Arty told me he planned to make good money because people in the United States wanted to pay him up to $6,000 for these hard-to-get black market two stroke sport bikes. He said confidently, "I know I'll make tons of money selling these bikes cause everybody wants 250cc sport bikes, and as long as I can get them titled by Charlie, I can get them all sold. That's why I'm here; I heard that your dad is the hook-up on paperwork deals."

Arty gathered his things, and we climbed down the ladder from the smoke room. I was startled when Pin Head jumped out from behind the corner and said, "I knew I smelled something really good back here. Next time you guys better invite me too."

As Arty and I walked by him, Pin Head said bragging, "Charlie never knows when I'm smoking weed here in the back and I don't need to use your secret smoke room to hide." Pin Head motioned for me to look at the side of the metal building where he cut a hole and pushed a rubber motorcycle hose through the hole while he said laughing, "I made this set up here so I can inhale a toke of weed then blow the smoke through the hose to go outside the building so Charlie never knows when I'm smoking pot because it never smells like dope in here."

After Arty left, I walked in the office and grabbed my lunch out of the refrigerator. Charlie and Pat still had the maps on the desk, planning out their motorcycle ride. Charlie talked to Pat about a ride they were taking with Mikey and Petey that would start out on the Sunday morning ride in Marin County. One of Charlie's friends then came into the office, and Charlie said out loud with a smile, "Hey, its Cal the car guy."

Cal was the latest addition to Charlie's network of friends who met in the office more frequently. He wore a thick white mustache that matched his shinny white hair which he kept neatly clipped. He was a few years older than Charlie, and he also retired from his line of work and was involved full time with his hobbies riding bikes and playing with cars. Cal joined Charlie and his friends on their sport bike rides every weekend. He recently upgraded to a near new condition BMW K1100RS. Cal and Charlie were also participating in 24-hour rallies and long distance rides together since Charlie had recently acquired a built up BMW K1100 from Ed Woo.

Pat also became a fixture with Charlie and his riding buddies. He would go on their Sunday Morning rides with them every weekend.

He was now coming to work in the mornings with a new bike about every two weeks. Pat always said he acquired his newest ride by finding a great deal in the classified section of the newspaper or through a friend, or by luck cleaning out someone's garage. I was puzzled because most of the bikes Pat showed up on were pristine condition bikes from the 1980's. He even showed up once on a mint condition 1984 Yamaha RZ350 Kenny Roberts replica. I questioned him about where he bought such a hard-to-find bike in such great condition and he answered, "Oh, this old thing. I just bought it from an old lady who wanted to get it out of her garage because it was taking up too much space."

One morning a rider pulled up on a 1988 BMW K75 and I saw it was Ed Woo. He asked, "How do you like my latest Beemer kid? I just finished putting it all together, I came by this morning to see Charlie about getting it registered and titled." As I checked out Ed's bike he said, "How's that new wife of yours doing? Tell her I need to get a haircut the next time she comes down to cut Charlie's hair."

Ed and Pat were in the office socializing when Charlie arrived. He walked in with somebody I was surprised and happy to see. It was my grandfather, visiting from Connecticut to see my mom. He and my grandmother came to California once in a while and stayed a few months at Charlie's house.

Charlie was happy to see Ed, and they talked about Ed's BMW while I greeted my grandfather and showed him around the shop catching up on old times. My grandfather said, "I've been waiting a long time to see you. When will I see your new wife?" I told him that I would bring Bert over to the house this week.

A few days later, Ed visited the shop with a black Porsche. The window rolled down to expose a smiling Ed with sunglasses on. He said, "I'm here because today Bert's supposed to come by and cut my hair, right?"

I answered Ed while checking out his newest Porsche 911 "Yes, you're right. She's coming in the afternoon to cut Charlie's and Pat's hair too."

As Ed closed the door and began walking into the shop I said, "Damn. This is a nice car, are you still hanging with those big boys?"

Ed smiled while waving hello to Charlie, "Fuck, yeah. I just put that car together, and I already have somebody who wants to buy it."

Later in the afternoon, Bert arrived after she got off work. She walked into a busy office crowded with Charlie's riding friends and Ed, while Pat was occupied talking at the front counter with the last few customers of the day. Charlie smiled and said, "Hey, its haircut time. I'm first." Charlie spun around in his chair, and Bert began to cut his hair and said, "Guess what, Charlie? I quit my job at the salon I work at, and I'm opening my own small two-chair salon and will be my own boss."

Charlie asked Bert as she continued to cut, "That's great news. Where's your new shop located?" She answered, "Marin County, across the Golden Gate Bridge."

Ed interrupted and said, "I can come by and check out your new place and get my hair cut because I'm in Marin County all the time."

She turned and said to Ed, "Great, I'll be in San Rafael. Do you know where that is?"

Ed smiled at Bert while flipping through a motorcycle magazine and said, "I know where San Rafael is, and let's just say I know my way around every square inch of Marin County, from Sausalito all the way through Petaluma to Tomales Bay on the coast." Bert smiled as she finished up Charlie's haircut and said, "Well, you can come by any time when I have the place open. I'll be happy to see you there."

Bert always interacted well with all the guys from the shop. She was nice to all of them even though she knew some were shady. She could hold her own in a conversation with the motorcycle guys, especially Pat. They would go back and forth with their wit, laughing with each other. After all, she was around the shop since the beginning when she was married to Joe.

Haircut time would put Charlie and the gang in a good mood at the end of the day. Charlie stood up from his seat and brushed himself off and said, "Okay, now I know that you charge those other assholes downtown a lot of money for a haircut, but I'm still free, right? After all, I'm your new dad." She agreed and giggled while Charlie gave her a hug.

Ed jumped up and said, "I'm next" as he sat down in the chair and Bert finished up his haircut in a short while.

When Ed was done, he said to Charlie as he was leaving, "I'll let you know when I have that new BMW I'm building ready. Give me a call anytime when my paperwork is done." Ed said goodbye to us and left the office at the same time Pat walked in, now finished with the day's customers and ready to have his hair cut. Bert took one look at Pat's dirty hair and tossed him the bottle of shampoo kept on Charlie's desk because she insisted that everyone at least have a clean head at the time of the haircut. The only water spigot was on the side of the building so Pat walked outside to wash his hair.

Pat returned and sat in the chair while Bert started to cut his hair. He said looking up at her, "How are things going downtown in the hair business? I eat dinner in San Francisco all the time downtown at a restaurant called Stars. I know the owner there, and they always treat me like a VIP."

Bert found it hard to believe that Pat frequented high-end eating establishments, based on the fact that most of the time Pat's wardrobe consisted of dirty pants with holes and old shoes with no laces. On some days Pat wouldn't even wear socks. She said while cutting his hair, "You're just kidding me, right? I seriously doubt that you eat at Stars in San Francisco dressed like you do and unshaven as you are. You look like you'd be hanging out at a biker bar in Brisbane instead."

Pat wise-cracked and said laughing, "Like I said, I know the owner at Stars, and they always have a booth reserved for me so I don't have to wait." We all doubted him.

When she finished all the haircuts, Pat said he was leaving for the night. He grabbed his helmet and jacket, said goodbye and walked out the door.

With Pat gone, Charlie sat at his desk counting up the day's receipts. He turned and looked at Bert, put his hand on her shoulder and advised her while laughing, "You can't believe everything Pat tells you because he thinks he's been to the moon and back without a rocket ship. Don't listen to a word he says because he's full of shit. A guy like Pat is a manipulator who learns to control people by finding what their weaknesses are and then exploiting them. Kind of like, what you would call mind control. That's why I have him working around here, because he can get into a customer's mind and make them believe they need to buy junk. Hey...Pat can sell fucking ice cubes to an Eskimo."

As we all laughed, Charlie packed up his money and some other things and said while leaving the shop, "Okay, you guys are coming over to the house tonight to see grandma and grandpa and give him his haircut, right?" I told him we would be there.

A few days later, it was a quiet weekend at my house in Fairfield when Bert said she had some shopping she wanted to do in Sacramento and asked me to come along. It was mid-morning when Bert and I climbed into the car and headed east on interstate Highway 80 toward Sacramento. Bert was driving, and I was fumbling with the radio about twenty minutes into the drive. As we rolled along the freeway I noticed something out the front window of the car. We were traveling in the left lane while gaining steadily on a vehicle in the center lane pulling a trailer with two small road racing motorcycles.

As we approached and drove along the left side of the trailer, I noticed the road racing motorcycles were Yamaha YSR50 bikes that were heavily modified for racing only. When we passed by the car towing the trailer I saw that the car was a Pontiac Fiero. When the driver and his passenger turned their heads and looked at me, I was very surprised and said to Bert, "Those two scruffy surf dudes are Ben and Eric Bostrom. They must be racing around here somewhere because those YSR50s are not usable on the street anymore because they look as if they've been transformed for racing purposes only." As we pulled away in front I wondered about Ben and Eric and those YSR50s.

Ed Woo screeched to a stop in front of the shop one morning on his Yamaha FZR1000. He said, "I have to pick up my paperwork from Charlie. Is he here yet?"

I told him Charlie was in the office and Ed suddenly dropped the clutch on the FZR and shot through the front door of the shop and skid the bike to a halt next to the office door.

Ed met with Charlie for 15 minutes and then climbed on his bike. Standing near his bike, I asked him if he planned to ride his FZR1000 on the Sunday ride with Charlie. He answered as he strapped his helmet, "I can't go riding with Charlie and his gang tomorrow because I have a ride planned out with my friends." I asked him who he was riding with and as Ed fired the engine and proceeded to do a large burnout in the shop he said, "With the big boys, kid. Who do you think?" Ed disappeared in an instant.

I was finishing up with a customer when I walked in the office. Charlie was happy, bragging loudly to his friends, "The good news is that Ben Bostrom is now the new AMA 600cc dirt track champion with my shop sponsoring him."

Charlie's friends were all happy as well. Charlie said he was sponsoring the Bostroms now for years and that Eric was really kicking ass as well in the dirt track ranks around the country.

One morning in the later part of the year, Charlie came to work with some bike magazines saying, "Here's the latest editions that I'm finished reading so you can have them to read."

He looked at me and said as he handed me the pile, "Remember when world champion motorcycle road racer Wayne Rainey crashed a few months ago in Italy? I read that he's now paralyzed and will never walk or ride again because his Marlboro Yamaha race bike ran over him while he crashed and his back was broken."

Charlie sat down at his desk as I said to him, "Man it would be cool if we could get the salvage wreck on that bike, right Charlie?" He smugly replied, "No chance on that one because Wayne Rainey's wrecked race bike would still be worth one million dollars and nobody can get their hands on those bikes because they are only made and owned by the factories that race them."

Wayne Rainey's career ending motorcycle accident was a shock to racing fans in the United States and fans around the world. The future of the Marlboro Yamaha Kenny Roberts' Evil Empire race team was in doubt because of the crushing and tragic results.

1994

Charlie honked the horn a few times one morning at the shop, around the beginning of the New Year. I slid open the side door to see him sitting in the driver's seat of a brand new 35-foot-long motor home. The vehicle's blue and white finish gleamed in the morning sun. This motor home was unlike any of the junky ones that Charlie had in the past. Charlie yelled out, "I just bought this because I want to take it traveling to the races on weekends with my friends."

Charlie parked the motor home and said he only could stay a short time because he had to store it at an area nearby. Pat walked out the side door and asked Charlie, "Wow. How much did you have to pay for that?"

Charlie responded, "I made a great deal and only had to pay them $40,000 for it."

I was surprised because Charlie never paid high money for big ticket items and still always complained about having no money around the shop. I asked Charlie, "Are you making time payments on it?"

He answered arrogantly, "I don't make time payments on anything. I pay cash because I don't believe in any of that credit and time payment bullshit." I thought even if you added up the money from all the good and bad days around the shop, it would be a very long time before he could come up with $40,000 cash for a motor home. I started to wonder where Charlie found that kind of money if he wasn't making it in the shop.

With Pat running things, Charlie planned most of his weekends that he wasn't riding sport bikes around his other interests. He and his friends were involved with motorcycle trials riding and vintage racing. Events were held around the state, so Charlie took some Saturdays off, leaving Pat and I to run things around the shop with Pin Head.

One morning after a long weekend, Pin Head came to work looking awful. He had open sores on his arms and face. Pat looked horrified and said, "You look like shit. What the hell have you been doing to yourself?"

Pin Head walked past Pat into the back of the shop, and Pat said to me, "I know Pin Head's high on speed and lying to us about not using drugs. He's taking that shit, and it keeps him awake for days. He gets agitated and picks his skin himself and that's what causes all that damage. The problem is that some customers are coming in with children, and Pin Head will scare the young kids with his fucked up appearance."

Laughing while he puffed his cigarette he said, "How am I supposed to sell junk to a guy, who doesn't need junk, when the guy sees Pin Head working on the junk in that condition?"

Charlie was working the telephones one afternoon while Pat went across the street to get a hamburger at a small café. Charlie hung up the telephone after speaking with a customer and walked into the back saying eagerly, "The Germans are coming, the Germans are coming. Get ready because some guys from Germany are coming to buy old bikes and parts to take back home to Germany."

Charlie told me the Germans were mostly looking for old Kawasaki KZ900 and KZ1000 bikes and parts. He said, "The old Kawasaki's are hard to find in mint condition, and that's what these guys are looking for."

Since I was familiar with almost everything Charlie had in his shop, I said to him, "We don't have any of those bikes in good condition. We only have loose engines and parts from a few wrecked bikes we broke down over the years."

He replied, "Well, these guys are coming in the next couple of days to look for all sorts of parts like carburetors and wheels and things like that."

As Charlie walked away I said, "Hey, Charlie, maybe the guys from Germany can find some old used Kawasaki's up at Mission Motorcycle's in Daly City."

Charlie turned to me and said, "Oh yeah, I forgot to tell you. The good news is, Mission Motorcycles is now a full on Honda and Yamaha dealership again, but Dave doesn't have anything to do with the business. Honda and Yamaha wouldn't let Dave have a dealership anymore, so they put the dealership in the new owner's name."

I said, "Did Dave sell the building to the new owners?"

He answered, "Dave still owns the building, but nobody knows it, and the good thing is the new dealership still pays Dave rent."

A few minutes later, Dave and Eric walked through the side door to visit with Charlie when he said, "I have to meet with Dave and Eric in the office a while and talk turkey before the Germans get here. I need you to answer the phones and keep an eye on the front counter while I'm busy in the office and until Pat gets back from lunch."

Sitting at the front counter, I thought that Charlie seemed almost over-excited that these Germans were coming to spend a bunch of money. We never before had a group of guys from Germany visit the shop and Charlie never had much success in the past selling large amounts of junk from his shop to any of his international clients. Most of the European customers only bought small amounts of parts. They were mostly fond of the California model igniter boxes and would try to collect as many as they could find.

Many times Charlie was busy doing paperwork deals for Dave and a variety of different characters. This included Dick, the customer who bought bikes and sold them out of his home. Dick would also give Charlie paperwork to do for him for motorcycles he said he purchased from other people. I wondered why Dick wouldn't just get the paperwork from the people he was buying the bikes from. Charlie would process the papers for him all the time.

In addition to these paperwork customers we were seeing more of Arty, the parts guy at Dave's old Honda dealership. Arty was now riding his black market two stroke engine sport bikes down to the shop frequently. Charlie verified the frame and engine number so Arty could register his motorcycles in California even though Charlie violated many EPA and DMV laws on the books in order to do this for Arty.

While looking through the small glass windows of the office I could see Dave and Charlie talking excitingly about something I couldn't hear. Eric was seated in the office, listening.

Pat returned from lunch and asked me how things were going. I said, "Everything's running smoothly, I'm helping customers and Charlie is in the office talking with Dave and Eric." Pat fired up a Marlboro, walked in the office and closed the door. I saw through the window that Dave was very happy to see him while Pat said a friendly hello to Eric and joined in the conversation.

After the four of them walked out of the office and the Bostroms left, Charlie began fumbling with some things and said, "Okay, let's get to work around here so we can make some fucking money."

Pin Head wasn't working today because he became less dependable due to his increasing drug use so Pat and I made ourselves look busy so Charlie would be happy.

In the afternoon, Charlie left to go to lunch with a few of his friends, and I heard that familiar bellowing from Pat up in the front: "Tire change!"

As I worked on the bike, Pat fired up another Marlboro and watched. I said to Pat while loosening the rear wheel, "You know, some time last year I saw Ben and Eric towing a trailer loaded with two Yamaha YSR50 race modified bikes with a white Pontiac Fiero, driving on Interstate 80 towards Sacramento."

Pat arrogantly replied, "You're wrong about that. It's a black Fiero." He turned and abruptly walked off up front. I thought, how could he know what color the car was?

Over the course of the next few months, Pat constantly talked about his motorcycle sport bike riding trips with Charlie and his other friends. Pat also showed up to work in the mornings on a different motorcycle all the time.

One bright summer morning, I pulled up to the shop and noticed Pat was washing down yet another bike. I said, "Hey, you're here early. Is this your newest bike?"

Pat told me he recently purchased the bike saying, "This is my new 1978 Kawasaki KZ750 twin cylinder bike, and it runs great." I was surprised to see Pat with such an old bike; it wasn't like the other bikes he recently showed up with, which included a 1988 Honda CBR1000 Hurricane and a Yamaha Fazer 750, both in near perfect condition. As Pat finished hosing down his bike he said, "My new bike has good torque and handles great on tight roads. The narrow engine gives the bike good balance, so it drives well on dirt roads or on the street."

This wasn't the first time I saw Pat washing down his bikes in the morning. Charlie gave Pat his own set of keys so he could open the shop if he arrived first. On certain mornings Pat would already be in the process of washing dust off his bike by the time I arrived. I wondered how he was getting his street bikes so dirty all the time during the spring and summer weather when it didn't rain.

I thought I would inquire further about Pat's newest bike as he rolled it to the side to dry off in the sun. "I can't believe the condition your bike is in. It almost appears original, like you just bought it off a dealership's show room floor. Where did you find it?" Pat said, "Oh, I found a great deal on this one from an old lady cleaning out her garage. She just wanted to get rid of the thing."

Doubting what he said, I replied, "Yeah right. That's where you tell me you find all of your bikes. You seem to know a bunch of old ladies cleaning out their garages."

Pat laughed and said while lighting up a cigarette, "Well...I do know a lot of old ladies, and they all need to be cleaned out, if you know what I mean."

I said, "These bikes that you show up with are always dirty and need to be cleaned, so I guess all the old ladies have dirty garages then, right Pat?"

Pat puffed his cigarette and said, "Some I buy dirty, but this one is dirty because I used this bike to race Ben and Eric up the dirt driveway to their house. And since this bike handles so well I can defeat the both of them easily."

Pat claimed that he grew close to the Bostroms and Ed Woo since he started working at Charlie's shop. He began to talk openly about life up at the house he called Verna's place. Charlie stopped talking about Verna years before, and Verna wasn't mentioned around the shop for a long time until Pat showed up. Now Pat and Charlie talked about Verna as if they were visiting her frequently. I wondered how long Verna's driveway could possibly be if they were racing full-sized bikes on it, and where it was even located.

I got the impression that Verna's place might not be too far away from Charlie's shop. Charlie used to talk about Verna having a place in the country with large barns for bikes. I recalled when Steve said that Ben's mom Verna stashed all her good bikes in the country when she closed her Honda dealership in Oakland years back.

Charlie was excited one day about a ride he was planning. After he invited me along he told me where the ride would take place and who was coming. Charlie said, "Mikey, Petey, Cal and I will meet at a gas station in Sausalito with a couple of other guys. If you're going, you should meet us there at eight in the morning and don't be late."

When the phone rang, Charlie said, "Why don't you and Pat help the customers and answer the phones, while I take care of some paperwork here in the office." As I picked up the phone I saw Pin Head walking into the shop.

It was a few days since he reported for work, so Pat jumped down his throat right away and said, "You look like crap. Where the hell have you been? Have you been shooting up again?"

Pin Head was holding an open quart of cream and after he took a big sip, he said angrily to Pat, "I'm not shooting up drugs these days. I'm only on methadone."

Pat started laughing and said, "If you're only using methadone then your face wouldn't be full of open sores. You're picking your face again and what's with the cream?"

Pin Head grew angrier and said, "The reason why I haven't been here working isn't because of drugs; it's because my teeth are all fucked up and they hurt. I don't have any money to see a dentist so that's why I'm drinking this cream, because it's the only thing that relieves the pain in my mouth."

Pat said, "Your teeth are only rotted out because you've been shooting up speed for thirty years. If this was my shop, I would've fired your ass a long time ago."

Pin Head smirked as he walked in the office to see Charlie and said, "Well, I only work for Charlie, not you."

I woke up on Sunday morning to have an early cup of coffee with Bert. She decided to stay home with our daughter while I got ready for the ride to Sausalito. It was cold in the early morning as I pointed the bike west and opened the throttle for a quick ride to meet up with Charlie in Marin. When I arrived at the gas station, I found Charlie and his group but was surprised when I didn't see Pat among them. I asked Charlie, "Where's Pat? Isn't he coming on the ride?"

Charlie said, "He is, but he had a few things to do this morning so he's meeting up with our group on Highway 1 in Marshall on Tomales Bay."

We all rode up Highway 1 on the twisting, tight coastal road. Charlie and Cal led the way, followed by Mikey and Petey. They were setting a brisk pace as I followed along on my ZX10, staying close to the fast-moving group of bikes in front of me. The morning coastal air was thick with fog as I rode along carefully on the wet pavement. A while later, Charlie pulled over on the side of the road in Marshall and said, "We'll wait for Pat here. This is the intersection where he's meeting us."

Charlie pointed at a small side road and said, "That's the road Pat's riding down, it's a shortcut back to Novato."

As we sat on our bikes and waited for Pat to arrive, I looked up the small side road and noticed an old red church a short distance up the hill. I remembered as we rode into Marshall I saw a small ghost fleet of boats in the water, and I thought it could be the side road that Pin Head talked about when he needed to ditch the police and hide behind a little red church just outside of Marshall.

Charlie interrupted my thoughts and said, "We should only have to wait here about twenty minutes. Pat left his place in Alameda a while ago and should be here soon."

Three minutes later, the morning silence was broken by the sound of a fast-moving motorcycle coming down the hill. I could hear the bike's engine before I saw it pull into my sight. A moment later, a near new condition black BMW K1100RS motorcycle with bright yellow wheels and no front fairing came zooming down the hill. The BMW stopped in front of Charlie, and the rider pulled his helmet off. It was Pat, and he looked like he just woke up. He wore no socks with his shoes, and his shoelaces were not tied.

Charlie said to Pat, "Hey, you're early. We didn't expect you for another twenty minutes."

Pat answered arrogantly as he pulled out a Marlboro, "It only took me thirty minutes to get here from Alameda, and I even made a gas stop and had a cigarette." I thought it was virtually impossible for Pat to make it all the way out to the Marin coast from the Alameda/Oakland area in only thirty minutes. Pat rode fast, but nobody was that fast.

Cal and Charlie led the way up the tight dangerous winding road of the California coast, with the rest of us following along at high speed. It wasn't long before Pat wanted to take the lead and he raced past Cal and Charlie on a sweeping high speed turn at close to 90 MPH. Pat pulled away from the group as we continued riding for the next two hours. After we stopped for a break and for Pat to have a cigarette, Charlie said to the group, "We're going to take this small tight road back over these mountains to go inland and have some lunch." We all followed Charlie east with the group dicing back and forth at high speed on the twisting tree lined road meandering through the woods for the next hour until we arrived at a small forest café.

Once our party was seated for lunch outdoors on a shady terrace, I said to Pat, who sat next to me, "Let me guess: Another old lady with a garage that needed to be cleaned out, right? Just get this BMW sport bike out of here with the rest of the trash."

Smiling, Pat said, "No you're wrong about that. This BMW was just built for me by Ed Woo."

I said to Pat, "What's with the small headlight and no fairings on your BMW?"

He answered as he devoured his food, "It's a street fighter; that's the new style."

After we finished eating, Charlie said, "Let's hit the road because we still have a long way to go on today's ride before it gets dark."

For the next hour Charlie led all of us on unfamiliar hidden roads that most people wouldn't even know existed. Winding down through the woods, we finally came to a part of the road we couldn't cross because a stream was blocking our way. The narrow road was submerged under a foot of fast-moving water. Mikey and Cal were immediately worried because Mikey didn't want to get his motorcycle dirty by riding through the stream, and Cal also thought it was a bad idea as Charlie talked about an alternate route. Riding the ZX10 to Fairfield during the winters I rode through rain storms and flooded streets many times. I knew I could easily cross the stream and said to the gang, "I'll give it a try, and show you guys how easy it is when I make it to the other side."

I pulled in my clutch, dropped the bike into first gear and charged my ZX10 into the stream. The motorcycle was submerged up to the wheels as I applied more throttle to drive through the water. Once on the other side, I gassed the bike and the rear wheel spun on the wet pavement as I rode to a stop. I turned around and yelled to the group, "It's only about 10 feet across and not too deep. I'm sure all you guys can make it fine." Pat confidently charged his bike into the stream after me and made it easily across.

Cal elected to try next and gingerly entered the stream. He was successful in his crossing, but when he attempted to gas the bike spinning his rear wheel like Pat and I, the power of his BMW took Cal by surprise, and his bike snapped one way and then the other as he tried to steer the machine. He lost control of the bike, and his BMW slammed on the ground at low speed, depositing Cal on the wet pavement. I jumped off my bike to assist him as the others quickly rode across the stream without incident. Cal was very upset because one of the expensive mirrors broke off and his nice bike was scraped up due to his attempted hot-dogging.

The next leg of the ride was an uphill section of tight road. Cal figured since his bike wasn't new anymore because of his crash, he would ride faster. He was in the lead climbing up the hill, with me right behind him and the others following, when Cal lost control and drifted off the road. His bike went off the side and down the mountain, crashing into a large pile of tall grass and dirt. Cal was thrown over the handlebars when the bike abruptly stopped in the mud and thick brush.

I stopped and looked over the embankment and I saw Cal's bike locked in some bushes but still in an upright position. Charlie and the rest of the guys parked their bikes and proceeded to climb down the hill. Cal was upside down in some bushes and lucky to have no injuries because of his durable riding gear. He was angry by now and said with a growl, "I don't even know what happened. I just blanked out and went right over the side."

We helped Cal out of the tangled branches and leaves and over to his bike to assess the damage. I was amazed that Cal wasn't hurt; he was several years older than Charlie, who was sixty.

Cal thought we would have to call a tow truck and that his day was finished, but I said to him, "I don't think your bike has any damage. We can just push it back up the hill all together because it doesn't have any vital parts broken off."

We pulled in Cal's clutch lever and pushed his bike in reverse up the steep hill on the same path it took. We worked together to get the bike up a distance of 40 feet. Once back on the road Cal fired the engine and even though the bike was now all muddy and scraped up, the dependable BMW ran well and was still okay to drive.

We continued on our journey until the afternoon, when we all pulled to a stop just outside of Petaluma. We just finished riding on a bumpy, narrow road that traversed through open country landscapes, with many cows grazing on grassy green hills as far as the eye could see. While stopped in the center of a quiet intersection late in the day, Charlie lifted up his visor and said to me as he pointed down the road, "If you ride down this road east it'll take you to Novato for your trip back to Fairfield."

With his gloved thumb, Charlie pointed west toward the other road and said, "The guys and I are riding to the coast and then back home." He and his friends rode away, heading west into the setting evening sun. I thought it would be nice if I could follow them out to the coast, but it was the end of the day and I was ready to get home because it was getting dark and I still had another hour and a half to ride.

Back at the shop the following week, Pat pulled up in the front, driving an old Dodge pickup truck I never saw before. He had two motorcycles in the back as he pointed to the bikes and said, "This one's a 1986 Yamaha SRX600 single cylinder, and the other one's a Honda Helix 250 scooter."

As I checked out the bikes Pat said to me, "I have to get these unloaded and clean them up because I'm selling one and keeping the other." When Pat finished unloading them I checked out the SRX600 because they were rare, and it was in near pristine condition with barely any miles on the odometer.

Both of the bikes appeared dusty and needed to be washed down so Pat quickly rinsed the dust off and fired up the SRX. He rode the bike back over to where his pickup was located and raced it up a ramp into the back of his truck with no problem. He turned his head and boasted, "I picked up that trick hanging out with Ben and Eric Bostrom."

In the heat of the racing season, Charlie came to work and said, "I'm leaving tomorrow on a motor home trip to watch Ben and Eric race. I'm going away for a two-week racing trip with some of my buddies."

Charlie said he would bring the motor home to the shop and have Pin Head help him install a small bike-carrying rack on the rear of the motor home so he could carry his brand new, recently purchased Gas-Gas trials bike along.

Charlie left and returned with his motor home while Pin Head was out to lunch so Charlie pulled the motor home in the back to install the rack. He wanted to start the work right away without Pin Head so he called for me to help him hold and position the rack.

While we worked together, Charlie said, "Hey, I was up at my friend's shop, and one of the guys who works there told me you're selling him your ZX10."

I told Charlie that a guy was interested in it and offered me $4,500. I said, "I wore the bike out these last few years commuting, and I could really use the money for paying bills. I'm using my old pickup truck for commuting now."

He looked back at me as he attempted to line up the holes of the rack under the motor home and said, "Without a motorcycle you won't be able to cut between the cars to get here to work on time. You'll be stuck in traffic like all those other assholes on the freeway."

Charlie continued to fumble with the rack and said, "Well, I need you here on time in the mornings because this place needs to be open at nine sharp, especially with me taking off for a few weeks."

I said, "I'll do my best to be here on time in the truck, but I can't help it if I'm stuck in traffic."

As Charlie pinched his finger badly on the rack he yelled out angrily, "Hey, you bought the fucking traffic when you bought that house far away, and you'd better be here on time because this place needs to be open!"

I snapped back, "I wouldn't have bought a house far away if I could have afforded to buy one closer to the shop."

Charlie threw down his wrench and stormed in the shop, saying, "Well, like I said, you bought the fucking traffic!"

About a week into Charlie's motor home vacation things were running fairly smoothly around the shop. Pat and Pin Head dazzled for the affections of the customers constantly. Pin Head, with his self-imposed wizard-like skills in working on customers' bikes, felt he was one up on Pat, who only possessed his gift of gab and mind control on the customers. However, things didn't run smoothly concerning a small group of Charlie's other friends who came in to whine and complain that Charlie wasn't there to do their paperwork deals. Arty, Dick and Ed Woo were the most problematic.

One afternoon, before Charlie returned from his vacation, Arty rode up to the shop on one of his black market Japanese bikes. He pulled off his helmet and said, "Hey, I came by to see if Charlie is here and show you guys my newest bike I smuggled into the country."

Arty gestured to his bike and said, "This is a Honda VFR400, which isn't available for sale in the United States anywhere, except my new shop I opened in San Francisco called Smarty Sports."

I told Arty, Charlie wouldn't return to the shop for a few more days. He said to me, "Damn, that's no good. I really need to get my paperwork picked up from Charlie, so I can get these bikes registered. I have buyers waiting who want to pay me six grand per bike." Arty rode off back to San Francisco disappointed.

When Charlie returned from his motor home race trip, he was already in the process of planning his next trip because he needed to get his traveling done before the weather turned cold and rainy for the year.

Near the end of the year was when Charlie ceased his traveling and settled down. The people who were happiest about that were Ed, Arty and Dick. Ed and Dave were coming around on a regular basis since Charlie returned from his travels. They discussed paperwork issues with Charlie and the status of the next BMW sport bike or Porsche automobile Ed was building.

Dick, on the other hand, was an entirely different deal. Dick wasn't even a motorcycle rider; he only sold bikes and acted like he was an expert in the field in order to impress young girls and make money selling bikes out of his home. He was always whining to Charlie because he would have his bikes ready for sale before Charlie processed his DMV paperwork for him.

I walked in the office one afternoon where I saw Dave Bostrom and Charlie sitting around talking about racing. Dave was telling an excited Charlie how well Ben and Eric finished the year out racing and how proud he was that both Ben and Eric were now professional racers for Harley Davidson. As Dave finished with his visit and said goodbye, I noticed he held a small stack of blank receipts from Charlie's shop in his hand. After he was gone, I asked Charlie, "Why does Dave have a stack of your shop's blank receipts?"

Charlie spun around in his chair and barked, "None of your fucking business. Like I told you before, why don't you get to fucking work and stop asking questions about my deals with Dave?"

Many years later I would find out why Dave needed the blank receipts more than he needed the bottles of oil and cans of chain lube which became a staple in the Charlie sponsored Bostrom racing program.

1995

During the early part of the year, Charlie came into work and told me that my mother was flying to the East Coast with my grandparents and Charlie was taking the motor home on a cross-country drive to Daytona, Florida. He was driving to the AMA races to watch Ben and Eric race and then travel up the eastern seaboard through Washington D.C. Afterwards he would head north to New England to meet up with her in Connecticut.

The early spring months around Charlie's shop were slow for motorcycle business, so Charlie knew he could take time off, with Pat running the shop. Charlie also made more time available to be with his own children, who were young adults by now. His oldest son was married and divorced, with a young son whom he was raising. He was recently remarried to a girl with a couple of children, and the two of them moved to Reno, Nevada a while back and they were now expecting a child of their own together. Charlie visited Reno frequently to see his oldest son so they could ride dirt bikes all over the hills around Reno and the eastern Sierra Nevada mountain range. Charlie was still athletic for a guy his age. He also enjoyed snow skiing with his kids in the Reno and Lake Tahoe areas.

A week before Charlie was to leave on his Florida trip he walked in the shop one morning and said, "I'm picking up the motor home from the storage facility to prepare it for the trip, I want you to tell Bert I'll need a haircut before I leave for Daytona."

Pat was standing nearby holding a smoldering Marlboro, and said, "I can use a haircut as well if Bert is coming by. Look at my hair; it's so long and wild now, and with it being white like it is, I look like Albert Einstein."

At lunch time I called over to Bert's hair shop in San Rafael to check in with her and tell her Charlie and the gang was waiting at the shop for haircuts.

A little while later, when I walked outside I noticed Ed Woo pulled up to the shop on his Yamaha FZR1000. I asked him how he was as he walked by saying, "Everything's fine. I'm just riding my

Fizzer and hanging with the big boys. I need to see Charlie because I want to install a new rear tire on my Fizzer."

Bert arrived at the shop a short time later as the gang gathered around for the haircuts to begin. Ed was happy to see her and said, "Alright, haircuts. I'm in."

Charlie took a seat in the middle of the office for his haircut. While Bert started to cut Charlie's hair, Ed said, "Well I guess I better tell all you guys the good news. My wife is pregnant with our first child."

Charlie was very surprised and said, "Wow! When's your baby coming?"

Ed said with a smile, "It should be around the end of this year." Bert and I were surprised as well. Bert said, "How nice! I can't wait to see the baby."

Bert proceeded to finish Charlie's haircut, and over the course of the next hour she completed haircuts on Ed and Pat as well.

After the junk bikes were rolled in and the shop closed, we were standing in the front lobby area when we suddenly heard a voice yell out from the back of the dark shop. It was Pin Head saying, "Hey, who turned off all the lights? Where'd everybody go?"

As Pin Head walked among the tightly packed bikes toward the front, Pat shouted out to him "Where the hell have you been for the last hour and a half?"

Pin Head walked closer to us while dry shaving his face with a disposable pink ladies razor. Pat said, laughing, "What the hell? Why are you shaving your face with a pink razor?"

Pin Head answered, "Why didn't you guys tell me my face was so dirty?"

Pat said sternly, "Your face is not dirty. I'm asking, why were you in the can for the last hour and a half. Were you shooting up?" Pin Head said he wasn't shooting up drugs in the bathroom and was upset he missed his chance at getting a haircut. Pin Head grabbed his riding gear and left the shop in a hurry.

Pat said, "He's been shooting up in the can again. He's lying to us because he's using the razor to relieve the itching sensation he feels after he shoots up. The razor gets the itch satisfied without gouging too deeply into his skin's surface."

Pat looked at Charlie and said, "I can't believe you still want him working here when you know he's using speed and heroin on a regular basis. Pin Head's high all the time, and people know it when they look at him. They wonder if he's a leper because of the way he looks."

Charlie said, "Hey, I've known Pin Head since he was a little boy, and I still know his dad and the rest of his family real well. We need Pin Head around here to be the mechanic."

Charlie left in his truck, and Pat rode off on his Honda Hurricane 1000 while I parked my pickup truck on the side of the shop overnight and drove home with Bert. When we were in the car driving home together, Bert asked, "What does Ed Woo do for a living with a wife and new baby on the way?"

I answered, "He says he builds and sells Porsches and BMW motorcycles with the big boys."

Bert asked, "Who are the big boys?"

I answered her, "I don't know who the big boys are, but Ed talks about them being his friends. He says he hangs out with them all the time in the motorcycle and automobile racket."

While Charlie was gone on his trip to Daytona, Pat grabbed as much control as he could around the shop. He orchestrated the customers like a symphony conductor, directing them where to go in the shop to search for parts they needed, then they would pay Pat at the cash register. While this was going on it afforded Pat plenty of time to sit around and smoke cigarettes with some of his new friends.

One afternoon when Pat was sitting at Charlie's desk, he introduced me to a pair of his riding buddies. He said, "These are my two friends who ride Ducati motorcycles."

Pat was telling his friends how great life was up in the country where Verna lived. He bragged, "It's beautiful cow country up there; they've got hundreds of acres of cow trails, so you can ride for days. They have one giant barn for all the bikes and another large barn they call the trophy barn because it holds nearly every trophy the Bostroms ever won. When you open the door, it looks like a sea of gold and silver, like a pirate's treasure. They have lots of motorcycles and acres of land as far as the eye can see, but the living conditions are pretty basic."

Pat embarrassed me as I walked out of the office. He said, "You've known those Bostrom boys for years; you've been up there in the country to their place, haven't you?"

Wondering why Pat would ask me such a question in front of his friends, I answered, "Nope, never been up there but I hear Ed is up there all the time."

A couple of days after Charlie returned from his trip, Pat and I stood at the counter reading a few free local motorcycle newspapers and drinking coffee. I said to Pat, "Listen to this article I'm reading. It's about a Kawasaki dealership in the East Bay that's closing down, and this letter in the newspaper was written by the owner of the shop."

The owner wrote in to explain why his Kawasaki dealership was going out of business. He wrote that due to slow sales he was forced to close his doors, even though he ran a racing team to help promote his dealership. It said despite his best efforts to keep his dealership afloat financially he couldn't make ends meet and subsequently apologized to the motorcycling public for his abrupt closing.

Moments later Charlie walked in the door holding a cup of coffee and said, "What the fuck do I pay you guys for, to stand around all fucking day and drink coffee? Let's get some work done and make some money."

Pat said, "Hey, Charlie's back. Vacation is over, for all of us."

Charlie said arrogantly, "Vacation? You guys are supposed to be working and making money around here to pay the fucking rent."

Charlie and I went in the office and he was anxious to see how much money we made while he was away.

As he was counting the money on his desk I was still holding the newspaper and said, "When you were away, the big Kawasaki dealership over in the east bay closed down, and the owner wrote this letter stating why he was closing."

Charlie said, "They must have had slow sales, high bills and overhead for them to close."

I said, "What happens to the motorcycle inventory from a large dealership like that when it closes?"

He answered, drinking his coffee, "That's what I hate about all that credit crap. You either have to give the money back or you have to give the bank back all the new motorcycles. The Bostroms did it right. When the banks were trying to collect from Dave when he closed his dealership, they either wanted the money or the bikes. Dave said he didn't have the money, so when the banks wanted all the bikes back, Dave took them to where they were located and when they rolled up the warehouse door there were no motorcycles there."

Charlie smiled saying, "Dave said he was ripped off."

I doubted Charlie and said "That's bullshit. No bank would ever believe that crap."

He said with a cocky smirk on his face, laughing, "Hey, all you gotta do is say the niggers did it."

He started laughing out loud and said, "Hey, no money, no motorcycles. What can you do? You can't get blood out of a turnip."

I walked out of the office, not thinking too highly of Dave and the Bostrom family. I wondered if Verna did the same thing when she closed her dealership since her shop was located in the heart of a black neighborhood in Oakland. I thought maybe the Bostroms stated the motorcycles were stolen and then hid them out in the country like Charlie boasted in the past. I grew suspicious about all the bikes Pat and some of Charlie's friends owned and many of the bikes Dick was selling. I thought maybe Dave and Charlie may have been doing illegal DMV paperwork for a long time on the Bostroms' hidden bikes that were said to be stashed away years before in the country.

Moments later, a shiny gold Porsche 911 pulled into the driveway. Ed Woo rolled down the window and said, "Hey, kid, why don't you jump in and let me take you for a ride in my new car?"

I never drove or took a ride in a Porsche car before so I decided to go. I opened the passenger door and climbed in. Ed said, "You better put your seatbelt on kid, because I have to test this thing out to make sure I have it together good and tight."

As I clicked the seatbelt Ed backed slowly out of the driveway and once he straightened the car out on the street he revved the engine to red-line and dumped the clutch, throwing me back against the seat as I felt the car leap forward under full power. Ed didn't shift the car to second gear until we reached nearly 60 MPH. As the car continued to accelerate I could feel the surge of the twin turbo engine spinning wildly as the tachometer reached the red-line zone through the first three gears. Ed was now traveling down a 35 MPH street at 85 MPH. My body cringed in the passenger seat at the thought of somebody pulling out in front of us from a driveway, because we would be killed for sure at the speed we were traveling.

He said we were heading to the freeway to test the car as he jumped the Porsche into the air, traveling over a small cement bridge which crossed a drainage canal. He quickly danced on the clutch and gas pedal using the engine to slow the car like a racer. Ed turned right and slid the car, drifting sideways onto the freeway entrance. When he had the Porsche pointed in a straight line, Ed quickly red-lined the engine in fourth gear before shifting to fifth, while slamming the accelerator pedal to the floor.

I looked over to see the speedometer sweeping past 100 MPH and continue to rise. Ed saw open road in front of us on the freeway and took advantage while I looked over at him and said, "Is this thing a five-speed?"

As the car reached close to 140 MPH Ed threw the shift lever again, looked over at me and said smiling, "Six speed, kid." I tried to hang on the best I could for the remainder of the wild and dangerous ride.

One morning, Charlie was planning for the upcoming Laguna Seca AMA road races in Monterey. He said, "I'm taking my motor home to Laguna Seca with my friends, and I'll be hanging with the Bostroms in the pits." I asked Charlie who he was taking to the races with him and he said, "Mikey and Petey are going, naturally."

Pat walked into work that morning with a middle-aged man with a pronounced limp. Pat said, "This is my new friend, Dieter. He's come here all the way from London, England." Dieter said hello with a strong British accent. Pat said, "Dieter is living with me because he has no other place to stay while he's visiting."

Dieter said, "Yes, we're living together at Pat's, and he's even doing all the cooking. Pat whips up a mean hot plate since he doesn't have a bloody kitchen."

Dieter limped over to my desk and dropped himself down in the chair. When Charlie turned around he noticed Dieter had an odd type of prosthetic lower leg. Charlie asked him, "How'd you lose your leg?"

Dieter said, as he knocked his knuckles against his prosthetic limb, "Let me tell you Yanks, London's a crazy town for motorcyclists. Back home I ride a Honda CX500 motorbike and had a serious crash; that's how I lost the lower part of my leg."

I was familiar with the motorcycle Dieter was talking about because occasionally we would get in a CX500 in junk condition that needed to be dismantled and thrown away. Since there were no customer demands for the parts of this old bike in our area I said to Dieter, "I can't believe they're still riding those old CX500s over in England and they're still popular."

Dieter was surprised and laughed saying, "We're fond of the old CX500 back home; we affectionately call it the Tea Pot." Dieter told us that back home he ran a small motorcycle shop that specialized in old Honda's.

Pat said Dieter was interested in searching around Charlie's shop for as many old CX500 parts as he could find. Dieter said he was looking for hard-to-find electrical parts for the bike because these would burn out and need to be replaced for his customers back home. Pat threw his arm around Dieter's shoulder, and the two of them proceeded to walk in the back of the shop, looking for parts.

After Pat and Dieter left the office, Charlie said, "He's not here just for parts; he's trying to find late model CX500's to fill a shipping container to send back to England. That's why he's staying with Pat for the next few weeks."

I said, "I guess Pat and Dieter can look around for parts, but if they want running bikes, Dieter will have to look around somewhere else."

Back out front, I noticed the mail was delivered. As I gathered the mail, I gazed at the see-through transparent window on an envelope. It appeared to be an official vehicle title from the DMV. I could see the name on the title certificate. It read James Brown, with Charlie's shop listed as the address.

Charlie insisted he was the one who opened the mail, so important documents wouldn't be lost. As I handed the stack of mail to him I asked, "Who the hell is James Brown?"

Charlie said, "Oh, that's Ed Woo's friend."

I told him, "Well, tell Ed his friend James Brown has some mail in the pile I just gave you."

Charlie looked quickly through the stack of mail and removed the DMV envelope for James Brown and set it to the side while saying to me, "I just got off the phone with someone who wants to have some work done on his bike, so I want you to make yourself useful and help Pin Head finish up that tire change he's working on."

I walked to the back of the shop and saw Pin Head was halfway done. He appeared angry because he was having a problem lining up the rear wheel on the customer's bike while re-installing it. I assisted him and asked, "Do you know Ed Woo's friend James Brown?"

Pin Head busted out laughing and said, while doing his best Donald Duck voice impression, "Stupid dummy. Ed Woo is James Brown."

When Charlie returned from the Laguna Seca race weekend, he was with some friends in the office along with Dick talking about the races. I heard him say, "Ben did great down there at Laguna, and my little Speedo Eric was kicking ass as well."

Dick acted as if he was a regular around Charlie's shop and thought he should be in the center of things with Charlie and his friends. Dick was far younger than Charlie or Pat and since he was living a boring life as a non-rider employed as a busboy before coming to Charlie's shop, he figured he was included in the group of Charlie's tight circle of friends and developed an attitude about it.

The funny thing was, Dick was never in, he only thought he was and we knew he wasn't.

To make matters worse for him, one afternoon Dick walked in the shop to get his usual order of a few motorcycle batteries on credit and pick up his paperwork deal from Charlie. When Dick approached the counter, Pat said laughing, "How are things down at Dick in the booty motors?"

Dick became angry and attempted to brush Pat off arrogantly while demanding Charlie's whereabouts. Pat dropped his smile and jumped right down Dick's throat and said, "Don't you take that fucking attitude with me because before you found this place a while back, you were just a loser busboy who sold cocaine at the restaurant you worked at. You even suffered from a serious drug problem yourself. Hell, this place has done a lot to help straighten out your sorry-ass life, so don't cop an attitude with me or I'll kick your scrawny ass out of here." Dick walked off angry looking for Charlie.

Pat said to me, "I know he's taking martial arts lessons because he feels he needs that sort of thing since he's such a small wimp, but if he pisses me off again, I'm going to kick his fucking ass biker style."

Pat struck a rather imposing figure while keeping Dick in check. I felt Pat could easily wipe the floor with Dick even though he was much older. Pat was well over six-feet-four, 280 pounds, and Dick was short and only weighed in around 150 pounds.

There was another time when Pat displayed his temper and his inability to control it. Next door to Charlie's shop was an older Italian man, an independent ornamental iron worker. His shop was something right out of the old blacksmith days: this Italian man would fabricate iron for his clients' houses and he also assembled other structural steel projects.

The old iron worker and Pat were constantly locked in a battle over where the customers should park in front of the two businesses. The old man would come out of his shop and hassle our customers about where they parked. Things boiled over badly after an argument grew into a violent fist-fight between Pat and the iron worker which broke out in front of the customers. Pat was much larger than the iron worker and a few years younger, so when the fight began, Pat was getting the better of it when the iron worker grabbed a pipe and smacked Pat on the wrist in an attempt to ward off the raging Pat. Soon the police arrived, and when things were sorted out, the iron worker was arrested and put in the back of the police car and driven away to be charged with the crime of assault. Pat said roughly, "I told that old guy not to fuck with me."

One morning, Charlie was at his desk planning his end of the summer motor home trip. Charlie made plans to take a trip to Arizona to visit relatives and do some land speculating. He said the high point of his trip to Arizona would be at Firebird Raceway in Arizona to watch Ben and Eric road race in the AMA National race.

While Charlie was making some reservation calls, I walked out of the office and heard a loud rumbling motorcycle that pulled into the shop. The rider revved the motor several times before shutting the engine off. It was Pat who said as he removed his helmet, "Harley, dude." He recently acquired a Harley 1200 Sportster.

The phone rang and while on the phone with a customer, I looked over at Pat's Harley. I noticed the bike wasn't new. It was an older 1980's model, but it was in good condition, with hardly any wear or mileage. I also saw the bike was dusty, as if Pat rode it down a dirt road to get to Charlie's shop.

Charlie walked out of the office and asked me, "Today's the day Bert's coming to do my hair, right?"

In the late afternoon she showed up, and the ritual quickly began. Bert brought us some lunch so I looked in the bag and grabbed some food and sat down in the office to eat. Pat walked in with a cup of coffee in one hand and a lit Marlboro in the other. He plopped himself down and joined in on the conversation. Bert said to Charlie, "I see a nice Harley out there. Are you guys starting to sell Harley bikes and parts now?"

Charlie said, "I don't sell Harley; we only sell Jap junk, you know 'gook' bikes."

Bert stopped cutting Charlie's hair momentarily and said, "Hey, that's mean; you shouldn't say that. First of all, I'm half Asian and you sell Japanese products in here, and that's how you make your living."

Charlie answered back laughing, "Well, you forget. I'm James Duck, and I don't give a fuck."

Pat interrupted: "That's my Harley out there; that thing's a chick magnet."

Bert was surprised and looked at Pat while finishing Charlie's hair and said, "I thought you looked like a Harley guy because I've been around a few sport bikes in my time and you don't look like a sport bike rider. You look way too old for sport bikes, like an old biker from the seventies."

Pat set his coffee on the desk and sat in Bert's chair. She began to cut his hair and pestered him saying, "You look like an old tough ex-biker. Were you in a biker gang when you were young?"

Pat smiled and answered in a rough tone, "I don't like to talk about my past with anyone."

Bert said, "Well, why don't you tell me what you did for a living before you started working here?"

Pat answered, "That's easy. I used to sell guitar parts at a guitar store: you know strings and guitar picks."

Bert found Pat's answer hard to believe, and while she was looking at a tattoo on Pat's arm she said, "Guys in biker gangs usually get in trouble. Were you ever in prison?"

Pat smiled slyly at her while changing the subject and said, "So Charlie, how's Eric Bostrom's deal going with Harley? I heard he's working for a Harley shop part-time, stocking parts on shelves."

Pat smirked and said to Charlie, "You should've given Eric a job working here at your shop, he could've filled in for Pin Head stocking parts on our shelves while wrenching on bikes and dismantling."

Charlie said arrogantly, "Eric doesn't have to work. Remember, we sponsor Eric. Most motorcycle racers don't work for a living. Ben and Eric don't work; they just race, then they sign autographs for the rest of the day for the losers who do have to work."

One rainy morning, Pat was late arriving so I had Pin Head push out most of the bikes while I helped Charlie take care of some other things. It was a quiet morning because no customers came in when it rained. Charlie and I were standing by the side door, when I saw a Pontiac Fiero pull quickly up to the side entrance. The car door swung open, and a struggling Pat attempted to extricate himself from an automobile that he appeared too large to be driving. Pat tried to step out of the car, but because his large belly was pressed so tightly against the steering wheel he couldn't free himself easily. As he finally pulled away from the car he said, "How do you like my new car?"

Wondering why Pat would buy a used car in which he couldn't even fit comfortably in, I grew suspicious and said, "That looks just like the Fiero I saw Ben and Eric driving while pulling the trailer with the Yamaha YSR50 race bikes a while back."

Charlie said proudly, "Ben's driving a brand new Hummer now that he's making a ton of money racing professionally. Dave and I tried to talk him out of blowing his first paycheck on a new Hummer and we told him that you don't want to draw attention to yourself, but he bought it anyway. Now that the race season is over, Dave and the boys are up skiing in Tahoe, testing out the new Hummer. The Bostrom boys ride snow boards, but Dave doesn't. Davey skis."

I couldn't stop thinking about where Pat picked up that Fiero and when I asked him he said the usual answer of stumbling across it on a good deal. I wondered if it was the same car I saw Ben and Eric driving with their YSR50 race bikes.

1996

Charlie came in one morning and said, "Ed's supposed to help me install a new tow rack on the back of my motor home for my trip to Daytona next week. Is he here yet?" Charlie still had his old rack but felt he needed to upgrade, even though he carried the same small trials bike.

While in the office, he asked me, "Do you still have that 357 magnum handgun my friend sold you several years back? I want it for my trip back east because I'm towing valuable stuff and I don't want to get ripped off when I'm parked in the middle of the night. Make sure you bring it to work tomorrow."

Driving a Porsche 911, Ed arrived at the shop a short time later. He and Charlie crawled under the motor home to see how the new tow rack would be mounted. They decided they needed some welding work done in order to install the new heavy-duty rack so Charlie said, "I'll drive my motor home up to my friend the welder, and he can do the work for us." Charlie and Ed piled into the motor home and drove away.

Twenty minutes later, I walked up front and noticed Pat was socializing with a friend of Charlie's I didn't see in many years. I remembered him from when Charlie used to have his jet boat, when he first met and married my mother back in 1977. His friend visited Charlie's vacation lake house years ago, and strutted around topless on the beach flexing his small physique doing his best to attract young girls with his old body. He was an ex-dirt tracker friend of Charlie's about the same age who made his living as a butcher. Charlie and I always had a free sandwich after Charlie was finished servicing the cash registers for the market. His name was Fred the butcher.

I didn't see Fred for nearly 15 years; his appearance changed but his demeanor didn't. He said he was still busy chasing after young girls, and now that he owned a Honda sport bike, he could give chicks rides. Fred told me he rode his bike down to Charlie's shop and asked me to take a look at it with him. I noticed Fred walked with a pronounced limp because of old injuries sustained in his dirt tracking days.

I was amazed at Fred's bike. It was a mint condition 1983 Honda VF750F Interceptor V-4 which looked like it was stored in a museum for the last 15 years. It barely had any miles on the odometer and the paint gleamed like a new bike. Fred didn't tell me where he purchased his bike, but he did say it handled great.

Pat walked outside and said, "That's a nice motorcycle, Fred. I hear those handle good around tight turns but not as good as the bike I just purchased."

I knew Pat was driving the white Fiero I thought he scored from the Bostroms when he said proudly, "I just bought a rare Suzuki Bandit 400 that's very hard to find and is great for riding around corners fast. I want to take my Bandit 400 to a track day coming up to hone my street riding skills with Ed."

Later in the afternoon, Charlie returned to the shop with the motor home. Ed said goodbye, and Charlie asked me, "How do you like the new rack on the motor home?" It appeared to be heavy duty and over-built for carrying one small trials bike. Charlie also had a tow ball installed on the motor home. I said, "What's the tow ball for?"

Charlie said, "That's just in case I have to tow something with my motor home later because I may have to tow a car one day."

Charlie's friends Mikey and Petey stopped by at closing time to say hello and Pat invited them to join him on his sport bike track days. Pat and his friends were now renting a professional racetrack for themselves where they could hone their street riding skills. Pat was always egging people to go with him and he bragged about his riding skills from hanging out with Ed, and training and riding with the Bostroms.

Charlie returned from Daytona after watching the Bostroms race. One morning he came in the office saying, "There's been a large rip-off up at Mission Motorcycles in Daly City. A while back they re-hired Dave's old saleswoman from the past. They said she took a credit card phone order for thousands of dollars worth of brand new Honda generators."

As I finished changing my boots Charlie continued, "Once all the generators were picked up by the customer, a short time later the credit card transaction was rejected by the bank because the card was bogus. I guess Mission Motorcycles are now out all that money and all those new Honda generators." I found it strange and wondered why anyone would buy more than just one generator because the price was nearly $1000.

Around closing time, a shiny black BMW convertible pulled up. Ed stepped out and said, "I'm here to see Charlie, am I too late, did he leave already?" I told Ed that Charlie already left for the evening for his pizza night.

Ed was in an upbeat mood as he pointed to a woman in the driver's seat and said, "I don't think you've ever met my wife." I said hi while Ed pointed to a small baby sitting in a child's car seat in the back. "This is my new baby daughter. Isn't she a cutie pie?" Ed patted me on my shoulder and asked, "When are you and Bert having a baby?"

I said, "We don't have any plans to have a baby because Bert and I are already very happy with her daughter we're raising together." As I continued to admire Ed's BMW convertible he said, "This is my wife's new car, she can afford to drive a car like this because she has a career as a businesswoman."

Ed told me they were leaving for the evening as he said, "Tell Charlie I'll be back next week to check in with him on some paperwork things." After Ed was in the car, he rolled down the window and asked me, "Are you coming to track day this weekend with Pat and Charlie to watch me tear up the track? You should see Pat and his friends try and keep up with me as I blast around them. They should learn by now that I'm a lot faster than they'll ever live to be." I told Ed I couldn't make it.

About a week later, I arrived to work late one morning. Charlie was seated at his desk and said, "Hey, you're fucking late again. I need you here on time because I have things I want to do before I head up to my lake house with my kids this weekend." I looked down at the side of his desk and noticed a brand new Honda generator. I asked him, "Where did you get that Honda generator from?"

Charlie said, "That's my new Honda generator that I'm taking up to my house at the lake to store there, just in case the power goes out."

It was only a short time since the giant Honda generator rip-off at Mission Motorcycles. I asked Charlie where he acquired his generator when he interrupted me. "I bought this generator for a good price from my friend that works at a shop in San Francisco. He said he was walking down a street in Napa this past weekend and when he saw this generator sitting on the porch of an old lady's house, he couldn't resist the temptation and stole it. He said the generator was heavy and as he ran down the street, he tripped and fell, fucking up his leg on the generator."

I left the office doubting every word he said.

Later in the day, Ed came in to visit Charlie. I was surprised to see Ed with many serious fresh burns and abrasions all over his upper body, barely scabbed over that appeared to be very painful. He wore a short sleeve, thin T-shirt that allowed me to see the severity of his wounds. However, Ed moved around and spoke openly as if his injuries weren't affecting him at all.

I walked behind Ed as he stood in the office doorway, shocked at the sight of his grotesque injuries, I said, "Wow, Ed, that's a horrific case of motorcycle road rash you have...I think it's the worst I've ever seen. Did you do that on your Fizzer at track day?"

Ed appeared annoyed at my question and abruptly said, "Not my Fizzer, kid, my Yizzer." He grabbed the doorknob and stepped into the office closing the door behind him as I wondered what kind of bike a Yizzer was.

I looked through the office window and saw Ed describing how he was riding a motorcycle and crashed. If Ed could ride a Fizzer better than a professional, then what kind of bike was a Yizzer that caused him to lose control, seriously wounding him?

After Charlie returned from the races at Laguna Seca, Pat and Charlie planned a Sunday morning street bike ride around Marin County. Fred pulled into the shop on his Honda Interceptor and was happy to hear Charlie and his friends were organizing a ride and he enthusiastically said he wanted to join them.

Charlie looked at me and said, "If you want to come along tomorrow, you can ride my Suzuki GS1100E."

I said, "Okay I'll take your Suzuki home tonight in my truck and meet up with you guys tomorrow." At closing time we decided where to meet in the morning.

I still had to load Charlie's Suzuki in my pickup truck so I dropped the tailgate and set up my ramp while Pat jumped on the bike and rode it over. Pat yelled, "Stand back as I jump this thing right up that ramp and in the back of your pickup, Bostrom style."

The next morning, I met Charlie and Fred at a gas station in Marin County. A few minutes later, Pat showed up and we rode off up through north Marin, heading west to the coast with Charlie leading the way on tight, winding roads. We rode for about two hours when Charlie pulled over and signaled for us to do the same. Pat decided to head home early, so he split off from us. Charlie said he and Fred were continuing up the coast for a while and I should come along. As Charlie, Fred and I rode north, Charlie suddenly turned right onto a side road that climbed a steep mountain and headed back inland.

Fifteen minutes into riding up the road, we pulled over and Charlie said the next section of road was very narrow and didn't have a center line painted in the middle. Charlie rode up the hill first and disappeared from sight. I was the next to take off as Fred was still strapping his helmet. I knew Fred would catch me in a minute because he rode his Honda Interceptor very fast and took many dangerous chances.

I was lost in thought trying to catch up with Charlie as I whipped the 1100 Suzuki through the tight turns and short straights. After a few minutes, I was overcome with a feeling that something might have gone wrong. I didn't see Fred appear in my rearview mirrors and was beginning to think he might have missed a turn and gone over the cliff. I continued to ride at a slower pace, and when Fred still didn't appear I knew something was definitely wrong. I hit the brakes and turned around in the middle of the road, riding back down the mountain to find Fred.

I rode back about one mile when I came around a turn and saw Fred smashed his Interceptor into the front grille of a small car in a head-on collision. The Interceptor was completely destroyed, and Fred was launched through the air and over the car. I stopped my Suzuki and ran over to Fred, who was barely conscious and in very bad condition. I lifted the visor on his helmet and looked in his eyes. It appeared as if he was looking right through me.

A woman was with him who was from the car behind the one Fred hit, she told me she had a cell phone and called the sheriff. She was a nurse and said Fred needed to get to a hospital right away because he suffered multiple injuries. I told her my dad was up the road and I would find him and return while she said she would stay with Fred until help arrived. I jumped on the Suzuki and raced up the road to find Charlie.

I found Charlie sitting on his bike with his helmet off, waiting for Fred and me at the end of the road. He said, "Where the hell have you been and where the fuck is Fred?" I explained to him as my heart raced Fred was wiped out in a head-on collision and was badly hurt. Charlie and I rode back to where Fred crashed at the same time the sheriff pulled up to the scene.

Due to the serious nature of Fred's injuries a helicopter with a medical team was called in to fly Fred to the nearest hospital. Charlie said, as the CHP cleaned up the scene and towed Fred's bike away, "I'm riding to the hospital to see Fred, and you should head back home; it will take you a while to get back to Fairfield." As I pulled my helmet on, I could hear the elderly male driver of the car Fred hit complaining to the sheriff saying, "I was only going 20 MPH and that maniac came barreling around the corner in my lane and drove right into the front grill of my car. My wife is traumatized!"

The next morning when Charlie arrived to work he said, "Fred's all fucked up and he needs lots of blood transfusions. He also needs a few surgeries because he has lots of broken bones. He'll be recovering for a long time."

The next week Ed came by and spoke to Charlie about some of the BMW motorcycles they were working on together. Charlie owned a few BMW bikes and decided to sell one or two at the shop to make room for his new one Ed was building.

Ed told us the Bostroms were making a special appearance at Lodi Cycle Bowl that weekend because they were in between road races and were home to race dirt track. Charlie said to me, "We're going to Lodi this weekend, and if you want to come, you can ride a shop bike up there." Ed finished up business with Charlie and told us as he left he was going to Lodi with the Bostroms.

The night of the races, when we arrived at Lodi, the racing program already began. Charlie led us around, walking in between the various trailers and transporters, looking for the Bostroms.

Charlie recognized the Bostrom pit from some dirt track race bikes and Dave's truck, but there were no Bostroms in sight. He unpacked some of his things as the race announcer yelled out, "Let's all give a big hand to Ben Bostrom tonight for winning that heat race." Charlie became excited and said to me, "Okay, you can hang out and do whatever you want while I try to find Dave. They may be calling his race to the line any minute." Charlie ran off into the crowd and I walked to the track for the next race.

Dave was indeed on the starting line ready to race. The starter threw a green flag, and Dave shot to the lead. The race was held on a small hard-packed oval dirt track which was brightly lit by large lights around the track. As Dave came by I could see he was riding a chrome-framed dirt tracker equipped with a Honda XL500 engine. Dave was riding so far on the ragged edge the dirt tracker appeared completely sideways, even on the short straights between the turns. Dave easily won the race, and I saw Charlie dart off to find him in the pits.

After the green flag flew to start the next race, I was surprised when I saw the rider in the lead speed past me. I could see he was wearing a black leather racing suit with three large red letters on the back that spelled WOO. It appeared Ed was riding Dave's bike and it was the same dirt tracker Dave just won his heat race on. Ed appeared fully healed from his crash on his Yizzer and I was impressed Ed could ride a dirt tracker so well, since his specialty was road racing.

Ed continued to slide Dave's dirt tracker around the oval track, leading the group of racers behind him. After a few more laps, he took the checkered flag and an easy win. He led the other racers off the track and back to the pits.

Once the next race started, I walked down by the track and found Charlie standing near a staging area, cheering wildly for a green Kawasaki KX motocross bike that was converted to a dirt tracker and leading the race. The rider of the KX led from start to finish and then rode a cool down lap. The winner rode right over to where Charlie was standing and parked the bike. Charlie was excited as the rider pulled off the helmet and said, "Hi-yah, Charlie. What's doing?"

Charlie could barely contain himself as he blurted out, "Hey, it's Verna!" Charlie congratulated Verna on her win in the women's division of racing, and they gave each other a very tight and long hug. Charlie released Verna from his grasp and turned to me. "This is my kid," he said. We shook hands and Charlie said, "Verna and I are heading back to the Bostrom camp, and I'll meet up with you later." She rolled her Kawasaki dirt tracker back to the Bostrom pit area with Charlie walking along beside with his arm around her.

During intermission I was surprised when I was tapped on the shoulder from behind. I spun around and saw that it was Charlie's friend who sold him the stolen generator. He told me he rode to Lodi that night alone and wanted to know if I would like to hang out with him for a while and smoke a joint.

We climbed up a small hill overlooking the track and he pulled out his joint, lit it and said, "Pat was supposed to ride over here with me tonight, but he didn't call me. He wants to hang out with the Bostroms; he thinks he's a cool racer dude like Ben, Eric and Ed."

I asked him, as I took a hit, "Do you know Ed? He's down there riding and training hard with the Bostroms on their dad's dirt trackers."

He said, "Dude, its known Ed Woo builds and drives stolen Porsches and motorcycles. He's also all coked out."

I handed him the joint and said, "Charlie told me Dave and his boys knew Ed for years, and they came around Charlie's shop since the beginning. Charlie's shop is the sponsor for Ben and Eric since both of them raced as children. After all these years of watching Ben and Eric grow up, it seems weird they're still hanging out and riding with Ed. I guess training with Ed really works because you learn how to be a fast racer from practicing with Ed Woo"

With the racing finished, I rode out alone because I didn't see Charlie or Pat for the rest of the night. It was a long ride back home to Fairfield.

A couple weeks later, Charlie was happy when he heard Fred was healing fast from his accident even though he faced a long rehabilitation.

Ed walked in to see Charlie for paperwork again, and Bert walked in soon after to give Charlie and Pat their regularly scheduled haircuts.

She gave me a kiss hello and when Ed saw Bert he said, "Do you have extra time to give me a haircut today?" Bert said she could fit him in after Charlie. Bert and I were in the office alone and a short time later Ed burst in the office, grabbed a spare motorcycle helmet off the desk and said to her, "I'll have to take a rain check because I have something important to do." He pulled the helmet quickly onto his head and without strapping it ran out of the office toward the back of the shop.

We wondered what Ed was doing and as I followed Bert to the door, Pat suddenly jumped in the doorway and blocked her path with his large belly. He said to her, "There are certain things you're not supposed to see right now, so why don't you stay in the office for a while?"

I instantly grew agitated with Pat and pushed my way past him. "I need to know what's going on, so get the fuck out of my way," I said. Bert remained in the office, and I walked toward the back of the shop, and saw nothing out of the ordinary.

Then out the side entrance, I saw Ed in the lot next door, sitting inside a newer model Porsche 911, with the motorcycle helmet still on his head. It appeared Ed was trying to start the car as I wondered why he parked his Porsche in the parking lot next door. After a few seconds, Ed rolled the car in neutral, coasting directly to the side door of Charlie's shop in reverse.

Ed jumped out of the car and worked on the engine furiously in a further attempt to get the car started. Charlie tried to help Ed start the car and told Ed he had a battery charger they could use to get it started. Ed thought a battery charger wasn't the answer and said, "I'll call my friend who has a tow truck and he'll help me get the car out of here."

In a few minutes a yellow tow truck showed up, and the driver jumped out to help Ed. The driver and Ed realized they couldn't start the car so Ed climbed back in the Porsche while the tow driver pushed the car with the truck, subsequently caving in the entire back end of the Porsche. The driver continued pushing the car as Ed steered the Porsche out on the street. I watched as the tow truck pushed the Porsche down the street at 30 MPH, further crushing in the back of the Porsche while they disappeared from sight. Ed wore the helmet on his head the whole time.

As the summer turned to fall, Charlie and his friends parked their street bikes for the year and pulled out their dirt bikes. They prepped their trials and vintage bikes to get ready for the upcoming weekends.

One morning, as Charlie hung up the phone, he said, "Petey didn't wake up this morning; he was found in a comatose state, and they think it's his heart." I was shocked to hear the news because Petey was much younger than Charlie and only ten years older than me.

Charlie and Petey were very close and Petey even came to my house with Charlie when he dated my mother and they both rode Yamaha RD350s in 1976. Charlie acted as if Petey was a son to him along with Mikey and Davey because Charlie rode with them since they were young boys. Petey was a happy red haired, freckled face guy and nice to be around. He also participated for years in salvage squad racing with the gang around the shop.

Charlie told me Petey was in the hospital, and the doctors were monitoring him to see if he has any brain activity. Charlie said angrily, "The doctors say they'll only keep Petey on life support for two weeks, and if there's no improvement, he'll be considered brain dead and Petey will be unplugged."

Over the course of the next two weeks Charlie kept track of all the friends who called and wanted to visit Petey. One night, Charlie was organizing which friends were visiting Petey. He said, "Now it's real hard to get in to see Petey because they're only allowing family and close friends. Dave and the kids are visiting Petey tonight, and I'll be there with Mikey and we'll try to wake Petey up."

I found it strange the entire time Petey was in the hospital Charlie didn't ask Bert or me to go to the hospital in an attempt to help wake him up. Many times I asked Charlie to put us on the schedule to visit Petey, but Charlie said there were no openings because they didn't want too many people in the room at once.

A few days later, Charlie came to work in the morning bearing bad news. Petey had shown no response during the past two weeks, so the doctors unplugged him. Petey was dead.

I expected to see Charlie saddened from the news, but he appeared very angry instead, and said, "The doctors could've kept him on life support longer, but all they care about is fucking money so they wanted to pull the plug on Petey. We have a memorial and funeral for him scheduled in a few days."

Bert and I arrived in San Francisco a few nights later for the memorial. Tons of bikes were parked out front. Charlie seemed to be the organizer of the whole thing and was standing in the doorway. The funeral home was very crowded, with many of Charlie and Petey's friends from the motorcycling world. There must have been one hundred people and many of them were guys dressed in black leather jackets and boots carrying their helmets. All of motorcycle vintage racing's elite were there because near the end of his life, Petey was very involved with vintage racing. Everybody seemed to know each other, and they all especially knew Charlie. One by one they lined up to greet Charlie and give their condolences.

When everyone was seated, the ceremony began. The crowd filled two large rooms that opened to a small area where Petey's body laid. I sat with Charlie near the Bostroms and I looked over and saw Ed sitting next to Eric. The funeral director said since Petey had so many friends he thought it was best if everyone came up to pay their respects one family at a time. Petey's immediate family walked up to the coffin first and then Charlie and our family was the next to pay our respects.

After we were seated and a few more families paid their respects, Dave Bostrom stood up and walked up to Petey with his family behind him. Dave was followed by Tami, his girlfriend, and his three sons, Tory, Ben and Eric. To my surprise I also saw Ed Woo, walking along with the Bostrom family behind Eric.

At the end of the night, as people were leaving, Bert and I stood outside. Mikey and Charlie were making travel arrangements for Petey's funeral as I grabbed Charlie's attention for a second and said, "Bert and I are leaving because it's a long drive back to Fairfield, what time should we see you tomorrow and where's the burial?" Charlie said, "Pat and I will be with the Bostroms at the cemetery tomorrow and I'll need you and Pin Head to get the shop opened." I was taken aback and hurt because I was not invited.

Near the end of the year, Dave came in the shop to visit, and proudly said Eric finished up the year by winning the Harley Davidson 883 championship. Charlie was very happy to hear this and said to Dave and Pat, "Eric is making a big impression in the world of racing because of all the riding and training over the years. I'm really proud of Eric"

I didn't hear Dave and Charlie talking about how well Ben finished out the year road racing. However, I did recall a while back when my fifteen year old daughter and I were watching television together. The TV was tuned to MTV, and they showed a very brief segment featuring a young motorcycle road racer with long hair riding talented standup wheelies on a Honda CBR600F3.

The show featured this young road racer as the next big talent to hit the motorcycle road racing scene. Wild guitar music played in the background of the segment while the racer was interviewed. The commentator held the microphone up to the racer as the new rider introduced himself to the world as Ben Bostrom.

As I stared at the TV in amazement my daughter asked, "Wow, he's cute. Do you know that guy?" I said to her "I've known him since he was a little kid, and his dad is a huge criminal."

1997

The year started off with Charlie making plans for another motor home trip to Daytona to watch Ben and Eric, now that they were both racing the 600cc super sport class.

After Charlie left, it was quiet around the shop. I answered a call one day that was not a customer. The voice on the phone recognized me, but I didn't recognize the voice until he said, "Hey, kid. Bostrom's flying to the races!" I immediately knew it was Ed. He didn't tell me what team the Bostroms were riding on, but he sounded a little depressed. I knew as he spoke to me about the Bostrom success that Ed rode and trained with Ben and Eric practically their whole lives. Ed's comments sounded as if he was somehow left behind while Ben and Eric climbed the ladder to fortune and fame. Ed told me he felt as if he was some sort of teacher or Sensei to the Bostrom boys.

While Charlie was gone, business was slow because it was the beginning of the year, and the wet weather didn't give way to the sunny riding season yet to come. Pin Head still showed up to work when he wanted, and Pat and Pin Head still competed with each other. During the struggle for power between the two of them, Pat always thought he came out on top by saying to Pin Head. "You're a junkie. You're always going to be a junkie. End of story."

One day started off unusually when I saw Pat sitting at the counter smoking a cigarette and drinking coffee. As I walked past him to put my things down Pat said, "Oh, by the way, Ed ran in here early this morning and took a DMV vehicle verification document off of Charlie's desk and stamped it with one of Charlie's DMV stamps. Then he left the office and ran out the door without saying anything to me."

I glared angrily at Pat because he was proud of the fact he was in charge of shop security. Because of his large size, nobody could steal anything on his watch. I said, "What the fuck were you doing when Ed stole the verification document? I can't believe you would just stand there and watch Ed steal the DMV papers. What the hell are you, an elephant in a pink tutu?" Pat sat expressionless still smoking.

Pin Head wandered in carrying some food and as he walked toward the two of us he said, "Mmmmm, prime rib!"

Pat said, "We're happy to see you showed up for work since you haven't been here for the last two days." Pin Head set the food container down on the seat of a rusty junk motorcycle and flipped open the Styrofoam top and began to saw through a two-inch thick blood-rare slice of cold prime rib with a white plastic fork and knife.

Pin Head smiled and shouted back to Pat, while slicing up and devouring a big chunk of the prime rib, "I gotta eat!!"

Pat fired back, "You come when you want and you leave when you want and this business doesn't even need you around."

Pin Head said, "You'll never be able to work on motorcycles the way I can, so Charlie will always need me around here."

Pat angrily said, "Well, like I've been saying, if this was my place I would've fired your ass a long time ago." Pat then cupped his hands to his mouth, simulating a bull horn, and shouted out as loud as he could to Pin Head, "Hellooooooooo. You're a junkie!!"

Pin Head wasn't smiling anymore while he applied too much pressure on the plastic knife and fork, breaking both utensils. He screamed out, "Motherfucker!!" as he slammed the container shut, picked it up and walked angrily to the back of the shop.

Pat laughed and said as he pulled out a cigarette and lit it, "Did you see the size of the piece of prime rib Pin Head was eating?" Trying not to break out laughing, I said, "That piece of meat was enough to feed four hungry men, and Pin Head puts it away like it's nothing."

Pat took a drag off his cigarette and said, "He eats that way because he's been up for the past three days shooting speed without sleeping or eating, then he's so hungry he could devour his own weight in beef." Pat said laughing, "Where does he put all that food? He stands nearly six feet tall and weighs about as much as a canary." Pat was right; I saw Pin Head in the past around the shop with no shirt, and he looked like a scared up living skeleton or even a rock star strung out on heroin.

I walked to the back of the shop where Pin Head was finishing off the cold slab of prime rib with a dirty metal knife and fork he found in the bottom of his tool box. He said, "He pisses me off. Pat thinks he's a big shot because he hangs out with the Bostroms and rides to Lodi once in a while. Charlie and my dad go way back at Lodi Cycle

Bowl, longer than any idiot like Pat could ever imagine. Even Kenny Roberts was only an ink spot racing at Lodi when Charlie and my dad raced there and won. My dad can even blow Dave Bostrom away any day of the week on a dirt tracker."

He started to work on a repair job saying, "In the old days at Lodi Cycle Bowl, my dad raced around on a Triumph dirt tracker in a tuxedo jacket and pants, beating everyone. Pat never raced a motorcycle in his life, so I don't know why he has such an attitude when he's not even a racer; he's a poser."

Charlie returned home from Daytona not a day too soon. Pat was ready to kill Pin Head by the time Charlie came back. Charlie wasn't happy when I told him it rained every day during the time he was gone, and we didn't make much money.

Bert and I visited my grandfather several times at Charlie's house when Charlie was away. He stayed at Charlie's since Christmas and took a turn for the worse health wise. He needed to be monitored by doctors, so he couldn't go back home to Connecticut. He was 85 years old and in great spirits mentally, but his body started to break down.

Over the course of the next few weeks, my grandfather's condition worsened, and he was admitted to the hospital for a variety of problems. Bert and I made trips to visit with him, and one night when visiting hours ended, we left grandpa quietly watching TV in his hospital room.

The next morning when I arrived at the shop, Charlie put his hand on my shoulder and said, "Well, Pops died last night at the hospital, and your mother and grandmother are not taking it very well. Now everything is all fucked up, and we'll probably have to go all the way back east for a funeral and family shit. I have a bunch of important things to take care of here and I don't have time to watch a bunch of people sit around and cry all day long."

I told Charlie I was shocked because we just saw Grandpa the previous night, and the doctor said he was fine. Charlie said the doctors thought even though he was in good shape, his heart gave out in the end and they could not save him.

Charlie was angry and said, "I'll need you to help Pat run things around here today, and you can come over the house tonight with Bert to see you grandmother and your mom."

A day before Charlie left to go back east for grandpa's funeral, I over heard Pat say to Charlie, "Why don't you just tell your kid? After all, he worked here with you since the beginning."

I heard Charlie respond, "I can't tell him the truth. If he knew the truth, he would want to kill me."

I didn't know what to think at first. I thought Charlie might have said he wasn't happy about dealing with my grandfather's death and flying back east for the funeral. I couldn't imagine what he could possibly have done to make me mad or why he was worried I would want to kill him if I found out what he was up to; it just didn't make any sense.

Charlie and my mom were gone a week when Dave walked in the shop and asked me if I would help him look for a part. While searching I asked him, "How's Ben and Eric doing with the racing this year?" Dave said, "The boys are fine, and now they're living part-time down near Los Angeles in a town called Granada Hills. That's where the entire motorcycle road racing action is centered down in the LA area."

Later on that day, Pat called me to the front counter because a customer arrived at the shop to pick up a rear wheel for a Yamaha FZR 1000. Earlier in the week I set the only FZR 1000 rear wheel the shop aside because the customer said on the phone he would come down to buy it in a few days. I greeted the customer and went to retrieve the wheel, but it wasn't where I left it earlier. I asked Pat, "Where's that FZR1000 rear wheel that was sitting here?"

Sipping his coffee he said, "Hmm. Let me think. Oh yeah. Ed came in the other day when you weren't here and told me he needed that wheel and he would settle up with Charlie later."

The customer appeared very agitated and said, "I just drove all the way over here from the east bay because you guys said you had the thing waiting for me. What kind of an outfit are you guys running here?"

He asked if we had another FZR 1000 rear wheel to sell him in our stock, but I told him we only have one for sale. I took the customer's phone number and said I would call him if I could get the wheel back from Ed.

While Charlie was away, I made a few visits to a local insurance salvage pool where Charlie would buy wrecked bikes. The place usually had five or six wrecked motorcycles for auction every week, along with wrecked cars. This was an insurance auction and only people who held a vehicle dismantler's or dealer's license could get in and bid on the items.

One morning I attended the auction sale and was surprised when I saw Ed in the yard viewing the cars. He was looking at a black Mercedes Benz sedan. The car was hit in the rear, and the whole back end was smashed in. Ed was surprised to see me and said, "Hey, kid. I'm checking out this car to build up for my dad."

I said, "How did you get in here?"

He answered, "I'm in here on Charlie's license, using his bidding number. I've been coming here for a while."

Ed walked around the car assessing things when I said to him, "Dude, I need to get that rear wheel for the FZR 1000 back you took out of the shop, so it can be sold to a customer it was promised to."

Ed was a little put out by my request and said, "Can't do it, kid. That wheel is already spoken for; it's gone."

I pressed Ed further, saying I really needed to get it back when his mood changed for the worse while he said, "Don't play into this all wrong because I'm telling you right now, the wheel is gone and I'm taking care of it with Charlie."

Shocked at the way Ed was talking to me, I demanded the wheel and Ed again said no. He finally said calmly with a smile, "You need to back off and not take things so serious, kid. After all, that shop isn't even yours and for the last time I'm taking care of it with Charlie." Ed turned and walked away while I was pissed.

When I arrived back at the shop, I was surprised to see Charlie there. He said, "I came back early from your grandfather's funeral. I couldn't handle all the crying and the grief. Your mother stayed behind with your grandmother and she's a little pissed off at me for coming home early, but hey, I have to take care of business." I noticed Charlie seemed more agitated than usual, considering he wasn't around the shop for a while.

I told Charlie how business was for the last couple of weeks while I was still angry about the argument with Ed earlier. I said, "I saw Ed at the insurance auction today, buying cars, and he said he's been buying vehicles in there for a while now on your license. What's that all about?"

Charlie brushed aside my statement and said, "What goes on between me and Ed is my deal, and I only need you to take care of things that are shop business."

I abruptly said, "I'm taking care of shop business, Charlie. Let's start with this one. While you were away Ed came in here and ripped off some DMV documents, and Pat didn't even do anything to stop him. Are you okay with that too?" Charlie looked like he was thinking about other things. I yelled, "What the hell's the matter with you?"

Charlie appeared to be lost in thought while I said, "Ed also stole our FZR 1000 rear wheel I promised to a customer, and when I told him to return the wheel, Ed said it's between you and him on the deal."

Charlie snapped back, "That's right. What's between Ed and me is nothing you need to be concerned about."

I said angrily, "If you want me to be concerned about shop business, I think the best thing for the shop is to keep Ed Woo out of the insurance salvage auction using your shop's license. I'm real tired of Pin Head, Pat and Ed saying they only work for you and answer only to you. Maybe you should have stayed behind to baby sit your own shop and employees and I could have gone to my grandfather's funeral." I stormed out of the shop.

A few weeks later Charlie pulled up next to the shop in his motor home to prepare it for the upcoming road races at Laguna Seca. He was especially excited because it was the weekend of the World Superbike races in Monterey. Pat was on the front counter having his morning coffee and cigarette, Pin Head was, as usual, nowhere to be found.

A quiet morning all of a sudden turned busy when I noticed a few people who didn't look like customers walking in. Soon there were more people and some of them held clipboards and walked around the shop. One of the guys identified himself to Pat as a police officer and asked if the owner named Charlie was available. Charlie walked in the side door and was puzzled at what was going on. He met with the officer in charge and together they went in the office and closed the door. Soon the place was crawling with a dozen undercover cops, searching around and writing down VIN numbers on their clipboards from as many engines, frames and junk motorcycles they could. Pat stood by smoking and watched.

I moved around the shop not paying too much attention to the police officers as I walked over to the office and looked in the window and saw a sergeant showing Charlie some papers and documents. Charlie sat at his desk with a blank look on his face, shaking his head from side to side, indicating he didn't know what the officer was talking about.

In a few minutes, the sergeant and Charlie walked out of the office, and the sergeant gathered his men and left. Charlie walked over to Pat and me and said calmly, "Those cops were looking for a stolen scooter they heard might be here. No big deal."

Pat seemed interested in what Charlie said; however, I was skeptical about what happened. It seemed strange it would require a small army of cops in order to chase down one stolen scooter.

I questioned things further and asked, "Why are they looking for a stolen scooter here in the first place?" Charlie didn't want to talk about the incident any further while his mood changed abruptly and he said angrily, "I don't care about any fucking stolen scooter. I need you guys to start making some money around here because you idiots didn't make shit while I was in Connecticut and I need to pay the fucking rent."

Charlie grew angrier and asked me if a motorcycle in the back of the shop Pin Head was working on was ready for sale yet. I said, "The bike is on the work table and almost ready to go; it needs a cracked steering stop re-welded on the frame to finish."

When we walked in the back to Pin Head's work table, Charlie was pissed off when he saw the motorcycle's front end was removed, and the bike didn't appear ready to go. I said to Charlie as he glared at the bike, "We're ready to load the bike in your truck so you can take it up to your welder friend to repair the steering stop."

Charlie instantly flew into a rage and suddenly reached down, picked up a hammer off the table and swung wildly away at the damaged steering stop. He shouted, "Motherfucker!" every time he missed the steering stop as Pat jumped back, saying, "Hey, watch out with that swinging, you're going to hurt somebody." Charlie wailed away with the hammer as he barked out like a rabid pit-bull yelling, "You don't need a fucking steering stop on this bike to sell it."

As the steering stop broke off the frame with the force of his last few swings, Charlie screamed out as he threw the hammer across the shop smashing it against the wall. "Now, get the fucking thing together so we can sell it!"

I was mad because Pin Head was working on this old Honda CX500 for a few weeks so I said to Charlie, "How the hell are you supposed to pitch it to the locks like a Bostrom if there aren't any locks to even pitch it to in the first place?" Charlie, with his face now beat red, yelled at me spitting, "Hey, I don't want to hear any of your shit!"

He seemed angry about something else other than the steering stop or an old stolen scooter based on his explosive behavior.

A short while later Charlie was in an odd mood when he came back from the World Superbike races at Laguna Seca. I heard him talk about how much he wished he could go to the road races at Pikes Peak if he didn't have to worry about running things.

The next day Bert and I walked in the office as Charlie said to us while he threw both of his hands up in the air, "Well, that's it. I'm retiring."

Bert and I were both shocked at the news, she said, "Wow, that's so sudden. Is everything okay?"

Charlie replied, "I've been thinking about it for a while since Grandpa died. I'm not getting any younger, and I want to spend more time going to the races. I'm tired of babysitting all these assholes around here and all the bullshit of trying to pay the rent."

Bert asked Charlie, "What are you going to do with the shop and all this junk?"

Charlie said, "Well, I was thinking I can give it to you two guys. I talked to my accountant, and I'm also out of the building rental business. I'm giving my building in San Bruno to your brother Garg. I figured since Garg's been living there for free and taking care of the place for the last 10 years, I'm transferring the title of the building to Garg's name and out of mine. So what'll it be? Do you want my salvage shop or not?"

I felt I couldn't run the shop by myself so Charlie said, "I know you're not capable of running things by yourself, but you have Bert to help you and Pat will stay on to run the place like he's been doing."

Bert said to Charlie, "What about all the DMV paperwork part of the business? We don't know how to do any of that stuff."

Charlie said, "I know learning that is complicated, so you don't have to worry about it at all. It will be taken care of by me like it's always been done in the past, so all you guys have to do is just run the shop. The good news is I'll still be here part-time helping out when I'm not going to the races, and you guys can start paying me a small salary now."

He looked me in the eye. "Well, yes or no? Do you guys want it or not? If not, I will shut this place down, and you can find something else to do." I told Charlie of course, we would try and take over his shop.

He answered back "That's great, now here's the deal. We need a new license for the place because the old license in my name won't be good anymore. The DMV is cracking down on giving new dismantler's licenses because of all the environmental bullshit, so the new license application will have to be in Bert's name for it to go through. With the new application submitted by a woman they can't say no and besides she's a minority, which gets it done for sure. Hey, they have to approve it because if they don't they can get sued, and then they have to approve it anyway."

Charlie walked over to Bert and put his arm around her shoulder saying, "Do you think you can handle being a female motorcycle salvage shop owner? I know you have your hair shop to run too, but I think you can do it. Besides, I'll take you around the next few months and show you the ropes, and you'll be a pro at running the shop in no time."

Bert was around motorcycles for a long time all the way back to when she was married to Joe. She always felt comfortable around the shop and knew about bikes.

She looked at me as Charlie held her and said, "Okay. I think I can do it."

Charlie insisted on Bert coming down to the shop so she could attend meetings Charlie made at the DMV when it was time to change over the license. Charlie also drove her around with him in his truck to all the different motorcycle shops where Charlie knew the owners. He would introduce her to all of his friends as the new owner of his salvage operation.

Charlie walked into different shops and told the guys Bert was his new Girl Friday. Sometimes they would stop for lunch, and Charlie would say to Bert, "Hey, now that you're the new boss you have to pay for lunch." After a couple of months with Charlie and Bert running around, the transfer of the shop was complete.

One morning when Bert and I arrived at the shop, Charlie and Pat already had the place open and were talking about life up in the country at Verna's place. Charlie looked at us and said, "Oh good, you guys are here. I went ahead and made a deal for Bert's new shop to buy a giant load of junk bikes and parts."

Alarmed, I thought his deal wasn't a good thing because Charlie brought in way too much un-sellable junk in the past, and Bert and I already decided to run the shop with less junk coming in. Charlie said, "Now I need you guys to give me $6,000 in cash to seal this deal I made."

The price of Charlie's deal almost knocked me over. I said, "We're not spending $6,000 on anything because we don't have that kind of money."

Charlie became angry and said, "I already made the promise I would take all the stuff because they need to get the place cleaned out."

I said, "I want to see what the hell they're selling for $6,000 because if it's just a bunch of crap I don't want it. Where's this shop located?"

Charlie fired back at me, "Where it's located is none of your business because you're not allowed up there anyway. You just need to give me the money, and Pat and me will get the parts and junk bikes and bring them back to you."

By now I was real pissed off and curious whom Charlie made his deal with. I asked him, "Who are you buying all these bikes and parts from?"

Charlie said loudly, "Verna, naturally."

Bert interrupted and asked, "Who is Verna?"

Charlie said, "Verna and Dave put away a bunch of bikes in the country when they owned motorcycle dealerships a long time ago. They have lots of junk parts and parts bikes left over they need to get rid of because they're cleaning the place out now that their boys Ben and Eric are famous."

After I heard that, I shouted to Charlie, "Fuck, no! I'm not buying any crap from Dave Bostrom. He's a shyster. He probably doesn't even have any legal paperwork for any of his bikes, and if the cops were just in here looking for a stolen scooter a little while ago, I can't even imagine what the cops would do if they found a bunch of Verna and Dave Bostrom's bikes here with no paperwork, bikes which have been missing for the last twenty years."

Charlie became angrier and yelled, "I want that money because you're buying those parts from Dave and that's that."

I held my ground with Charlie and yelled back, "I don't want any of the Bostrom junk in here, and I wouldn't give them $6,000 even if I had it."

Just as Charlie became so angry he couldn't see straight, Pat jumped into the argument and said, "Okay Charlie, the Bostroms mostly do have junk left over up at their property now, so if your kid doesn't want to buy it, I guess it should be alright with you."

Charlie yelled out, "Fuck it then. I have some other things to do today, so I'm leaving for the rest of the day." Charlie stormed out of the shop in a huff and drove away in his truck.

Pat laughed to break up the tension and said, "Well, I guess you won't be too popular up there at the Bostroms' place now that you're not buying their shit."

I said to him, "I don't give a fuck. I already know I'm not well liked by those Bostroms for a while now."

Pat said as he lit up a cigarette, "You're right about that, you're not too popular up there already. As a matter of fact, your name they made up for you at their place, according to Ben and Eric is Junk Yard Johnny, a guy who stole a whole bunch of pipes from their dad."

I knew Pat was talking about the time I crossed paths with a young Ben when his father was tanking his dealership. Pat wasn't in the picture at the time so I didn't say anything about it to him because it sounded as if Ben and Eric already told him their version of the story for the last few years. I knew by now Pat visited Verna's place regularly for a long time, and I couldn't understand why it was so important for the Bostroms to be cleaning out a place where they lived for years. I said, "What's the real story on Verna's place in the country? Are they selling the property?"

Pat answered, "I heard they are being foreclosed on by the bank."

The phone rang, and Pat answered it as I walked out of the office thinking; with the amount of money Dave had and the stories Steve and T used to tell me in the past I found it very hard to believe a bank could foreclose on anything the Bostroms owned. After all, Charlie led me to believe Dave owned his dealership building on Mission Street and the building next door so it appeared as if he had money.

A few days passed and tempers calmed down between Charlie and me. Charlie came to terms because I held my ground not paying the $6,000 for his deal with the Bostroms.

One afternoon, Bert and I were in the office listening to Charlie tell us the best way to run the business. Charlie's mood quickly brightened when Dave and Eric walked in. Charlie said to Bert, "I want you to meet my good friend Dave Bostrom and his son Eric. Eric is a racer, and you should be proud because your new shop sponsors him."

Not knowing how famous Eric Bostrom was, Bert said to Eric, "Since I sponsor you, do you have our shop's name on your helmet while you are racing?"

While Eric smiled Charlie interrupted: "I've sponsored Ben and Eric's racing since the beginning, and now you sponsor them Bert."

Bert and I left the office as Charlie talked with Dave and Eric in private. While in the back she asked me, "What does Charlie mean when he said I sponsor that Eric guy?

I said, "Eric is Dave's son and you should remember Dave because he's the guy Joe spent a lot of time with when you guys broke up. Charlie's been sponsoring Eric and his brother Ben racing ever since they were 10 years old, when Charlie first opened his salvage shop. Charlie usually gives them a lot of things to help them with their racing program. The last few years, instead of Charlie giving them oil and chains, he gives Dave blank receipts from the shop as part of the sponsorship deal. But that ended now since we're running the shop."

The riding season slowed as the year wound down. It rained almost every day since Bert and I took over Charlie's shop. Customers weren't coming in and due to the continuous rain the roof leaked, flooding the shop with an inch of water on the floor in several areas.

Just before the Christmas holidays, Charlie said, "I'm planning my Over the Hill Gang Christmas dinner party, and I need to know what you and Bert want to order, fish, beef or chicken?"

Charlie's annual Christmas party grew in popularity over the last several years. This particular year was no exception. Everyone showed up, including Charlie's old dirt track buddies like Pin Head's dad and Dave Bostrom. By the time the event started there must have been more than one hundred people who crowded into the small restaurant, drinking cocktails and sharing racing and riding stories.

Charlie introduced Bert to his buddies as the new owner of his salvage shop. While Bert and I were standing with Charlie by the bar, Pat and Dave were at the other end of the bar talking about how Eric won the Harley Davidson 883cc road racing national championship and Ben was riding for the Honda factory team next year. Ben was now ranked as one of the top racers in America and had his grasp on the coveted Honda factory Superbike ride, the ride of a lifetime. He was expected to do well.

1998

Nothing changed on the surface with the shop when Charlie retired and transferred the business over to Bert. Charlie still controlled the office and used the same desk. Even though he was running the DMV books portion of the business, he didn't do any of that work in the office; he took care of all that paperwork at his home office.

Charlie was making plans for his annual trip to Florida to see the AMA road races at Daytona to watch Ben and Eric race when Bert and I were in the office as Charlie said to Bert, "I paid for my ticket to Daytona this year with a business check from your shop's bank account. I'll advertise the shop when I'm down there, and you can use the expense as a tax write-off."

While Charlie tore out the check from the shop's business checkbook, one of his friends hobbled in the office. I was surprised to see it was Fred the butcher. I didn't see him since he was nearly killed some time ago on the ride with Charlie. Fred walked with a cane and extended his hand for me to shake while he told us more about the accident and the extent of the injuries he went through.

He suffered a broken pelvis and a badly broken leg as well as other internal injuries. He told us the motorcycle was in a storage yard since the accident and he wanted to give it to the shop for salvage. He said the Highway Patrol report stated the car he hit entered the roadway from a private driveway after Charlie and I passed it. Once the car turned onto the road, Fred and the car were on a head-on collision course. He said he would have a tow truck deliver his destroyed Honda Interceptor to the shop.

With Charlie away on his trip to Daytona things ran smoothly, except in the paperwork department. Dick had a hard time understanding his paperwork deals would no longer be processed through the books of Bert's salvage yard.

One afternoon, Arty pulled up on his latest black market two stroke sport bikes. He wanted to know if Charlie was around so he could have some paperwork done. He was upset to hear Charlie didn't own the place anymore, and when I told him Bert was the new owner, he wanted to know if he could have his paperwork done the same way it was by Charlie in the past. I told Arty it wouldn't be possible to have his paperwork processed at our salvage yard anymore, because we weren't running the shop the way Charlie was running it. Arty became angry and said, "I've been selling these bikes for $6,000 each, and now you're telling me I won't be able to anymore because I can't get the paperwork for them?"

He tried to con me further saying, "I used to give Charlie $100 per motorcycle he would paper for me. How about if I double what I gave Charlie and offer you $200 for each bike?"

I grew aggravated with Arty pestering me and said, "I won't do your deal for $300 or even $1,000 per bike. I can't do your deal because it's illegal and you violate EPA and DMV laws every time you bring one of these bikes in the country to register." Arty said, "Your dad has always been the hookup on the paperwork deals so I'll just wait until he gets back from Daytona to talk to him about my bikes." Arty left in a hurry.

I thought to myself the only reason that guy ever came in here was because he wanted to have other people make money for him. I recalled when he only worked at Dave's Yamaha-Honda shop, slinging parts over the counter and weed on the side. Now he walks around thinking he's a big shot import/export dude.

A while later an insurance adjuster called me for a bid on a crashed 1998 BMW K1200RS. We were awarded the bid and the bike was delivered by the insurance company.

Once Charlie returned from Daytona, he agreed to keep an eye on the shop with Pat so I could take a small two-day trip with Bert and our daughter. When I returned, I walked in the shop and saw the BMW K1200RS was gone. Charlie and Pat told me when I was away they traded the 1200RS for another, less desirable BMW model bike and a little cash. Charlie said, "The 1200RS was sitting here not doing anything, and since nobody was buying it, we made you some money and you have another bike to sell as well. Hey, you weren't here at the time so If you don't like the trade, then I'll buy the new BMW for myself when I come back from my trip to Hawaii."

Charlie added, "You shouldn't complain about how I run your shop when you're not here. I went over the books from when I owned the shop, and I sold over sixty Ninja motorcycles. You and Bert should try and run the place more like I did in the past." He walked out saying, "I have some travel plans I have to make."

After he left, I thought about what he said selling sixty Ninjas. Since the beginning of his shop, the Kawasaki Ninja was a motorcycle he didn't get in for salvage often. The only Ninjas that ever came in the shop were customers' bikes, for tire changes and repairs. I remembered over the years only a few old wrecked Ninjas came through the shop, but they were dismantled for junk, not sold. If Charlie sold sixty Ninjas in the past, where were they located and whom did he sell them to?

Charlie came in the office two weeks later and said, "I'm leaving for Hawaii in a couple of days, and while I'm gone, I need you to pick up a motorcycle from my friend in San Francisco because I don't have the time to do it before I leave. It's a BMW that Ed and I built, but I couldn't get it started so my friend, who works at a BMW shop, has the bike to get it running."

Charlie gave me directions to his friend's house and said, "I'll be back from Hawaii in time for the Laguna Seca races, and if you want to, you can ride my new Ed Woo built BMW around to check it out until I get back."

A few days after I picked up the Ed built BMW I decided to try the bike out on a ride to work. It felt pretty good considering it was put together by Ed and Charlie. The BMW felt smooth at 80 MPH. When I pulled in the driveway, Pat walked over to me and said, "I see you have the new BMW that Charlie and Ed put together, it's good to see the thing's all done."

Charlie arrived back from Hawaii but he didn't stop by the shop before he left for the Laguna Seca races. When the weekend was over, Charlie came back to work and was talking to Pat and some of his friends, describing the highlights of the race. Charlie was excited as he spoke to Pat about Ben's new girlfriend saying, "Hey, the girl Ben's dating is a supermodel. Ben has really come a long way, and now that he's a chick magnet at the races, all the girls want Ben and all the guys wanna ride like Ben."

The following week, I made a trip back to the insurance salvage auction. There were a few crashed newer bikes, and one destroyed and melted frame and engine for an old Yamaha FJ1200 which was completely burned in a fire.

I waited for the sale to begin and gazed around the yard. I was happy to see Ed was nowhere to be seen. I removed Ed's name from our account at the insurance auction. Changing the shop's license and removing his name from the auction account was hopefully enough to keep him out of the place.

When the sale began, it took a while before the auctioneer arrived at the motorcycles. Once he sold the bikes, the prices were all too high, except for the burned up Yamaha FJ1200 frame and engine. I placed the minimum bid of $25 on the burned piece of salvage, and when there were no other bidders the auctioneer slammed his gavel down and awarded me the hulk. When the sale was over, I paid and returned to the shop.

When Charlie came back from Hawaii, he was only staying a few months before he was leaving again on a scheduled cruise to the Panama Canal and other Central American countries. Charlie was living a life of leisure, traveling around and enjoying his retirement.

Because it was the middle of summer Charlie wanted to do some sport bike riding around the usual area of west Marin and the Petaluma countryside, where he commonly rode. He didn't ride for some time because he was traveling so much and felt like he was missing out on the season with Pat and his other friends.

Saturday afternoon, Charlie and his friends were assembling in the office with Pat, making plans for a ride in Marin. Charlie said to me, "We're riding tomorrow and you and Bert can come along if you want to. I haven't had a chance to try the BMW that Pat and I traded the 1200RS for so how about if I take it on the ride and you guys can use my Ed Woo built BMW?" I told Charlie it sounded like a good idea, and we would meet him in Marin.

The next morning, Bert and I pulled in the gas station where Charlie and his friends were assembled. Charlie was in the parking lot with Pat and Mikey and Cal the car guy. We all rode out to the coast and then north for some time until Charlie pulled into a café for breakfast.

After we ate, we rode north for an hour along the coastal route as the weather turned cold from the fog. We took a small break along the side of the road for Pat to have a cigarette when Bert said, "I'm cold, do you think we can head inland where it's hot, and it won't be foggy and cold?"

Charlie, Cal and Mikey followed a fast-riding Pat inland over the mountains from the coast, while I did my best to keep them in sight and follow along with Bert on the back of my bike. We rode east for about two hours, following the group along fast, dangerous, twisting roads, leading through the woods of Sonoma County.

In the afternoon we found ourselves riding down a mountain on a winding road, leading to a large, beautiful lake. At the bottom of the hill Charlie signaled for our group to pull over and rest. Pat quickly pulled off his helmet, sparked up a Marlboro and sat down on the dirt. He bragged how fast he rode and how the rest of the group couldn't keep up with him while he was riding like a Bostrom.

Not wanting to listen to Pat's rambling, Bert and I walked down by the water's edge and sat down on a bench. Bert said, "I almost forgot this weekend would be my dad's birthday."

I said, "You're right. How many years has it been since he died?"

She answered, "9 years ago."

I said, "I know you must miss your dad, but I guess the next best thing is you have Charlie to call your new dad like I do. It's not much, but it's all we got." We laughed. After ten minutes, we gathered our helmets and walked back up to the group.

As we prepared to ride, Bert said, "Hey, Charlie. Can we try out the new BMW for a little while?"

Charlie said, "Well, I guess so, since it's really your shop's bike." We switched bikes, and while riding it, I could feel a huge difference between the BMW I now rode and the Ed Woo-assembled bike Charlie was now riding. We continued to ride away from the lake for about thirty minutes until we entered northern Santa Rosa.

Charlie and the gang pulled into a gas station, and everybody pulled off their helmets and purchased sodas. Pat enjoyed an energy drink while the gang finished topping off their gas tanks and started to plan their route home.

Bert said to Charlie, "I like this new bike way better than the Ed Woo one you're riding. This bike has a back seat that's much more comfortable. Can we ride this new one home for the rest of the day?"

Charlie said, "I guess that won't be a problem because I think I feel a small vibration with this Ed built BMW anyway, so I should take it home and check it out."

Pat, Cal and Mikey already put their helmets on and fired up their bikes ready to ride down the 101 freeway south. The three of them rode out of the gas station and onto the freeway, thinking Charlie and I would catch up to them. Bert finished her drink and put her helmet and jacket on while we started up the bikes, and I followed Charlie onto the 101 freeway.

It was mildly congested with Sunday afternoon traffic as Charlie and I rolled down the road at 65 MPH. Pat's group wasn't in sight; they must have rode faster because we didn't catch them. I continued to cruise along behind Charlie for about a mile and nothing seemed out of the ordinary as we rode along in the right lane.

Just as Charlie switched on his left turn signal to merge into the faster lanes, the rear wheel from the Ed built BMW he was riding suddenly shook violently. In a split second the rear wheel exploded from the motorcycle and shot right past me. Charlie instantly attempted to control the broken motorcycle, which slid wildly from side to side at 60 MPH with no rear wheel as I slowed my bike to warn drivers behind me of the accident. Charlie miraculously rode the Ed built BMW like a veteran dirt tracker with both of his feet dragging on the freeway pavement, eventually slowing the motorcycle to less than 10 MPH on the right shoulder of the freeway. Sparks flew everywhere as the bike's rear swing arm dragged like an anchor along the tarmac. Charlie appeared to have controlled the accident brilliantly.

But then, just as the motorcycle was coming to a stop, it flipped over on its side, taking Charlie with it, smashing his right leg between the engine and the concrete curb which ran along the freeway.

I quickly pulled my bike to the side of the road, and Bert and I ran to help him. He couldn't get the bike off, so I lifted the motorcycle away from his leg as Bert helped Charlie and asked him if he was okay. Charlie told her to pull his helmet off while he said, "I think I'm okay, but I know my lower right leg is broken. I can feel it's all fucked up and it hurts like a motherfucker." He started to sweat profusely all over his sparsely grey haired bald head.

Motorists stopped to inquire if we were okay, and someone called 911. Soon the Highway Patrol and fire department arrived to the accident scene followed by an ambulance crew who worked on Charlie's right leg. The paramedics confirmed Charlie's leg was broken, and they loaded him in the ambulance for a trip to the hospital.

After speaking briefly to the Highway Patrolmen, Bert and I told them as they finished taking our statements we needed to go to the hospital to see how Charlie was. We left on our motorcycle after a tow truck took the Ed built BMW away. As I rode off, I could see the Highway Patrol officer searching in the bushes for the rear wheel that blew off the Ed Woo built BMW Charlie was riding.

We arrived at the hospital in Santa Rosa a short time later. In the emergency room a nurse told us Charlie was having x-rays taken on his leg. While we waited, a doctor told us Charlie suffered a broken knee but the break didn't look too bad so we sat around for the doctor to verify the x-rays.

A few minutes later, the Highway Patrol officer from the crash site walked in the hospital and told me that he found the rear wheel. He said nothing looked out of the ordinary, and he couldn't explain how the wheel came off the motorcycle so suddenly. I remembered when I saw the rear wheel come off the bike it was just the tire and wheel assembly; no other parts of the bike broke off. The officer had a few things for me to sign, and left afterwards. Bert and I went in to see Charlie.

He was on a table in pain and said, "That would've been you guys out there on the freeway if we didn't switch bikes. Bert could have been killed. You two are lucky it was me who crashed because riding double you guys would've been all fucked up."

Feeling bad for him I said to Charlie, "The doctor told me that he thought the break wasn't too bad, and it might heal quickly."

Just then the door opened and the doctor walked in. He said, "Not good. I've been an orthopedic specialist for many years, and this broken knee is the worst I've seen in a long time."

The doctor said Charlie faced a few corrective surgeries and a long recovery. As they gave Charlie pain medication he said to Bert and me angrily, "Well, I guess that's it for my Panama Canal trip I planned with your mother, It looks like I just lost a whole year of my life."

Charlie said he would call my mom and let her know the situation. I told Charlie we would open the shop the next day as scheduled and let his friends know he was injured.

Once in the parking lot I talked to Bert about the accident. Bert and I felt Charlie took a hit we were supposed to take. We felt guilty because he was so badly injured and we were unscathed, we were shocked we escaped harm.

I fired up the bike, and Bert climbed on the back for the ride home to Fairfield. I pulled out on the freeway, thinking about how many tight winding roads and how many bumps the Ed built BMW went over for hours when Bert and I were riding it very fast earlier that day. I couldn't figure out how the BMW could hold us all day, riding on rough roads and fast twisting turns. When Charlie took the bike from us, his weight was less than our combined weight, and he only rode the bike a short time, compared to the several hours Bert and I were on the bike.

It just didn't seem logical the wheel would hold Bert and me and wouldn't hold Charlie by himself. When I thought about the accident, the fact Bert and I escaped injury, or maybe even death, almost made me nauseous. As I continued to ride, a chill came over me as I remembered Bert did say this weekend would've been her father's birthday if he didn't die 9 years ago.

The next day, when I arrived at the shop, Pat was there and already heard the bad news. He said the majority of Charlie's friends also heard he was in the accident. Pat lit up a cigarette and said, "Many of Charlie's friends and your own family members feel that it's your fault the accident happened, because you guys traded bikes before the crash. They feel you and your wife should've crashed, not Charlie."

I grew angry and said, "It's not my fault Charlie was hurt. The motorcycle was built by Ed and Charlie. They probably didn't put something together correct in the rear end of the bike because the wheel broke off."

I told Pat the accident happened so quickly there was nothing we could do to help. Charlie rode the motorcycle down to a slow speed with no injuries and was only hurt when the motorcycle slammed over on his right leg, breaking his knee. Pat had a hard time understanding the entire rear wheel could just snap right off and said, "All I know is you're not very popular right now in the Charlie circle, if you know what I mean." I was mad about what he said.

The next week, the shop seemed empty; there was a void with Charlie injured and none of his friends came by. One slow afternoon, I saw Dave and Eric Bostrom in the shop walking toward me.

They asked how things were and I told them business was slow since Charlie was injured. They told me they needed to buy a set of front forks for a small Honda motorcycle.

While the two of them looked through the pile of forks, Dave said, "Did you hear how well Eric is doing, now that he's riding for the factory satellite Honda team?"

I stuck out my hand to congratulate Eric and said, "Riding for Honda is good now that you're not a kid anymore. How fast does your Honda race bike go?"

Eric said, "I go 185 MPH on my race bike, but the mechanics can gear it to go 220. I just try to stay out of the way while the professional mechanics work on everything." For a moment I felt like Eric was downplaying his role on the Honda road racing team.

In all my years of being around sport bikes and being a racing enthusiast, I never saw anyone come up so fast to get a factory ride like the Bostrom brothers. Maybe the reason the Bostroms were faster than everybody else was because they were trained by Ed Woo since they were small kids.

While Eric and his dad continued to rummage around, I realized they didn't say anything about Ben racing on the full factory road racing Honda program. It was almost 9 years since Dave had all his problems with Honda when he elected to close down his dealership. I wondered if Honda even knew their latest road racing stars may have been trained by a Porsche thief like Ed Woo on a fleet of missing motorcycles stashed away in the country by parents who tanked their Honda dealerships. I wondered if Dave Bostrom would be considered a big disgrace in the eyes of Mr. Honda and the Japanese people.

I remembered long ago when Bernard and I rode to the city with Dark Ninja and joked around about Ben the Honda prince. I wondered how Dark Ninja would feel if he knew the little kid from Charlie's shop wound up being the fastest rider in the country with the highly prized Honda factory road racing contract. Ben and Eric's story was a real life ticket to superstardom.

A few minutes later, Dave found a set of old forks from a Honda CB175 and I said, "I guess you guys can just take the forks because that's what the deal has always been, since the shop sponsors Eric."

Dave said, "I think it's best if Eric pays you for the forks in cash on this deal."

I said to Dave, "No, it's cool. You guys just go ahead and take the forks and don't bother paying me because they're just old rusty junk forks anyway."

Dave and Eric insisted on paying but since I never charged Dave for a part in twenty years, I didn't know how to answer him when he said, "What do you think these forks are worth? How about if Eric gives you $100 and we call it a day?"

When we arrived at the front counter, I asked Dave if he needed a receipt for the transaction. He said, "No, thanks. We don't need any receipts from your shop right now."

I thought it was strange Dave was nice to me when all of Charlie's other friends didn't think so highly of me. I also wondered why Eric, who was working for Honda, needed old rusty forks from me when he should still have the parts Charlie tried to make me buy from the Bostroms for $6,000 when the bank was foreclosing on their property last year.

I wondered since Ben and Eric were making good money racing for the last few years, why didn't they help make the mortgage payments on the property where they lived in order to stop it from foreclosure? I thought Pat might have been lying about the property being foreclosed on and the Bostroms might still own the secret place in the country. Dave did tell me his two sons were living only part-time down in the Los Angeles area.

My thoughts were interrupted when Pat walked in and said, "Wow! It's really slow in here. Didn't anyone come in to buy anything since I was gone for lunch?"

I told Pat that Dave and Eric just left and nobody else came in. Pat said, "Well, if business doesn't pick up around here I guess I'll have to find a job somewhere else. That rival salvage yard across the bay is really jumping with business these days, and the owner told me while I was hanging out there he could really use a guy like me in the sales department."

A few days later, Ed walked in the shop and looked strung-out on something and I noticed he was dressed in dirty clothes from head to toe, sweating while talking fast. He walked around and then pulled me over to a pile of junk bikes in the corner and said, "This burned up Yamaha FJ1200 frame and engine is exactly what I'm looking for, and I need it right now. I have to get it from you today."

Ed jumped in the pile and using all his strength, pulled the burned Yamaha wreck out. Ed stared at the bike sitting next to the burned Yamaha and said, "I want to take that wreck out of here too."

Ed pointed out Fred the Butcher's wrecked Honda Interceptor 750 sitting in the pile. He pulled it out with the help of a friend who came with him in his van. In no time Ed and his equally strung-out-looking buddy, loaded the wrecked Honda and burned up Yamaha frame and engine in Ed's old black van. They slammed the door closed and I noticed the van was wearing license plates from the state of Nevada.

Ed asked me how much I wanted for the salvage and before I could answer him, he produced a large wad of cash and peeled me off a few hundred dollars saying, "Here, this should be enough for both of these wrecks. I'll see you later, kid."

One Sunday afternoon, Bert and I took our daughter around the neighborhood to teach her how to drive. We drove to an area near our home where newly constructed commercial buildings were available for lease. As she slowly drove the car around the streets, Bert saw a phone number to call for inquiries about renting a unit. The sign advertised units for $1,000 a month as I said "Wouldn't it be nice if we could get one of these small units and downsize the shop? We're struggling to keep the place in South San Francisco open at $5,000 a month. We're also paying those losers Pat and Pin Head too much money when they're just a bunch of monkey asses anyway."

The following week, I called the number and found there were a few 2000-square-foot units available for immediate occupancy. I told Bert the units were a good idea and we both decided moving and scaling down the costs of the shop and commute times was the best idea.

A few days later, I told Pat I was closing the salvage yard in South San Francisco after all these years. Pat said, "I already thought this place wasn't staying afloat much longer, so I went ahead and took that job across the bay. I start tomorrow at the rival salvage yard."

As soon as he found out he wouldn't be paid for the day he said smirking while standing in the front smoking his cigarette, "Well, I guess that's it then. I'm out of here. Lot's of luck, Junk Yard Johnny. It'll take an army of men to clean out all this crap." He turned and walked out.

Fifteen minutes after Pat rode away, Pin Head walked in and I told him I decided to close down. He said, "That's okay because I'm not able to work for a while anyway. I'm having all my rotten teeth that are remaining pulled out at one time and replaced with phony teeth. I'm applying for the state to pay for my new teeth, and they have to give them to me because I'm poor and don't have the money to pay for it myself." Pin Head said goodbye and walked out of the shop.

And all of a sudden it was over.

I stood in the warehouse all alone, and the only thing I could hear were my own thoughts bouncing off the metal walls. I wondered how I would ever clean out this huge warehouse, nearly full of rusty junk, undesirable Dave parts and old Verna-mobiles.

I picked up the telephone to call Charlie, who was now home from the hospital, to see how he was and tell him of my decision. As I predicted, Charlie wasn't too happy about the news and said, "You can't close, how in the hell are me and my friends supposed to get bolts and nuts for things we want to put together after my leg gets better?"

I told Charlie I had no other options because we ran out of money. He was silent for a moment and then said, "Well, I think you're making a big mistake because that place I gave you guys is a million dollar gold mine."

I said, "Most of the parts and junk we have in our shop taking up space and collecting dust were in there for the last 10 years, and nobody ever came in to buy the junk we had."

Charlie attempted to interrupt me, but I said, "The shop turned into nothing but a huge dumping ground for all your friends to dispose of their crap when they tanked their dealerships over the years."

Charlie backed down a little and said, "What about the license? You have to keep the license."

I told Charlie I researched the subject of the license, and the DMV told me it was okay to move the shop and keep the same license we already had. He said, "Good, that's the most important thing. You need to not change the license around."

Over the course of the next month my attempts to sell the entire stock to another shop in bulk for one price proved fruitless. A few buyers came to look at the undesirable parts, but they quickly decided they didn't need the old junk inside their shops either.

After I took out what I thought I could sell in the new Fairfield shop, I was lucky to find some guys who said they opened a new salvage yard in the central valley of California. They said they would take everything they needed and offered me only $9,000 and said they would leave behind what they didn't want.

When they finally took out their loads, the shop was still more than half full, with tons of old motorcycle engines, rusty frames and every other conceivable junk part as well. The day the guys left with the last load the leader of their team handed me $9,000 and said, "You're lucky to get this much out of me because your place was full of undesirable junk and I feel like I'm paying you too much." They drove off with their trailer and I thought the only way to get the rest of the place cleaned out was allow anyone to take anything they wanted for free.

The next day, after he heard I was giving away what was left for free, Ed Woo walked in the shop and said he wanted the cash register. Ed reached up and grabbed the two hundred pound 1950's vintage cash register and carried it outside to his Porsche saying, "I'll come back in a few days to get more stuff, and I'll let Dave know you're giving everything left away for free."

Dick walked in the next day, and started to grab as much free junk as he could carry out to his small Ford ranchero pickup. Dick said, "Since it's free, I'm taking as much as I can because I want to stock up at my place."

Later in the day, after Dick returned and trucked out another load of junk parts, Dave walked in with one of his sons. The son appeared much taller than Dave and at first I didn't know who he was, then Dave said to me, "Hey there, you remember my oldest son Tory?"

I realized I didn't see Tory in almost 9 years, since Dave tanked his Honda dealership. Tory said hello and they walked around the shop evaluating the junk that was still in the building. Dave yelled out as he was standing in the middle of a large pile of old parts, "So, everything goes out and everything's free, right?"

I was busy breaking down the large wooden shelves while Dave and Tory looked around the shop for the next half hour. Later, Dave said, "Tory and I have seen enough for now; I'll get back to you if I need to get anything later." Without taking any parts, Dave and Tory walked out and left in Dave's old truck.

As I came closer to closing the shop, I worried where I would move the old junk truck we used for towing bikes. Ed was in the shop one day collecting more free stuff when he asked me, "What are you doing with the old pickup?"

I answered, "I'm not sure what to do with the thing right now because it's not running and I'm so busy and bogged down trying to get this place closed down and cleaned out by the end of the month because the landlord will want to collect more rent."

To my surprise Ed quickly and happily volunteered his services saying, "How about if I help you out by towing your truck over to my storage yard I share with Dave in Oakland. I'll even let you store it there for free because we're all brothers here and family has to help family out...Right?"

I jumped at the offer.

The next week as I worked in the afternoon cleaning up, Dave walked in and asked me how things were with the closing. I told him I wasn't doing that well as he helped me load some junk in a dump truck I rented.

I thought it was strange Dave was the only one of Charlie's friends to help out after Charlie was injured. He acted like he was the only one who didn't blame me for Charlie's crash.

Once we loaded the dump truck to capacity, Dave rummaged around and loaded various parts he wanted to take home in his truck. He said, "If you're still getting rid of all this stuff, I'll load my truck with some of these free parts."

With the evening winding down a light rain began to fall as I walked outside to see how Dave was doing loading his truck. He was tying down his load of junk as I assisted him when he said, "Thanks for all the free parts. I'm sure I'll find a good purpose one day for all this stuff you gave me."

I said to him, "I read Ben won the AMA Superbike championship riding for Honda this year. What's on tap for next year with Ben and Honda?

Dave smiled proudly as he continued to tie down the heavy load and said, "Ben's not riding for Honda this coming year, but the good news is he recently signed up with the new Ducati factory Superbike team. This weekend Ben's trying out the new Ducati Superbike at the Daytona tire test in Florida, and everyone expects him to do well on his first outing with the team."

Dave maneuvered the truck out of the driveway with the rear bumper scraping the ground. He waved goodbye as his taillights disappeared down the street.

It was dark outside as I stood in the rain wondering where Dave was taking all the junk if the Bostroms didn't have their property in the country anymore. I found it hard to believe Dave would unload all that junk in the garage of his home in Brisbane.

I locked up the front of the shop and walked to the back. I stared in silence at all the remaining junk in the shop as the rain started to pound harder on the metal roof. In an instant the sound was interrupted by the familiar distinct noise of a small four-cylinder engine puttering along on three cylinders. I looked outside to see it was the old black men who collected junk metal for a living. One of the old guys stepped out of the truck and said, "We hear you're closing, and we're here to help."

I invited the guys in to look at all the remaining scrap metal and junk in the building. They were surprised to see so much stuff in the shop and told me they could return with other guys with more trucks to help remove the remaining loads of junk, which they could sell to metal recycling yards. I told them I was happy they could help and I only have one week left to get it all done.

I also told them after I cleaned out the junk I still needed to clean the oil and grease off the entire floor. In all the years it became caked on the floor, up to one inch thick in some areas where the engines and junk frames were piled. One of the men said to me, "We don't have anything on the truck tonight, so we'll get a load of aluminum engines now and we'll come on back with our friends tomorrow."

Once they were loaded the old man said, "When we get it all cleaned out, I got a friend who'll stay in your shop and steam clean all night long. All you got to do is buy him some cheap food and all the booze he can drink while he works on the floor." I told the old man I would go along with his idea and rent a steam cleaner.

After the loads of junk were removed and taken away, with all of us working all day long for a week straight, the job was finally finished. I felt I hadn't slept in days. I rented the steam cleaner and gave the old guy's friend a fast food dinner and enough alcohol to drown a horse. He was so happy he started to steam clean enthusiastically while he said, "Shit, I'll have this motherfucker done by tomorrow morning."

I returned the next morning to see the floor almost clean and the dude lying on a piece of plywood, passed out cold with all the empty alcohol containers around him. He woke up when he heard me and said, "It's mostly done. I ran out of gasoline on the sprayer around four o'clock in the morning, so I just drank up the rest of the booze and kicked back till the sun came up."

Just then the old black man pulled up to see if his friend finished the job. He said, "Well, it looks like he got most of it done for you. They didn't want to give me any good money on the all the loads at the metal recyclers; I was happy just to get enough for some beers to go with my steak."

Laughing, I said, "That's funny because my step-dad is mad at me for closing down, saying this place was a million-dollar shop and I threw it all away."

Both men laughed and the old guy said, "Million-dollar shop? I was lucky to sell all that shit at the metal scrappers for just a few hundred bucks. If your ol' man thinks this place was worth a million dollars, then you need to go and get him some serious medication, because that boy is trippin'." The old man picked his friend up off the floor, and they walked out to the truck as I thanked them graciously.

1999

The first week of the New Year was quiet, and I couldn't have been happier. I was still in a state of winding down from cleaning and closing the salvage shop in South San Francisco. I settled in with Bert at the new Fairfield shop, planning on running a cleaner operation with no junk bikes and parts.

One morning I drove to the local Honda dealership in Fairfield to pick up a few small parts. While waiting at the counter, I noticed some copies of a motorcycle publication lying on the counter. I thumbed through one and noticed an article on the Bostrom brothers: Ben recently won the AMA Superbike championship. As I looked through them I saw several pictures of Ben and Eric posing with their expensive automobiles. I noticed a small sidebar that mentioned Ben was seriously injured at the Daytona tire test at the end of last year.

It reported that Ben was blowing everybody away on his new factory Ducati at the tire test, and then, out of nowhere, the rear wheel suffered a catastrophic failure at close to 170MPH on the high banks of the Daytona circuit. The article reported Ben was in the hospital in Florida with serious injuries from road rash but was lucky enough to have no broken bones. I found it very strange Charlie and Ben were both wiped out by rear wheel failures. The good news was Ben would be healed and ready to race when the season began.

The first few months around the new shop were very slow. Nobody knew where the place was located and customers were not walking in the door.

One morning, Charlie called to tell me something very bad happened the night before. He said in a subdued voice, "Pat was nearly killed last night on his bike. He crashed hard into a telephone pole." Charlie said after Pat left a friend's house in Oakland, riding a Suzuki Katana 1000, he lost control on wet pavement and impacted the telephone pole at high speed. He was practically pronounced dead at the scene.

Charlie told me paramedics transported Pat to a local hospital that was equipped with a trauma unit. Pat suffered broken bones and serious internal injuries. Before Charlie hung up, he said, "You two better get your asses down to the hospital in Oakland to visit Pat because he's in a coma and they're not sure if he will live or die."

While Bert and I were driving to see Pat, I said, "You know, for all the times Pat was an asshole, I still feel sorry for the dude."

Bert agreed and said Charlie and Pat working together at the old shop was lots of laughs and it would be sad to see Pat die.

When we arrived in Oakland, Bert and I walked into the hospital and located the ICU. The nurse told us we could visit Pat because no one was currently visiting him. We were shocked to see the condition Pat was in. He was lying on a special bed, monitored by several machines with tubes, wires and hoses running in and out of his body. He was unrecognizable, bloated and swollen with severe black and purple bruising all over.

While we stared at Pat, the short middle aged female nurse with a thick Filipino accent said, "It is okay for you to say hello to your friend, Mister Pat. He can't hear you, but it's good for people to interact with him while he is unconscious."

I noticed the bed was moving around and rotating slightly. I said to the nurse, "I've never seen anything like this before. Why's the bed moving around?"

She said, "The bed moves to keep Mister Pat's fluids moving around inside his body. It rotates to keep him alive. Without the movement his body fluids would cease to flow and Mister Pat would die."

I asked the nurse what were Pat's chances for survival at this point and she said, "Technically he is dead; the machines are the only things keeping him alive right now. He's in a drug-induced coma so he can heal faster. We are hopeful that Mister Pat will recover."

I reached out and touched some of the white hairs on Pat's swollen left hand, which felt like steel wool and his hand was icy cold. The nurse looked up and said with a kind face, "Mister Pat appears to be a strong man; we're hoping for the best." After thirty minutes visiting, Bert and I left the hospital.

In the truck I said to her, "Wow. First Fred was wiped out, next Charlie was smashed by the Ed built BMW, and now Pat is near death after a bizarre crash."

Charlie called one Saturday afternoon and asked if I wanted to go to the AMA Superbike races at Sears Point Raceway in Sonoma the next day. He would be at the track with his gang of friends, watching Ben and Eric race. He had an extra ticket to the races on Sunday and said he would leave it at the front gate for me to pick up. Charlie said, "I'll be hanging out with Dave and Paul Bostrom, and you can find me by the Ducati pit with Ben and the racers." I told Charlie I would be there.

Sunday morning, the trip to Sears Point was only a 30-minute drive from my house in Fairfield. I drove my truck up the hill above the race track to park and soon found the entrance to the racing pit area. I walked around the various displays looking for a familiar face in the crowd, wondering if I would find anyone I knew.

Suddenly, I saw a familiar face. He looked just a little bit older and the hair was just a tad grayer, but there was no mistaking Dave Bostrom, walking right in the middle of the crowd of people. Dave mingled through the crowd without anyone knowing he was the father of the two famous racing brothers.

As I drew closer, Dave recognized me and said hello. I asked him if he saw Charlie around the races yet. Dave said, "Charlie was walking around earlier, but I don't know where he is right now." It was a while since I saw Dave so I asked him how he was.

Dave said, "Everything's just fine, no problems at all. I'm just watching my boy's race." All of a sudden he said, "Okay, I have to get going now, so I'll see you later."

Dave vanished into the crowd as I walked around, and before I knew it, I was standing in front of Eric Bostrom's racing pit. There was a mechanic holding a race bike while he revved the engine and warmed the bike up and I knew it was Eric's bike.

A few minutes later, Eric emerged from a team transporter truck wearing his racing leathers. He walked over to the mechanic holding the bike directly in front of me and spoke to the mechanic about the race bike while I said hello and asked him if he saw Charlie around. Eric was surprised to see me and said, "I haven't seen your dad around today, but I think he's hanging out with my dad." Eric climbed on the race bike, threw his helmet on, and after his mechanic gave him some instructions, he rode off to attend a practice session on the track. I continued to search for Charlie.

After a short time, I found the Ducati road racing pit, but there were no race bikes or racers present. I thought Ben and his Ducati were out at the same practice session for the Superbike race Eric was in.

I decided to get a snack, so I walked over to the concession stand and stood in the long line. I suddenly saw Charlie ahead of me and said hello. He said, "We can have some lunch before the Superbike race starts."

While we ate, he said, "My leg still hurts, but now I can walk without my crutches and my recovery is ahead of schedule. I'm riding my bicycle every day to condition my knee. Oh yeah, I have good news on Pat. He's healing faster than the doctors thought and he should be on the road to recovery soon. He'll be riding again in no time."

We talked for 20 minutes until the announcers said the Superbike race was lining up on the grid. Charlie said, "Let's go over to the fence by the starting line to watch Ben get the hole-shot. He has a front row spot on the starting grid." I followed Charlie through the crowd and over to the fence where we could see Ben on the front row on the Ducati Superbike, ready to go.

I could see the enthusiasm in Charlie's face suddenly turn to horror as the race started and the entire field of bikes took off, leaving Ben Bostrom sitting on the starting line in a state of panic. Ben's factory Ducati Superbike cut-out right as the race began. Ben fumbled quickly with various parts of the bike, trying to get it to start. Within seconds, some Ducati mechanics ran out to the starting line with a battery charger and quickly jump-started the Ducati. The bike roared to life as Ben dumped the clutch and took off up the hill after the pack of bikes that long disappeared.

Charlie and I left the starting line and walked to an area where we could watch the racers pass by through the turns. Ben, in last place, was riding like a man possessed. The announcer stated Ben was shredding through traffic in a desperate attempt to catch up to the leaders while knifing through the lappers.

After many laps, Ben managed to break into the top ten by the end of the race. Once the checkered flag flew, Charlie said, "Let's go down to the Ducati pits and see if Dave and all of my friends are there."

When we arrived at the Ducati pits, Charlie's friends were waiting there. Charlie introduced me to Dave's brother, Paul Bostrom, for the first time. He stuck his hand out for me to shake and I immediately noticed one of his hands was missing the thumb. I remembered Charlie told me years ago that Paul chopped off his thumb while riding Charlie's bike when they were young. Moments later, Charlie's friend Mikey appeared with Dave, and everyone waited together for Ben and the other racer on the Ducati team to emerge from a team meeting in the transporter truck.

Five minutes later, Ben walked out of the truck with his teammate, over to where Charlie and I were standing with the rest of Charlie's group. Ben and his teammate, Anthony Gobert, mingled with Charlie and his friends. Dave and Paul stood around shooting the breeze while Ben produced and signed several Ducati hats for Charlie's group.

Ben handed one to Mikey and another hat to one of Charlie's friends. Ben then signed a third hat and with a sly smile on his face, handed a Ben Bostrom signed Ducati hat to me. Along with the signature Ben also scribbled a large number one on the hat signifying he was defending his 1998 AMA Superbike Championship.

I took the hat from him and I shook Ben's hand while Anthony Gobert shook hands with Charlie and his friends. I put the hat on my head and looked back at Charlie, standing right next to me. I was shocked to see Ed Woo about 10 feet away, circling on a very expensive-looking Cannondale mountain bike. Ed pedaled the bicycle around quietly and didn't approach us or act like he knew any of us.

I thought Ed might have been under instructions to not interfere with the Bostroms when they are in the public eye. Charlie tapped me on the shoulder to get my attention and said, "This is Anthony Gobert. He's on the Ducati Superbike team with Ben." Anthony Gobert shook my hand, and by the time I turned around, I was astonished to see Ed vanished. I then looked back at Ben to see him smiling at me.

When the race day wound down, Dave and Paul Bostrom headed over to see Eric, and Charlie's other friends left on their motorcycles. Charlie said, "I came in my truck because I'm not riding yet. I'm parked up on the hill."

As we walked to the trucks together, I said, "I saw Ed behind you guys in the pits on an expensive mountain bike. What's the deal with that?"

Charlie said, "Ed has to stay out of the limelight when the boys are racing so he's riding around on Ben's bicycle. Ed came to the races with the Bostroms."

One afternoon while I was standing outside the shop and Bert was in the office answering the phones, I noticed a motorcycle riding toward our shop. The rider pulled into the parking lot and took off his helmet to reveal his thick white hair. He introduced himself and said he owned a small motorcycle repair shop right down the street and was there for many years. I told the man I recently moved in my shop after closing down a large motorcycle salvage operation in South San Francisco.

He said, "Is that the place that was owned by a guy named Charlie?"

I told him it was. "He's my stepfather."

The old white-haired man cracked a smile and said, "Well your dad's a real asshole. A long time ago he fucked up my deal."

At first, I was taken aback, even though Charlie was called an asshole by many unsatisfied customers in the past. The old man climbed off his bike and came in our small shop to check things out. I asked him, "Where do you know Charlie from?"

He answered, "I've known Charlie for years, and he pissed me off when I made a deal with a woman who closed down her Honda dealership in Oakland."

He said hello to Bert and took a seat on the second-hand sofa we installed in the office saying, "Way back in the mid-80's I made a deal with a woman to clean out a bunch of parts and shop equipment from her dealership in Oakland, which was going out of business. Charlie showed up and attempted to unravel my deal with the woman, saying he wanted to buy the parts from her as well. I was angry because Charlie tried to coax Verna into giving me half of my money back so he could pay her the other half and get a piece of my deal for himself."

The man surprised me when he said the name Verna so I said, "I think I know the Verna you're talking about. Years ago Charlie made a deal with a woman named Verna who owned a Honda dealership in Oakland. Charlie bought junk bikes by the truckload for us to dismantle and throw away after Verna tanked her dealership. Charlie told me Verna went out of business because motorcycle sales back in the 80's were slow."

The old man laughed and said, "I don't know if I believe that story. Do you know what I heard Verna's real problem was?" I watched as the old man raised his finger to his right nostril and sniffed, indicating cocaine usage.

He checked the time and said he should go. As I watched him ride off I wondered what he said about Verna and drugs. I thought maybe Verna didn't have a drug problem at all; maybe she was just as sly as Dave when it came to closing down the dealerships and hiding the motorcycles away.

About a month later, the phone rang at my house. It was Charlie in one of his grouchy moods, complaining about the old shop being closed. He said, "You know, I can't even get a fucking headlight screw for my bike because everything at the dealership has to be special ordered and costs too much; they don't keep anything in stock. If you still had the shop open I could just get my screw for free like I used to." As I listened to Charlie I realized, even with the broken leg he was back to being his old self, complaining about a screw that cost less than a dollar.

I told him he could buy a screw for his headlight anywhere and it wasn't necessary for me to keep a warehouse full of junk open for him and his friends to do so.

He asked firmly, "What happened to all my stuff in the office? I had a bunch of things in my desk and my red tool box. I also had a box of my shop's blank receipts sitting under my desk. I hope you didn't throw my things away when you moved because I need my stuff."

I told Charlie I put all his things from the office and his desk in a few large boxes and left them in the garage at his house while he was in and out of the hospital with surgeries and physical therapy appointments.

Charlie was happy to hear all his personal stuff was safe. "Good. I need to give some of my old receipts to Eric. Dave said Eric made lots of money racing last year and he's making close to $300,000 this year, so he needs receipts again for tax write-offs."

I listened to Charlie boast about Eric's salary and tax woes, and I became agitated. I said, "I thought I told you to stop all that receipt shit when we took over back in 1997. You can't let Eric use the receipts because Bert and I own the shop now and it's not cool to keep Dave's deal going. We have our own taxes to worry about and I don't think we should have to carry a big motorcycle racing star like Eric Bostrom along with us while we file our income taxes for our shop."

Charlie became angry and said, "Hey, my receipts show the address of my old shop, and if I let Eric use my receipts for his taxes, I see nothing wrong with it. There's no shop located there anymore, so you guys don't have anything to worry about with the IRS." Holding my ground I told Charlie I was against it.

Charlie appeared to accept my decision about not letting Eric use the old shop's receipts, but he said, "Well, if that's the way you want it then, fine! Okay, well, I have to go to a physical therapy appointment now."

Charlie abruptly hung up the phone while I thought about the receipts. Charlie never listened to anything I ever told him to do in the past, and when it came to the Bostroms and Ed Woo, Charlie never said no to a request.

A few weeks later, the phone in the office rang. It was a woman who identified herself as an agent for the State of California Department of Insurance Fraud Investigation Unit. She told me she was working on a case involving the shop's old receipts that were used for collecting insurance money on items which were supposedly purchased at the old shop in South San Francisco and then reported stolen.

She asked me if I would make an appointment to answer some questions and identify the receipts. She felt they were used fraudulently by someone. I immediately thought Charlie used the receipts when I told him not to, so I made an appointment with the woman to go to her office.

The next day I walked in the building, located her office and took a seat in the waiting room. After a few minutes, she walked out to greet me. She was a stern woman with a serious look on her face. She was well dressed in a blue suit and had dark hair tied up in a bun. We walked to her office and sat down while she produced a few receipts from Charlie's old shop after the time he turned the place over to Bert. The receipts were submitted to an insurance company for items reported stolen.

Her first question was whether I could identify the name of the customer who supposedly purchased the items listed on the top of the receipt. I immediately recognized the name as a good friend of Dick, the guy who ran what Pat called Dick in the Booty Motors down the street from the old shop. The woman's next question was whether the items listed on the receipt were actually purchased at the shop, because the receipts showed the purchase of a few expensive leather jackets and helmets totaling hundreds of dollars.

I told her the purchases were not made at the shop. She said, "If the items were not sold by your shop, is it possible someone stole the receipts from your shop and made them out to show items they never purchased?"

I answered, "Yes those are probably stolen receipts."

I told her the shop was mostly a salvage yard and high dollar items like jackets and helmets were not sold there.

The woman's final question I found rather bizarre. She said, "This gentleman reported all of these jackets and helmets stolen along with his Suzuki GSXR sport motorcycle. He claims most of the jackets were stored under the seat. Is that possible?"

I laughed and told her you would be lucky to fit your wallet and a set of gloves under the seat of any Suzuki GSXR motorcycle. The woman didn't give me any details about the case, but by the time I left her office I suspected Dick stole the receipts from the shop and gave them to his friends for illegal purposes.

With the meeting over I pulled out my cell phone in the truck and called Dick. I said, "Hey, fucker. You and your asshole friends stole receipts from my shop and used them to make money." I demanded Dick tell me what they did and who he did it with. Dick didn't say anything at first then I said, "The State of California Insurance Crime Unit is looking for you and your friends. They know you guys wrote out receipts for stuff you didn't buy at my shop and they suspect your friends' claims are bogus."

Dick panicked when he heard he and his friends were investigated by the State of California, and said, with his voice shaking, "I didn't steal anything, dude. Honestly. I'll talk to my friends and let you know what's going on." Dick hung up the phone without saying anything further. I never heard from him again.

During the summer the phone rang and I was surprised to hear Ed Woo's voice. He said, "We have to get together because you need to get your old truck out of my yard. I repaired it with Pin Head, so your truck's ready to go."

I told Ed it would be a few days before I could get down to Oakland. He said, "I want to get it out of there. I need the room since they're giving me back all of my cars."

Ed gave me directions to his yard in Oakland, and I told him I would go to his place later in the week.

Bert and I met Ed at an Oakland gas station a few days later. Ed showed up driving a Porsche 911. He waved to us from his car and indicated for us to follow him to his storage yard and we soon found ourselves in a rundown neighborhood while Ed steered his Porsche over to the side of the street and parked. He climbed out of his Porsche and said, "This is the place. I'll unlock the gate and give you guys a tour, and you can get your truck out of here."

Ed walked over to a large sliding gate and unlocked the latch and the three of us walked in the yard. It was huge and encompassed an open area between the old houses on the street. There was room to park over twenty five cars in the dirt lot, which contained various junk cars and old trucks strewn about the yard, along with an old motor home sitting in the far corner of the property. He said, "It looks a little empty around here right now, but I need your truck out of the yard because I'm getting all of my cars back."

We followed Ed in a building with several big rooms the largest was used to hold a few Porsches in various states of assembling. One was only the body shell of a Porsche 911, with wires running wildly about the partially constructed car.

While I gazed at it, Ed said, "I had a bunch of Porsches parked in here, and the cops just showed up one day and towed them all away."

Following Ed into another room, I saw a wrecked motorcycle stored and what appeared to be years of junk and memorabilia lying all around the room. He said, "We've been fighting the San Francisco Police Department for a long time on my case, and now they have to give me back all my property because me and Dave Bostrom have that Sergeant Roccaforte eating out of the palm of our hands."

Ed laughed and said, "Dave and me have the whole entire San Francisco Police Department eating out of the palm of our hands."

I asked Ed, "Did you get in trouble for stolen cars?"

Ed answered quickly. "Hell no, all of my Porsches were legal, and they were wrongfully seized from this location by San Francisco cops."

I noticed the wrecked motorcycle stored in the room was Fred the Butcher's Honda Interceptor Ed removed from the shop last year. I said, "I can't believe you still have this old wreck. What are you doing with it?" Ed told me he had no plans to fix Fred's bike.

I walked over to a work bench and picked up a large trophy and read the inscription. It was a first place road racing trophy dated 1983. That was the year Charlie first opened his shop. I wondered how long Ed occupied the space.

I set the trophy back down and looked at some other odds and ends when I heard Ed say, "Think fast kid." I spun around to see a small black metal object flying through the air directly toward me. I tried to catch it, but it flew past my outstretched hands and hit me in the chest. I quickly grabbed the object and saw it was Ed's black Porsche wristwatch, which he wore many years ago at Charlie's shop.

He said, "You can have that watch for old time's sake. I used the stop watch feature on it to time Ben and Eric while they trained and rode with me. I want you to have it now as a keepsake. Hold onto it tight because it might be valuable in the future."

As the three of us left the room, I glanced in the corner and saw the burned up Yamaha FJ1200 frame and engine Ed removed from the old shop when he took Fred's bike as well. The junk Yamaha was in the same melted, burned condition as the day Ed bought it from me. I wondered why he wanted it in the first place if it was only sitting in the corner doing nothing.

We followed Ed back outside where our old truck was parked. Ed jumped in the truck and said it was ready to go while he turned over the engine and found the truck wouldn't start because of a dead battery. Ed said he would work on the truck further to get it running again and asked me if I would come back another time to pick it up.

He said, "Me and Pin Head had this truck running fine. I don't know what's wrong with the battery, but we'll work on it again."

As I gazed around the yard I asked him, "What's the deal with the old motor home parked in the corner?"

He answered, "That's Dave's old motor home from when he took his boys racing at Lodi Cycle bowl years ago. Come on, I'll give you a tour." We walked through the yard past a series of broken down fork lifts in different states of repair. I asked Ed, "Do you work on fork lifts too?"

He said, "Yes I'm an expert in hydraulics as well."

We arrived at Dave's motor home and Ed said, "Walk inside and check it out if you want. It's like a Bostrom time capsule in there." While inside he said, "I can't wait to get all my cars back because I know my lawyer is working hard against that Roccaforte."

I asked him, "Who is Roccaforte?"

He said arrogantly, "That's the cop who's up my ass on my Porsche cars, but that's all about to change soon because I have witnesses who will say the cops seized my cars illegally so they have to return all my stuff."

Ed escorted Bert and me back to the gate when we finished checking out the Bostrom motor home. He said as we left, "Don't worry about your old truck kid, I'll have Pin Head come back here and get it running perfectly and I'll call you when it's ready."

Since I didn't hear back from Ed for more than two months, I thought they were still working on the truck.

2000

Over the New Year holiday Bert was talking to me about how difficult it was for her to split her time between her salvage shop in Fairfield and the hair shop in San Rafael. Bert decided she would retire from cutting hair and put all her energy into the bike shop.

I was alone in the office one morning when a call came in from Pin Head. He told me he was in a bad motorcycle crash a few months back and he broke his neck. Shocked, I was surprised no one told me. I asked what happened and he laughed and said he crashed on a freeway entrance while rounding the turn. He wanted me to visit him with cigarettes and candy and gave me directions to a place in Redwood City, I told Pin Head I would come down to visit him in a few days.

A couple of days later when I was leaving to visit Pin Head, Bert stopped me and said, "Here's a bag of soft chocolate chip cookies I baked earlier for Pin Head, tell him I said hi."

I told Bert I was sure Pin Head would love the cookies because he was eager to eat as many sweets as he could get his hands on. I took the bag from Bert and kissed her goodbye.

The trip to Pin Head's in the middle of the day took me two hours because of traffic so I ate some of the cookies on the way. When I arrived in Redwood City, I looked for the place Pin Head told me to find. I followed the directions to a very old, dilapidated motel that was built in the 1930's. I couldn't believe it was a free out-patient facility because it seemed like a drug haven for addicts and other down and out people.

I parked my truck and walked to the room Pin Head said he was in. When I came to the unit with the number 9 on the door I couldn't tell if it was a six or a 9 because the metal digit spun around on a single loose screw. I knocked and found the door partially open so I stepped inside to find the worst-looking motel room I ever saw. Half the soiled carpet in the room was torn out and most of the ceiling was missing from water damage. There was a small black and white television turned on which sat atop a broken dresser with drawers missing.

I was shocked to see Pin Head's condition. He was laid out on a very dirty and worn-out blue-striped mattress with no sheets with a huge metal cage-like device bolted to his head and shoulders. I laughed when I saw him and said, "Wow, That thing looks like it hurts, I guess your new name should be Bolt Head not Pin Head."

Pin Head was very happy to see me but was upset at his living conditions and said, "The bathroom doesn't work because there's no running water. This place sucks, but it's the only place the state will pay for during my rehabilitation until I'm healed."

He was glad to see I brought him a carton of cigarettes, but even more happy to see the cookies and a quart of half and half cream. Pin Head munched down the cookies and then tore open the carton of cream and maneuvered it between the bars of the metal cage to his lips, gulping the cream, while it streamed down his cheeks and chin.

Once Pin Head devoured the cookies and cream, he lit up a cigarette and told me the halo apparatus he wore for the last few months gave him headaches, and he was having a hard time sleeping. He said, "I hate this fucking halo and it has to go. I think my neck is healed now, and I don't need this thing anymore so you have to help me remove it. Do you have any tools? I have to get it off because it itches badly and I can't stand it anymore. Go get some tools for me, kid."

I walked outside laughing and grabbed my tool box and walked back in the room. Pin Head took the tools from me and while looking in the cracked mirror, locked pliers onto one of the bolts that was drilled in his head and slowly turned the bolt outward.

I winced as I watched the screw back out of his skull. The skin appeared to have grown in around the screw and adhered to the twisting bolt. As the bolt continued to turn, the skin tore away and soon the first bolt was out of his head. To my surprise there was no blood, only dried crust around the hole in his head. He was feeling no pain as he unscrewed the second and then the third bolt. In no time at all, Pin Head was free from the halo cage and said, as he discarded it on the bed, "There, it's done and I didn't even have to wait for no stupid doctor to do it for me."

He said, lighting up another cigarette, "Now that I'm all better, I can't wait until I can get back to riding again."

After visiting a while, I told Pin Head I had to leave, and he walked me out the door, saying, "I'll talk to Charlie about getting another motorcycle. I'll ask him if he will loan me some money to buy a cheap old motorcycle because my dad won't help me out with anything. He won't even visit me."

As I drove away, I recalled Pin Head's dad always reprimanded him about his heroin and speed use. He never quite fit in with his dad's and Charlie's friends from the past. It seemed as if they didn't want him in their circle because of his wild drug use and dangerous riding habits. Every time Pin Head asked his father for money, the answer was always the same. His dad would say no and told him he should get his shit together because he was disappointed Pin Head shot drugs his entire adult life and was now close to 45 years old.

Ed Woo called one day and said, "Hey, kid. I know it's been a while, but I need you to come down and get your old truck out of my storage yard in Oakland since I'm getting my cars back." I told him I would make plans to pick up the truck.

I was in Oakland a few days later with Bert to meet Ed. I called him on my cell phone, and he told me to be at the same gas station as before.

We waited fifteen minutes in the parking lot, and Ed didn't appear. After waiting nearly an hour, my phone rang again and it was Ed, he told me he was in San Francisco and would be in Oakland to meet us in about ten minutes.

When Ed arrived, we were surprised to see he wasn't driving his usual Porsche 911 but an old beat-up 1978 Yamaha motorcycle. He was dressed in blue jeans and a worn-out, dirty shirt with no jacket. He also wore rubber beach thongs on his feet.

As we followed Ed I said to Bert, "Look at the way he's dressed and what he's riding. That's not the Ed Woo I know."

She said, "I see what you mean. Where do you think Ed found that old junky bike, and where did he ride it from? It wasn't from very far because the bike looks like its running shitty, and the way he's dressed looks like he just woke up. What's the deal with the thongs on his feet; where's his shoes?"

I said, "He kept us waiting for an hour and then he shows up like he just rode in from around the block."

When we arrived at Ed's yard, he swung open the gate and we walked over to my old truck to start it up. I gazed around his yard and realized nothing changed since the last time we were there. When Ed started the truck, I noticed the front tire was flat and when I brought this to his attention he said, "Damn. It wasn't flat just a short time ago when I was here last. The truck runs good now, so I'll fix the tire and I'll call you back again."

Ed felt bad we drove all the way from Fairfield and the truck wasn't ready. He said, "Let me make it up to you guys by taking you both out to dinner for some good Mexican food." I accepted Ed's offer because I thought he could tell me some of the latest Bostrom racing gossip since he was so close to Dave and his boys. If anyone knew about life with Ben and Eric, it would certainly be Ed.

As we walked out of Ed's yard, he noticed I was looking around and he said, "It's still a little empty in here because there's been a slight delay on the cops returning all my Porsches, but I'm expecting each and every one of them back because my lawyer has those cops going in every direction."

Ed told us to follow him on his motorcycle to the Mexican restaurant. While we drove, I said to Bert, "Do you think Ed is on some kind of drug? He looks all strung out and he's acting weird. He's talking so fast and sweating so much he looks like he drank 9 cups of coffee." I scoffed and said, "Or snorted 9 lines of coke."

She said, "Maybe he's just embarrassed he brought us all the way down here for nothing again."

Ten minutes later, Ed pulled his motorcycle into a Mexican restaurant parking lot, near the waterfront of Oakland. Together the three of us walked into the restaurant and were seated for dinner. When the waitress came over to the table, Bert and I ordered, and Ed said, "I'm not hungry, so I won't order anything."

The waitress collected the menus and left our table. We talked briefly with Ed about Charlie's rehabilitation and Pin Head's broken neck, while waiting for the food.

As we ate dinner, Ed leaned over and said to me, "You know, kid, if you ever want to sit at the table with the big boys, you have to know when to say the right thing and who to say the right thing to."

I said, "The big boys?"

Ed boasted, "I've sat at the table with the big boys for years because they know that I know when to do and say the right thing and who to say it to."

Bert was puzzled and said, "What are you talking about? I don't get it."

Ed leaned over to her and said sternly, "Usually the women are supposed to just sit there and eat their dinner and not ask any questions, so maybe that's a good idea for you to do right now."

I listened to what Ed said and grew angry. I said to him, "Hey, you can't talk to her like that."

It seemed Ed didn't want her to know what he was trying to tell me about the big boys. Ed apologized and said, "It's just I have to get things right for the big boys, and nothing can go wrong because I'm in the process of getting all my stuff back and I don't want to blow it now."

I thought Ed would tell me the latest news about the Bostroms' racing. Now, Ed behaved suspiciously and talked about the big boys again. The last time I heard Ed talk about the big boys was way back when Charlie was operating his shop. I wondered who the big boys were and why Ed looked up to them after all these years. I thought the best thing for me to do was to listen to whatever he had to say and remember every word he said. Ed never spoke about the big boys needing any help in the past. I also wondered why he thought I would be invited to sit at the table with these mysterious big boys because I was never invited before or ever met them.

With dinner just about over, Ed said, "I don't want you to get the wrong idea, kid. I just want you to say the right thing when the time comes." The waitress came over to the table and asked if there was anything further we needed. When she gave us the check, Ed grabbed the bill and said, "This one's on me and the big boys."

We left the restaurant and walked out to the parking lot. Ed stood at my truck door to say goodbye and I asked him before we left, "You've been mentioning these big boys for years. Who the hell are these big boys anyway?

Ed smiled and patted me on my shoulder and said, "Don't worry about that, kid. First you have to remember to play your cards right and say the right thing and then maybe one day you can find out who the big boys are."

As Bert and I drove home, she said, "I'm pretty mad at the way Ed talked to me tonight. He was always real nice to me in the past when I used to cut his hair. Ed didn't seem to be himself. He keeps telling you to say the right thing, but who are you supposed to say the right thing to and what the fuck is the right thing to say anyway? Do you think he's in some kind of trouble? I hope he doesn't have us mixed up in anything bad he's doing."

I said, "Ed's probably high on cocaine and still worrying about getting his Porsches back from the cops."

She said, "When Ed was talking about those so-called big boys, I thought he was talking about Charlie and all of his old friends from his past, but you can sit at the table with Charlie any time you want; I guess the big boys are dudes more important than Charlie."

I said, "I thought Charlie and Dave was the top of the food chain when it came to Charlie's group of friends. Maybe the big boys are professional racer friends of Dave's from the past. I don't care who the big boys are, he better not have us involved in any of his crap he's mixed up in with Dave or whomever."

One evening, while Bert and I were cooking dinner, the phone rang and I was surprised to hear it was Charlie because it was several months since he called us. He talked to me about his annual over the hill gang Christmas dinner, which was coming up in a few weeks. Charlie said, "If you guys want to go, you need to get there around seven o'clock."

Charlie paused for a moment and then said, "Oh yeah, I forgot to tell you. We're helping Ed get his bike back from the tow yard so I want you to say that you guys sold Ed his Yamaha."

I said, "I sold Ed a Yamaha FJ1200 frame and engine."

Charlie said, "Good...Now here's the deal. A cop who towed Ed's Yamaha away will call you and I need you to say that you guys sold Ed his Yamaha."

I told Charlie I would wait for the cops to call about Ed's bike, and then I asked him how he was doing with his leg these days. Charlie skirted my question and seemed to be in a hurry to get off the phone.

I hung up the phone and said to Bert, "I think Charlie's working on something with Ed concerning the old burned up Yamaha frame and engine we sold him a long time ago. Charlie said it was towed away and said the police will call here in a few days and ask whether Ed bought the burned up bike from me or not."

Just then the phone rang and I picked it up thinking it was Charlie again. An unfamiliar voice on the other end said to me, "Good evening. This is a call from the San Francisco Police Department. My name is Sergeant Roccaforte, and I'm calling you about a man named Edwin Nei Woo. Do you know him?" I answered, "Yes." He asked, "Do you recall Ed Woo purchasing a Yamaha from your motorcycle shop?"

I said, "Yes, Ed Woo did buy a Yamaha a few years back from my shop that was located in South San Francisco."

He then said, "Is there any chance you have a copy of the receipt that shows Ed Woo making this Yamaha purchase?" I told him I would try and find it.

Then the Sergeant asked, "Is it possible in your opinion to polish and repair a destroyed motorcycle that has fire damage?"

I answered, "It depends on how bad the fire is. Most of the time motorcycles sustain heavy damage in fires, and it would be difficult to repair any parts. They would all have to be replaced."

He asked, "Can a frame be polished to like new condition after it was burned in a fire?"

I said, "If a motorcycle frame is made of aluminum, then most of the time they melt and can't be polished back to perfection. I've seen many burned bikes and the only time a frame can be salvaged is when it's made of steel. Aluminum frames never stand up to heat, and they are easily destroyed and can't be repaired."

I told the Sergeant I would try and check any records I had lying around for the receipt. He thanked me for my time and as he closed the conversation, he suddenly said, "Oh, I have one more question before I say goodnight. Have you ever heard of a Rock motorcycle?"

I told him I didn't know what a Rock motorcycle was and I never heard of one before. He said, "Okay, if you get your hands on that receipt, I would appreciate it if you could let me know right away." He left me his phone number.

I hung up and said to Bert, "Ed must be up to something on that old burned up Yamaha FJ1200 frame and engine we sold him. That was the cops calling here, and I bet Ed used the burned FJ1200 frame to build up another stolen FJ1200 that must have been impounded or towed away. It sounds like he's trying to get it back from the police impound tow." I started to get real pissed off because I thought Ed and Charlie had me involved with something and didn't let me know what it was.

I grabbed some plates and set the table as Bert put dinner down and said to me, "It seems strange Ed has an old FJ1200 motorcycle when he's only associated with high-end, exotic bikes and expensive Porsche cars. Are you going to call Charlie back and ask him what's up?" I told her I didn't want to say anything to Charlie until I found out exactly what they were up to on my own. If I knew Charlie he would lie to me on anything I ask him concerning Ed Woo and the cops.

When Bert and I arrived at Charlie's Christmas dinner a few nights later there were many faces we never saw before. Charlie sat us at a table with people we didn't recognize. Charlie orchestrated his entire evening from the other side of the room and didn't talk to me all night. He was standing, making speeches directly in the center of the tables that seated the family of Dave and Paul Bostrom and the current owner of a large San Francisco motorcycle dealership.

I gazed over at Dave, who was engaged in conversation with the owner of the dealership. Bert reached over, gave me a kiss and whispered, "Do you think the table where Charlie's sitting with all those guys over there is the big boys table?"

I laughed and said, "I guess I didn't say the right thing to that sergeant on the phone because we're not sitting over there with the big boys."

Bert said, "I don't see Ed here tonight sitting over there with them. Maybe they're not the real big boys." I said, "Well, I see Dave and Paul Bostrom over there with Charlie and those boys are big."

I found it strange that Dave didn't turn around and make eye contact with me the entire night and Charlie also avoided us for most of the evening. I knew it was the last Charlie Christmas dinner Bert and I would be invited to. I stared at Dave thinking, *he's up to no good with Charlie and Ed*.

2001

A few months passed since Bert and I downsized our living conditions and moved to a smaller one-story house away from Fairfield. Business at the new shop was still slow, and we were always trying to find ways to decrease the monthly bills to make ends meet.

We found out running a motorcycle salvage shop in Fairfield didn't make us much money. Walk-in customers were rare and phone and email requests were mostly for newer parts we didn't have. I wondered how Charlie managed to stay in business through the slow season all those years when no one wanted to buy the junk he had in his business. We continued to struggle on for several months.

One afternoon, during the summer I located a decent condition Honda CBR600F4 at the insurance salvage auction and bought it.

Three days later, the Honda was delivered, and I noticed the left side engine cover was damaged and needed to be replaced, along with the gasket. After phoning around to several Honda dealerships and finding no one had the parts, I called Mission Motorcycles in Daly City. I was connected to the parts department and they told me I was lucky because they had one generator cover and one gasket in stock. I told them I would come down the next day to pick up the parts.

When I arrived, I was surprised to see a couple of people I knew from the past still working at the dealership. One was Dave's ex-saleswoman from his old shop. I asked the parts guy about her, and he told me she was now one of the owners of Mission Motorcycles.

While I was standing at the parts counter, I picked up a magazine and on the front cover was a picture of Ben Bostrom riding the Factory Ducati race bike. The headline read: 'Bostrom smokes 'em at Brands'.

The story was about how Ben recently won the round of the World Superbike racing series at Brands Hatch raceway in England, after he was moved up from racing in the United States to the international scene.

I was surprised to see Dave Bostrom walk into the parts department. He looked at me and said, "Hi there, how's it going?"

Dave picked up the entire stack of motorcycle newspapers on the counter and said, "I just got off the phone with Ben yesterday, and he told me to come down here and grab up all these issues that feature him on the cover beating the world."

I didn't see Dave since Charlie's dinner last year, when he was too busy to say hello to me. Dave told me how well his boys were recently doing in motorcycle racing. He said, "Ben just finished scoring a double win at Laguna Seca just a few weeks back and now he's showing the world how fast the Bostroms really are. Eric recently blew everybody away in the Superbike races at Laguna Seca in the AMA Superbike series."

Hearing all this good news about the success of Ben and Eric, I wondered just how far and fast an Ed Woo-trained Bostrom could go in the international world of motorcycle road racing.

Several of the parts department employees circled around Dave to congratulate him on Ben's success. Dave held the newspapers close to his chest as he greeted his friends and well-wishers. A parts employee gave me my parts, and I walked out the door. I could still see Dave engaged in friendly conversation.

A few weeks later, when I was home in the evening, the phone rang and it was Charlie. It was quite some time since I heard from him and he asked me numerous questions about how business was running for Bert. Our conversation also consisted of Charlie complaining he still couldn't find any small bolts and fasteners for things he wanted to build.

I asked him what he was up to, and he said, "I've been doing nothing except going to the road races. I enjoyed watching Ben and Eric win against the best motorcycle racers in the world down at Laguna Seca Raceway recently."

When Charlie mentioned the Bostroms, I thought about Ed's training, which now looked largely responsible for their meteoric rise. Thinking about Ed, I realized he never called me back on the old truck. I also remembered speaking with Charlie last year about Ed and his Yamaha FJ1200, which was stuck in a police tow impound. I said to Charlie, "Did Ed ever get his Yamaha FJ1200 out of the police impound tow yard?"

Charlie hesitated for a moment and said in a confident voice, "Yes he did because Dave Bostrom really saved the day on that one."

One afternoon, I was in the office of the shop when the phone rang and it was Ed. He told me he wanted to come by and see Bert's shop. He was in Sacramento and would stop by Fairfield to see me on his way back to San Francisco so I gave him directions to the shop, and he told me he would arrive soon.

An hour later, a sleek black Porsche 911 pulled in the driveway and a well-dressed and confident-looking Ed Woo stepped out of the car. He walked over to the front of the shop and said, "It looks pretty nice. Sorry I haven't been able to come by and check out your new place sooner." Ed and I walked in the shop, and I showed him the small operation Bert was running for the last couple of years.

Ed gazed around at the various wrecked bikes and parts and said, "I see you don't have too much stuff in here. That's good because it's finally time for you to get your truck back from me." He said in a cocky voice, "You know, I did work on and store that truck for a very long time, if you know what I mean, kid."

I asked Ed what he was talking about, and he said to me arrogantly, "I think it's only right if you pay me for some storage on it because of everything I did for you."

I became a little annoyed at Ed's request. I thought it was ridiculous for him to ask me for money when he drove up in a nice Porsche dressed in sharp expensive clothes. I said, "Business is slow around here and I'm very short of money, so if you want to be paid, you'll have to accept payment in the form of a piece of motorcycle salvage that's sitting on the floor in this shop."

Ed pointed to a frame and engine for an old Suzuki GSXR750 an insurance company sold me after it was recovered from the bottom of a lake. The wrecked frame and engine was under water for several days.

Ed said, "I'll take this as payment for the storage on your truck, but only if you're willing to deliver it to my house in San Francisco on Russian Hill." I agreed to deliver the wreck to Ed the next day, and together we walked in the office. He wrote down some directions on a piece of paper to his house on Union Street.

I said to him, "What are you doing in Sacramento?"

He said, "I was in Sacramento to see Dave. He's working with his brother on house deals up there."

I said, "I just saw Dave down at his old dealership a while back. How's he doing?"

Ed said, "Dave's doing just fine. I was over at his house last week helping him with the weed cutting on the mountain around his place in Brisbane." Ed told me he had to get back to San Francisco. He climbed into the Porsche and disappeared down the street at a high rate of speed.

That night, I told Bert I made a commitment to deliver a piece of salvage to Ed's place in San Francisco. She wasn't happy about going to San Francisco in the wake of the September 11th terrorist attacks just a week ago. I assured her it should be no problem to make a trip to San Francisco and we could go out to dinner after we delivered the salvage. She agreed, and we made plans to go to Ed's house.

The next day, Bert and I drove across the Bay Bridge heading towards San Francisco. When we were in the Russian Hill district near Coit Tower, I found Ed's house and parked the truck in front. The garage door opened, and Ed stuck his head out and said, "Let me pull this car out of the way and we can unload that wreck in my garage."

Ed backed a black Mercedes Benz out of the garage. It appeared to be the same car he purchased at the insurance salvage yard a few years ago. The car was in great condition with no damage at all.

Ed parked the car on the street and walked back over to my truck. We unloaded the frame and engine and walked into his garage carrying it. Once inside the garage, Ed said, "Where's Bert? I haven't seen her in a while, isn't she coming in?"

I told him she was waiting in the truck, and he walked outside to get her. Moments later, Ed returned to the garage with Bert and closed the garage door.

I noticed the entire garage was packed completely full of car parts and other junk. There was virtually no room to move about the garage at all. Upon closer inspection, I noticed there were piles of Porsche engine parts that were wrapped tightly with plastic wrap all around the garage. Bert asked Ed, "What are all these, cocoons?"

Ed laughed and told her the cocoons were to prevent his car parts from weathering. I looked over in the corner and saw an exotic motorcycle which caught my attention. I walked closer to get a better look because I never saw a motorcycle like it in my life. I could see that it was a special purpose race bike and not a converted street bike. I leaned over the motorcycle and placed my hands on the handlebar grips. I turned the steering back and forth and noticed the front forks only had a small amount of steering movement, as if the motorcycle was only meant to be ridden on a race track.

As I looked at the gauges, I noticed the cockpit of the bike was made for racing only and the front fork triple clamps appeared as if they were very strong and constructed of an exotic metal material. I looked down and checked out the front brakes on the race bike and I saw they were also made of an exotic metal or plastic. I wondered if the brakes were fabricated with carbon fiber material. The race bike had no fairings on it, so I could see the exposed engine and I knew it was special because I never saw this type of motor before. The radiator was the largest I ever saw on a bike and appeared to be hand-welded and constructed by a master craftsman.

While Bert was busy talking to Ed, I walked around the back of the race bike. I ran my hands over the plastic tail section while I noticed the red and white paint scheme resembling the logo on a Marlboro cigarette box. I saw two exhaust pipes exited the rear of the race bike through the tail section and on the right side of the bike were two more exhaust pipes, for a total of four pipes. The wheels were colored black and wore slick tires for racing only.

The frame appeared strong and was tightly built around the small engine. I stared at the head stock area of the massive frame when my eyes focused on what appeared to be a strange-looking series of digits stamped on the frame. I looked closer at the numbers and just as my eyes focused on the small digits Ed called out to get my attention and said to me, "Hey, kid, you like that bike?" I looked up and answered yes as he boasted, "That's the one you helped me get back from the cops. That bike is so fast when I was involved in a high speed police chase the other night across the Golden Gate Bridge, I blew the cops away on that bike, riding it on one wheel right through the toll plaza."

I gazed at Ed and said, "The bike doesn't even have a headlight on it. How can you see where you're riding at night?"

Ed laughed, "I don't need a headlight, kid. You're forgetting... Sensei Woo can beat them all night or day."

Ed gestured and said, "Come here. I have something special to show you." I walked away from the exotic race bike to where he stood next to a near new condition green Kawasaki KX250 motocross bike and said, "This is a nice KX250. I didn't know you rode dirt bikes too. Where did you get this one from?"

He said confidently, "Eric Bostrom tossed me this one because he gets new bikes from the Kawasaki factory any time for free."

Since I knew dirt bike riding areas were not available anymore in the bay area, I asked, "Where do you ride this thing around here?"

Ed's face lit up with a cocky smile while he said, "Bostrom ranch. Where do you think, kid?"

He told me how well his KX250 dirt bike handled because it had a special upgrade to the front end, enabling the bike to jump higher and land softer than a stock one. He said, "Eric and I have been training together since Ben's racing over in Europe in World Superbike. I usually can beat Eric most of the time when we race on dirt bikes all around Bostrom ranch. The best thing is when we settle in for the evening, with his mom making us home-cooked meals after a hard day of riding together."

Ed continued bragging, "I always like to say that relaxing on Bostrom Ranch after a long day of training Ben and Eric is the best way for Sensei Woo to unwind."

I said, "It sounds like Eric is fast, but it looks like your student Ben is the one who's showing the fans right now what a Woo institute-trained racer can do in the world of international road racing." I told Ed I was shocked Ben recently pulled off five World Superbike wins in a row and said, "I read Ben didn't stay with Honda because his manager asked for too much money so Honda fired Ben."

Ed said, "Yeah, I know. Believe me kid, there were a few tears on that one, and I was around to help Ben feel better and get over it. Ben's working for Ducati now, and he's finding more success than he did when he was with the Honda team."

Ed continued to brag about his life with the Bostroms, and he pointed to a signed poster of Ben on the wall, among the piles of Porsche engine parts and said, "Ben just gave me that poster you see there on the wall, and he signed it for me too. With Ben over in Europe racing, Eric's a little lonely without his brother to ride with, so I'm filling in the void training with Eric at Bostrom Ranch while Ben's gone."

We were at Ed's for some time now, and it was late. Bert and I were ready to get some dinner before heading home so the three of us walked out of the garage when Ed said, "I'll get back to you on that old truck as soon as I get a chance to fix that tire. I didn't get a chance to do it yet since I've been busy hanging out and training with Eric."

We said goodbye, and Ed said, "Keep a good watch for the Bostrom brothers on the TV. They're part of the new generation of riders who steer the bike with the rear end. Not too many people can do that like I showed them."

Once in the truck, I rolled down the window, leaned out and said smirking, "Okay, Mr. Sensei Woo, creator of Ben and Eric Bostrom. Tell me, what's next? What should the world expect next from the Bostrom brothers?"

Ed laughed and said, as he closed his garage door, "You'll have to wait and see what we're up to next, just like everybody else."

When we drove away from Ed's Bert looked up at his three-story Victorian house and said, "Wow, this is a big house Ed has, and we're in a really nice part of San Francisco, I think that giant house must be worth a lot of money. Ed's rich."

As Bert and I drove to the restaurant, I said, "You know, Ed talks about this place called Bostrom Ranch that Charlie and Pat used to talk about in the old days. I remember when Pat told me back in '97 the Bostroms moved out of their place in the country because they were foreclosed on. The way Ed was talking tonight it sounds like the Bostroms never foreclosed on the property and still own it today. Pat was lying the whole time."

When we arrived at the restaurant, I said to Bert, "It's hard to visualize Ben's mother cooking home-cooked meals for Ed and the Bostrom brothers together."

She said, "He sounded so happy to have a home-cooked meal at the Bostroms' ranch house. Doesn't Ed get home-cooked meals from his own wife?"

Laughing I said, "Ed has a wife to cook for him, and he also has a young daughter to take care of as well. I don't know where he gets all the time to ride with Ben and Eric."

Bert selected a small Japanese restaurant we frequented many times in the past. The waitress took our order and served us some green tea as we waited for our food to arrive. As I watched the coy fish swimming around the small Japanese garden and indoor pond, I couldn't stop thinking about the special race bike I saw earlier in Ed's garage.

I said to Bert, "That race bike Ed has in his garage is some kind of special racing machine. It's very exotic."

She said, "I heard Ed say the red and white bike you were looking at in the corner of his garage was the one that you helped him get back from the police. What's up with that? I thought he was trying to get an FJ1200 back. Do you think Ed put the numbers from the burned up FJ1200 on that red and white race bike you were looking at?"

I said to her, "I'm not sure. I did see a serial number on the frame of the race bike, but it wasn't seventeen digits long so it can't be the FJ1200 numbers. It seems weird a racing motorcycle like that would wind up in a police impound tow yard, when you're not even supposed to ride a race bike on the streets in the first place. What's funny is Charlie told me to tell the police I sold Ed a Yamaha. I sold Ed an old burned up Yamaha FJ1200 frame and engine, and I can't see why that has anything to do with the race bike Ed has in his garage."

Bert said as the sushi arrived, "I think its suspicious Charlie wanted you to say you sold Ed some junk in order to get a race bike back from the police impound."

I said, "Charlie and Ed are up to something real big on that race bike. I remember the police sergeant on the phone who called me about Ed last year asked me some weird questions. He asked me if it was possible to fix up a motorcycle by polishing and buffing the parts that were destroyed in a fire in order to restore the parts to original condition, as if they didn't burn in a fire in the first place."

She said, "The race bike you were looking at in Ed's garage doesn't look like it was in a fire. It was in real nice condition; maybe the sergeant was talking about a different bike that was involved in a fire and then repaired."

I said, "I don't know why a fire has anything to do with what we were contacted about. Charlie said Ed's Yamaha bike was towed away, but he never said anything about a fire or a race bike to me."

As we finished up dinner, I said, "That race bike in Ed's garage isn't the same bike I sold him. When we were at his yard in Oakland, I saw the burned up Yamaha FJ frame and engine I sold him and it wasn't repaired. I wish I could get another look at that race bike because just as I was trying to read the serial number on the frame Ed pulled me away from the bike and talked about Eric and him riding together at Bostrom Ranch."

We left the restaurant and drove home while Bert said, "I think Ed already had the race bike, and since it was towed by the cops, he needed you to say you sold him a bike to get it out of the tow yard.

Maybe race bikes don't have paperwork to be ridden on the streets so by you telling the cops you sold Ed a bike it was enough for them to release his race bike from the tow yard."

I said, "I don't know where Ed picked up that race bike from, but he must have acquired it from a motorcycle road racer. Only a racer would have a machine like that."

She looked over at me and asked, "Do you think Ed got that race bike from Ben or Eric, since they are professional motorcycle racers Ed knew personally for a long time?"

I answered, "He may have acquired the race bike from the Bostroms, but I don't know for sure. There's just something about that bike that keeps me wondering."

I told Bert since the Bostroms were racers for years they were given many bikes by the factories they raced for. I said, "That green Kawasaki dirt bike Ed has was given to Eric by Kawasaki, and since Eric and Ben have many motorcycles, Ed wound up getting that dirt bike from Eric. I guess it's possible for Ed to get that race bike from the Bostroms because they are probably the only people that Ed knows who has access to a race bike like it. If Ed got the bike from them and then he got in trouble with the cops on it, he would have to get it back from the cops no matter what. It would be a bad reflection on the Bostrom brothers because they would be associated with a criminal and that would be a detriment to both their careers. If he didn't get it from Ben or Eric then there might be the possibility Ed stole that race bike at the races one day when he was there watching the Bostroms, but the cops wouldn't have returned it to Ed if it was reported stolen."

We were almost home now, and I was lost in thought, trying to remember the night I spoke to the sergeant about Ed's bike. I tried to recall any other questions the officer asked me. Suddenly I remembered the last question he asked before he hung up the phone that night. I said, "I just remembered, right as I was hanging up the phone, the cop asked me if I ever heard of a Rock motorcycle."

Bert said surprised, "What's a Rock motorcycle?"

I said, "I don't know. I've never heard of a Rock motorcycle before, and I've seen a lot of old junk bikes in my time."

She asked, "What does a Rock motorcycle have to do with Ed and the police anyway?"

I answered, "I'm not sure, but I'm going to find out what Ed and Charlie are up to. Maybe I should try and get another look at Ed's race bike in his garage."

As the year wound down, business was slower than usual because of the aftermath of the 9/11 terrorist attacks in New York City. The holidays were exceptionally slow as well.

It was a cold Christmas morning when we were having coffee at my house and exchanging presents. My daughter picked up a wrapped box sitting under the Christmas tree, gave me a kiss while handing me the box and said, "I know you will love this because you love motorcycles." I opened the package, and it was a two-inch-thick 600-page motorcycle encyclopedia with information on almost every motorcycle ever built during the last 100 years. The book was filled with color photos of rare and vintage motorcycles from all over the world, photographed from private collections. I was very happy; it was a great gift.

Later in the evening, I sat in a chair and thumbed through my new book, looking at all the different pictures. The book was arranged in alphabetical order, and as I reached the end of the book in the Yamaha section, I noticed a color picture of a mint condition Yamaha YR5350. That bike was the first motorcycle I ever owned, after Charlie came home one day in 1977 and told me that he found it in an old guy's garage. Directly below the picture of the YR5350 I noticed a small entry for Yamaha YZR500. I looked at the opposite page of my book and saw a picture of famous racers standing with a Marlboro Yamaha YZR500 grand prix race bike.

Instantly, I realized after all these years that a YZR Yamaha race bike must be what Ed referred to as a Yizzer when he crashed and had all that road rash on his body in the early part of 1996.

I immediately read the text describing what a Yamaha YZR500 was. The book stated it was a 500cc V-4 two stroke race bike that produced close to 170 horsepower with a top speed of 190 MPH. The article said the YZR500 was used to win six world championships between 1984 and 1993. It also said it was used as the basis for the ROC and Harris framed Yamaha V-4's of recent seasons. The article finished by saying the most famous American racers of all time rode the Yamaha YZR500 in the international road racing scene in the past.

I was shocked when I saw the word ROC. I instantly knew a ROC was a Rock motorcycle. My spine tingled as I thought about the race bike Ed Woo had in his garage he desperately needed to get back from the police. Could it be a world famous ROC Yamaha YZR500 grand prix racing machine? I wondered what Ed was doing with a rare, un-obtainable race bike like that in his garage and how it wound up in the hands of the San Francisco police department.

I knew I had to get back into Ed's garage to see that race bike again no matter what.

2002

Once the New Year started, I was on a mission to try and get back to Ed's house to see his race bike again. Ed didn't call me or return my calls about the old truck he was still storing. I thought I wasn't going to hear back from Ed and maybe the old truck wound up towed away for junk.

One morning, Bert turned on the computer in the office, and we were surprised to see an email from Ed. He expressed interest in a wrecked Aprilia RSV1000R that was for sale on our web site.

I recently purchased the bike at the auction. I was able to get a good price on the Aprilia because it was broken in half and connected only by wires and hoses. The front end was ripped off the frame, but the Ohlins gas forks were in excellent condition.

Ed's email read he would pick up the Aprilia at our shop in the afternoon. He didn't mention anything about my old truck, so I figured I would speak to him about it when he came. I said to Bert, "If Ed buys the wrecked Aprilia I'll offer him free delivery so I can get in his garage and see that race bike again."

Later in the day, Ed showed up driving a gold-colored Porsche 911. I noticed the car wasn't as nice as the Porsches I saw in the past. Ed and I walked in the shop and I showed him the wrecked Aprilia. He said the bike would work fine for him since the forks were what he was looking for—they were the same forks that came on the recently released Ben Bostrom Ducati 998 Superbike signature series replica.

Ed told me he wanted to buy the wreck so I offered to deliver it to his house on Union Street when he said, "That's not necessary. I'll drive it home myself. I'll quickly dismantle it here and load the parts into my Porsche."

Bert was standing by and said to him, "You can't fit that huge motorcycle in that little Porsche."

Ed put his hand on her shoulder, smiled confidently while looking at me and said, "Just watch me. Show me some tools, and I'll have it apart in no time."

I directed Ed to a tool box in the back saying, "There's the tools, go for it." Ed wrenched away on the bike, and soon it was reduced to a pile of parts on the floor. The dismantled Aprilia appeared too big to fit in the car and he said, "I'll just remove the passenger seat from the car, so I can stuff all the parts in there." Within minutes Ed unbolted the passenger seat of his Porsche and placed it on the ground next to the car.

He loaded various parts of the Aprilia into the car and found it was a tight squeeze because the Porsche was a coupe with no back seat. As Ed was loading the car with parts he said, "That's a real big white pit bull you have there; how much does he weigh?"

Bert said "He's a hundred pounds and his name is Mr. Pink because his skin is so pink." Ed said as he picked up the front forks of the bike, "He's looking funny at me, like he wants to eat me."

I said, "It's the tire on the forks you're holding that Mr. Pink wants to eat."

As soon as I said the word tire, Mr. Pink lunged at Ed's front end, grabbed hold of the tire with his wide mouth and proceeded to engage in a tug of war, with Ed holding the handlebars of the front end as the dog locked onto the tire. Ed said he couldn't believe the strength of the dog and continued to play around and fight Mr. Pink for a while. It wasn't until Bert called the dog off when Mr. Pink reluctantly released his mouth from the tire and Ed quickly stuffed the front end into his Porsche.

Soon afterwards, Ed loaded the engine, frame and all the rest of the Aprilia parts in the small front trunk and passenger side of the Porsche. After it was all finished, Ed handed me $500 and said, "How about if I put the car seat in the back of your truck, and you can follow me back to San Francisco with it. I can pay you the remainder of the cash at my house." I was happy and thought, fuck yeah...Now I can see his race bike again.

Bert rounded up the dog and put him in the truck as I locked the shop for the day. We left for the trip to San Francisco, following Ed.

In 45 minutes, we arrived at Ed's house in Russian Hill. He drove around the back down a small street called Rockland alley. He parked and motioned for me to drive into the alley while he opened a different garage door. I parked the truck, and we walked inside with Ed. I gazed around the garage and didn't see the race bike. It appeared to be a second garage for the house because we entered from a back alley. I immediately noticed three sleek black shiny Porsche 911 cars that were backed into the garage.

Ed motioned for us to come over to where a pair of Ducati 998 sport bikes was located. He started one of the Ducati bikes, revved the engine wildly and yelled over the loud roar of the pipes, "This is my latest track bike for hanging out with the big boys."

I saw the bike was a Ducati 998, wearing a red fairing with a large number one emblazoned on the front. I thought it could be Ben Bostrom's bike wearing his AMA Superbike championship winning number one from the factory Ducati team.

Ed shut off the Ducati and said, "I rode this one down the freeway at 140MPH, riding to Dave's birthday party a few nights ago." Ed described his time at the party and said, "You should've been there, kid. All the big boys were there, and let's just say I saw more motorcycle racing talent in one room than I've ever seen assembled anywhere in all my days of riding."

Ed continued to brag about the big boys at Dave's party and said, "It's too bad you weren't there because I saw Charlie there, and he was having a great old time with Dave and Paul. Eric was there too while he was in between road races."

Looking at the Porsches I said, "Are these three cars the ones you were trying to get back from the cops all that time?"

Ed smiled and said, "I got all my Porsche cars back now from the police, and these three are just some of the cars they had to return to me. I don't need to talk about the cops anymore because all that's over now that I won the case. Come with me, and I'll give you a tour of my house."

Ed led us away from the black Porsches and the Ducati bikes, and while he walked past some boxes, he suddenly stopped and grabbed a motorcycle clutch basket and handed it to me. He said, "This is a factory Ducati clutch basket Ben gave to me as a gift. The piece is broken right here because Ben blew the clutch apart on his bike over in Europe. Feel the weight on this; it's made of special metal and weighs just a few ounces."

I held the clutch basket in my hand, and it was the lightest clutch I ever felt. Ed grabbed the clutch basket back from me and tossed it on the boxes as he continued to lead Bert and me through a small passageway and up a flight of wooden stairs lined with plastic-wrapped Porsche parts.

He walked us through the darkened hallways from room to room and I saw they were completely full of plastic-wrapped Porsche parts from floor to ceiling. After leading us through several rooms, we walked into a large cluttered kitchen. Ed tripped over some boxes as he kicked them to the side. He walked over to a refrigerator and opened the door of the freezer on top. He produced a large three-inch-thick stack of $100 bills, and after he pulled a few hundred dollars off the stack, he handed it to me and said, "Here's the rest of the money for the Aprilia, so we're all squared up on that deal now."

After Ed put his cash back in the freezer, he offered Bert and me something to drink. Ed handed me a soda, and as I gazed around, I realized the large Victorian house looked completely unlived in; most of the living space was occupied with plastic-wrapped automobile parts. I didn't see any beds in the rooms at all.

Ed continued to show us different rooms piled high, full of parts from Porsche cars and bikes. We followed Ed down a dark passageway with stairs that returned us to the rear garage where the three black Porsches were parked. We walked outside, and I asked Ed if he wanted me to help him unload his car as he said, "No, I don't need any help because I'm not unloading that car here." The three of us walked over to my truck, while Ed said, "I just have to get my Porsche seat back from you, and we can call it a night."

A few weeks later, I was looking through the latest edition of a local motorcycle newspaper. There was an article that featured a picture of Dave and Eric Bostrom at an exotic car store, attending Dave's 60th birthday party. I said to Bert, "Take a look at this picture of Dave and Eric it's the party the gang threw at a car place on the Peninsula. This must be the party Ed talked about riding 140MPH to meet up with the big boys. It says here Dave Bostrom used to be an ice delivery man when he was younger, before he went to Viet Nam. It also says Dave became hooked on buying land after he returned from the military. That's probably the property Ed brags about called Bostrom Ranch. Get this part: it says Dave and Paul didn't always see eye to eye on a few things in the past."

She said, "It's funny you find out about Dave's big party from Ed or by reading about it in a newspaper. Charlie should've been the one to tell you about the party but he hasn't called you for months. I bet Charlie sat with Ed and those big boys he talks about at the main table because Ed told you all the big boys were at Dave's birthday party."

I said, "Without a doubt Ed and Charlie sat with Paul and Eric and the rest of the Bostrom family celebrating the special exotic race bike returned from the cops. Charlie and Ed are practically members of the tight-knit Bostrom family."

During the hot summer, I was surprised when I received a rare phone call from my mom. She said, "This weekend is July 12th your ten year wedding anniversary. Charlie and I want to see you guys. Do you have any plans on that special day?"

I told her I made plans to go to a nice restaurant in San Francisco with Bert to celebrate, and if they met us there, we could all have dinner together. My mom said that would be fine.

On July 12th, Bert and I arrived at the restaurant and waited for my mom and Charlie to show up. I was concerned after 30 minutes when they didn't arrive. After nearly an hour, I noticed my mom driving past the restaurant, looking for parking. She was alone in the car. When she walked up to the restaurant, Bert appeared worried and asked her, "Where's Charlie?"

My mom shrugged her shoulders while rolling her eyes and said, apologizing, "Charlie couldn't make it because he went to the races at Laguna Seca instead of coming to your anniversary dinner." Bert was shocked and seemed disappointed.

I didn't say anything to my mom at first, but I already knew the races in Monterey were happening that weekend, and I knew Charlie would definitely choose to go to the races to see Ben and Eric race rather than to come to dinner with us.

The three of us went into the restaurant and were seated. After the waiter took our orders for dinner, I asked my mom, "So, who did Charlie go to the road races with? Dave Bostrom?"

She looked at me from across the table and said, "Oh, do you mean Mr. Clean?"

Surprised I looked back and said, "Mr. Clean? Who the hell is that?"

My mom said, "Oh, I thought everybody refers to Dave as Mr. Clean."

As I laughed out loud I told her I never heard that nickname for Dave before.

I already knew Charlie went to the races with Dave because Ben and Eric usually win at Laguna Seca and Charlie wouldn't miss Ben and Eric winning for anything.

Once the food arrived, I asked my mom, "How's Dave doing these days anyway? Do you ever see him anymore? How's his girlfriend Tami doing?"

My mom said, "Oh, didn't you hear? Dave has a new girlfriend in Sacramento. Apparently she's much younger than Dave." I was surprised because Dave and Tami were living together for a long time, nearly 20 years since back when my younger sister babysat for Ben and Eric.

I asked my mom, "What about Tami? Where did she go?"

She replied "Well, Tami is allowed to live at Dave's house in Brisbane for as long as she wants, but Dave and Tami are not a couple anymore."

I was irritated during the whole dinner and finally said, "That really pisses me off Charlie went to the races and didn't come; we haven't seen him in a long time. He fucking sucks." With a guilty look on her face my mom cracked a half smile, lifted her shoulders and said, "Well you know that Charlie and his motorcycle friends. It's like he's practically married to them. They call every day, and Charlie spends hours talking on the phone, or he's out all day riding around with them." As Bert and my mom talked about the war and weather I wondered, what's so important that Charlie would talk to his friends on the phone for hours at a time?

When dinner was over and Bert and I drove home, I said to her, "I wonder why my mom called Dave Bostrom, Mr. Clean. I bet it has something to do with his reputation in the past with cocaine. I remember T and Steve used to talk many years ago about Dave's involvement in the cocaine scene. I think the nickname Mr. Clean has something to do with Dave gets away clean, and never gets caught by the cops for coke and bikes."

Bert said, "I bet that ex-husband of mine is still hanging out with Dave being a loser. He never wanted to grow up when we were married. I can't believe that asshole hasn't seen, or made any effort to see his daughter one time in over 20 years."

I agreed with Bert. "What a loser. At least I love her and she has me for a dad."

I then said, "What about Charlie not showing up tonight? That really irks me. He sucks as a dad. I know he's done a lot of shitty things that have pissed me off before, but tonight really tops it all. What an asshole!"

It was nearly the end of the year before Ed finally called me about the old pickup truck in his yard. "Hey, kid. I'm ready to give you back the old truck."

I said, "I can't make it there to pick up the truck in Oakland until the weekend."

He said, "I won't be around this weekend because I'm going to Temecula down in southern California to dirt bike ride with Ben and Eric on their new 27-acre ranch they recently bought. We're all going, and Charlie said he's coming too." Ed told me he would deliver the truck to the shop on a day he was free after he returned from the dirt bike trip with the gang. The next morning I arrived at the shop, and I was surprised to see the old truck was parked in front of the door. Ed delivered it overnight.

Since I knew Ed and Charlie were down in Temecula riding on the second Bostrom ranch, I thought, Ed may have used me for something because it was strange the truck was returned in the middle of the night and then Ed was quickly off riding dirt bikes with Charlie, Ben and Eric.

I didn't get another look at his special red and white race bike and now I was more curious than ever. I wanted to know how Ed got his hands on that race bike and why it was so important to associate it with a burned up Yamaha FJ1200 frame and engine he bought from my shop. My mission was to find out.

I wanted to know if Ed, Dave and Charlie fucked me.

2003

Only a few weeks into the New Year, we received an email from Ed. He wanted to make sure the old truck was okay and if I received his business card he left on the dashboard of the truck. It was a short email which read he was back from dirt bike riding with Charlie and the Bostroms in Temecula. At the end, there was a strange statement: "Don't worry, kid. I still love you."

I went outside to the truck, I didn't move it since Ed dropped it off. I opened the door and looked on the dashboard, and there was a business card wedged between the corner of the window and the dash. On the back was his handwriting that read, if I ever needed to use 60-foot long shipping containers he had the connections out of Oakland to get things done. Ed listed his phone numbers and his address on Union Street.

I tucked the card in my wallet and closed the door. In all my years the only people I ever met who used 60-foot shipping containers were the people from Europe who came into Charlie's shop to send their U.S.-purchased motorcycles back to Europe for resale. I thought Ed might be using shipping containers to ship Porsches and Porsche parts.

After not hearing from Charlie in over a year, he called me at home one evening and told me he purchased a brand new Ford pickup truck. Charlie said he wanted to give Bert his old 1991 Ford truck since she didn't have anything to drive.

When Charlie and my mom arrived the next day, we checked out Charlie's new red Ford truck while Charlie said to me, "Nobody in the family knows we're out here visiting you guys. Garg found out I bought a new truck, and he was all over me about what I was doing with my old truck. I couldn't tell him I gave it to Bert because Garg will have a temper tantrum in the middle of the street." I found it strange Charlie was giving Bert his old truck in the first place but I did not say anything about it.

My mom carried a large white box in the shop, handed it to me, and said, "This box is full of old DMV forms and other shop things I thought you might want. I re-did our home office with new furniture and this box is the last of everything from Charlie's old shop I didn't think we needed anymore."

Bert and my mom sat in the office and talked while Charlie and I went into the back so he could check the place out. I asked him, "Have you ever been to Ed's house?"

He answered after hesitating. "Uh, no, I can't say I've ever been there."

I said, "He took me to his house and when Ed showed me around upstairs, the entire house was full from floor to ceiling with plastic-wrapped Porsche parts." Charlie looked at me with that same lying face and said with a coy smile, "I don't know anything about Ed's business. I don't even know what he's up to these days." Charlie left with my mom and headed home. I stood there watching him drive down the street, and I thought to myself, *I bet he's lying. He knows what Ed is in trouble for on that race bike and he's not telling me something because I think he and Dave are involved too.*

The year went by, with the old truck Ed dropped off still sitting in front of the shop. The truck had a For Sale sign on it, and I advertised it in the local newspapers. Many people called about it, but nobody wanted to buy it.

When the landlord came by one day he told me he wasn't too happy about junk vehicles stored on the premises, he also said, "I'm selling the unit space you occupy for $250,000 and unless you want to buy it, I'll need you to leave by the end of your lease, which is up at the end of this year."

Once he left, I said to Bert, "I don't think we should buy this space because the price is the same as buying a house." Bert agreed, and we decided we would close down the motorcycle salvage operation at the end of the lease since it never was a lucrative business for us.

The next day, the phone rang. It was Pin Head saying he was completely healed from his crash. He told me he was living in an old motor home parked in front of Charlie's old shop, and he asked me what I did with the truck from Ed's yard. I told him I was selling it. Pin Head said, "Why don't you make a deal with me on it kid?"

"I need to get some money on the sale of the truck," I told him. "You can't make payments like all the other deals you made with Charlie on bikes."

"I have cash this time," Pin Head said. "How's $500 sound?" I was surprised because over the years he never had $500. I told him I would accept his offer of cash, and he could come and pick up the truck anytime.

A few days later, Pin Head arrived in the afternoon. He looked around the shop for a while and said, "Let's do the money deal on the truck." We sat down to do the paperwork in the office and I produced a title for the truck while Pin Head pulled out $500 from his pocket. I said as I gave him the title, "The truck runs good. You and Ed worked well together on it." Pin Head scoffed and handed me the cash.

He said, "I'm really mad at Ed because I helped him out, and he never helps me in return. I helped Ed get all his Porsche cars back from the cops, now he acts like I never did anything for him. I really saved the day on that one for Ed by allowing him to use me to get his cars back." Pin Head and I finished up the truck business, and he left.

Sitting in the quiet shop I remembered when I asked Charlie if Ed ever pulled his Yamaha out of the police impound yard. Charlie told me Dave really saved the day on that one. I started to suspect maybe Pin Head helping Ed with his cars and Dave helping Ed with his exotic race bike was possibly the same case, because both of them are associated with saving the so-called day for Ed.

What did that special race bike and all of Ed's Porsches and a burned up FJ1200 frame and engine have to do with the San Francisco police department, Dave Bostrom and Pin Head, and how did Charlie fit into the equation?

2004

One spring morning, Charlie called. Since I hadn't talked with Charlie since he gave Bert his truck a year ago, I was happy to hear from him, but he didn't sound too happy to talk to me. He barked out and said, "I heard you and Bert closed down the shop in Fairfield! What kind of dumb shit idea was that?"

I told him about the landlord selling our unit, and he said, "What about the salvage license? You have to keep the license, I hope you weren't a fucking idiot and let it go."

I said, "We let the salvage license go. We didn't make any money in the motorcycle salvage business since you gave the shop to Bert, and we didn't want to buy the unit the Fairfield shop was located in."

Charlie said angrily, "I told your ass a long time ago that you should've never closed down the shop in South San Francisco."

I began to get irritated at Charlie's pestering and said, "The overhead running your old shop was four times the amount monthly as it was for us to run the shop in Fairfield, and we made no money. I still wonder how you made enough money to keep the South San Francisco shop opened for all those years because you had to pay the employees and the rent was much higher than our shop in Fairfield."

Charlie snapped back and said, "I did it the right way. I concentrated on the small sales, and I ran things efficiently. I took care of the pennies and let the dollars take care of themselves."

Angrily I said, "Apparently the right way was the illegal way with you and your gang."

He yelled back, "Hey, I don't want to hear any of your shit; so shut the fuck up."

Charlie abruptly said he had to go but before he hung up he asked, "Okay, I want to make sure what you said. The salvage license is gone now, right?"

I answered yes. Later I wondered why he needed to ask twice about the license.

The next day I received an unexpected call from Pat. It was a few years since I talked to him. He said he was healed completely from his accident and he was riding again. I heard him take a puff off of a cigarette as he said, "I hear you're on Charlie's shit list these days for letting your salvage license go."

I got mad and said, "Maybe Charlie should have never given the shop to Bert, and he could have kept the shop and license for himself if he has a problem with what we did with it."

Pat said, "Well...With that Ed Woo thing going on with the cops, Charlie had to give Bert the shop back in '97."

"What Ed Woo thing?" I asked sternly.

Pat hesitated. "You know...Don't you?" When I didn't answer, Pat quickly said goodbye and hung up the phone.

I looked at Bert and said, "I think we have a problem."

She looked back at me, puzzled, as I said, "I think Charlie fucked us on the shop deal by giving you the business back in 1997 because he was in some kind of trouble with Ed and the police."

"What? That's crazy," Bert said, shocked.

I said, "I bet there is something funny going on, and I want to find out what it is. I don't think I can trust Charlie or Ed and I don't know what I'll do first, but I have to get to the bottom of this and find out the truth."

A few days later, Bert and I were looking through some old boxes from the shop while cleaning out the garage. She dug to the bottom of the large white box from my mom and pulled out three hardback books. "What about this stuff? It's a bunch of old beat-up books. Should I toss it on the dump load?"

I said as I reached out my hand, "Let me see those. They look like Charlie's old DMV entry books he used to carry around years ago to record all the VIN numbers of the bikes that came in the shop."

Bert handed me the books and I opened one of them in the middle and started reading it. I said, "This seems strange because it shows here in this book that in the year 1994 a woman named Verna using Pat's last name sold Charlie's shop a few motorcycles with an address listed as 230 Marshall Street in Petaluma. Did Pat marry Ben's mom?"

I gazed at the name listed two lines up from the Verna bike sales and noticed another transaction that caught my attention. This time the book stated Charlie bought a motorcycle from Daly City Yamaha, Dave's old shop. The problem was Dave's Daly City Yamaha dealership closed around 1989, and the book said the transaction took place in 1994. Even stranger was the fact that both transactions took place on the same day. I turned a few pages and noticed several motorcycles listed in the book Charlie was selling to himself as the buyer and seller.

As I continued to look at the book, Bert said, "I remember that book. Charlie brought it in the office of the South San Francisco shop, before he broke his leg. Charlie told me to write down a few names and addresses with bike VIN numbers, while he stood above me dictating them."

I said, "I see many motorcycles sold to Charlie's shop when he owned it by people who are listed living at my brother Garg's building in San Bruno. The funny thing is I don't remember any of these people ever living at Garg's building, and whoever these people are recorded in this book I think they never sold Charlie a motorcycle."

She asked, "How do you know one motorcycle from another when it's just a bunch of VIN numbers listed with names and addresses in the book?"

I answered, "After all the years of working on bikes for Charlie, I pretty much know most of the models and the VIN numbers they carry. Each model is designated with a different set of letters and numbers. The numbers I don't know can be checked to my dealership books, which show exactly what kind of bike each VIN number is."

I grew concerned as I continued to examine Charlie's books. I said, "I see expensive sport bikes and dirt bikes I know never came through Charlie's shop,"

I flipped through the pages to the summer of 1997, which was the time Charlie told us he was retiring from the shop. "Here's a VIN number I remember well because a long time ago I used to own a beat-up Yamaha YSR50. The prefix of the VIN number on an YSR50 is always JYA2RR. On this one page I see two Yamaha YSR50s sold to Charlie's shop, with Charlie himself listed as the seller and the buyer and the address listed in this book for the seller is Charlie's own shop. I know I never saw those two YSR50s come in the old shop. I need to take a closer look at this book and try to match some of these odd-looking VIN numbers to my dealer books." We walked in the house, and she put together lunch as I settled down at my desk.

I didn't even know where to start so I decided to start at the beginning of the book and work my way to the end. Since I wondered about the pair of YSR50s, I decided to count how many times I saw the VIN number JYA2RR listed in Charlie's books.

After reading quickly through the books, I walked in the kitchen, where Bert made lunch and said, "You'll be shocked to hear twenty four Yamaha YSR50 mini-road racers are listed as coming through the books of Charlie's old shop. Even stranger is every one of them showed coming through the books after Pat started working there."

"Where do you think all those YSR50s in Charlie's book came from?" Bert asked.

I said, "I don't know, but I'm certain they didn't come through the shop. Charlie had one a long time ago we used to race with the salvage squad, and that became mine. Since then I never saw another one come in. Remember many years ago, you and I were driving on Highway 80, and I pointed out Ben and Eric driving a car pulling a trailer with two YSR50s that were modified for racing?"

She said, "Yes, I remember when you pointed them out to me a long time ago, right around the time we were married. Do you think those YSR50s we saw the Bostrom brothers with are the same bikes that are listed in Charlie's book?"

I grew puzzled and said, "I don't know for sure, but I wonder how the Bostrom brothers acquired those Yamaha YSR50s for racing. Their father closed down his Yamaha dealership years before we saw Ben and Eric on the freeway towing the bikes."

I wondered if some of the bikes listed in Charlie's books were the secret fleet of bikes rumored to be hidden away by Dave and Verna. Bert set lunch down on the kitchen table and asked me to put Charlie's books away for a while and have something to eat.

After lunch, I decided to jump right back into checking the VIN numbers in Charlie's books. An hour later, Bert walked in the office while I said, "A while ago Charlie told me he went over his books and said he sold sixty Kawasaki Ninja motorcycles before he gave you the shop. Now, after looking at the books, I see over 150 Kawasaki Ninjas. We never had any nice Ninjas come through the shop we only had a few junk Ninjas we dismantled after they came in."

Bert said, "I thought you said Charlie spoke of selling sixty Ninjas. The book shows he brought the Ninjas in for dismantling, not that he sold the Ninjas."

I said, "You're right. Charlie did tell me he sold the sixty Ninjas, and it says here some of the Ninjas were sold to Charlie by people who lived at Garg's building. Only I think these people never existed or ever lived there or sold a Ninja."

Over the course of the next few weeks, I checked nearly every VIN number Charlie recorded in his books. I found hundreds of high line sport bikes, along with many other rare vintage bikes and a few Harleys. I also found dozens of scooters, dirt bikes and several automobiles I knew didn't come through Charlie's business. Most alarming was a fleet of BMW motorcycles which were favored by Charlie's gang.

I wondered how the vehicles could be listed in the books over the years without ever coming through the shop itself. I couldn't understand the junk bikes we did dismantle which were supposed to be in the book didn't appear on the pages of Charlie's books at all.

I found it strange Charlie had hundreds of bikes in the books from the 1980's which were coming through his business in the 1990's. During this time the books should have shown most bikes from the 90's; instead, the book was filled with bikes from the 70's and 80's. I remembered many dealerships in our area went under in the 1980's.

After Bert and I worked together on classifying the different categories of the books, I realized there were dozens of Honda XR and XL series dirt bikes listed in Charlie's books that never came through Charlie's shop. There was also a large fleet of old Yamaha XT and TT series dirt bikes, as well as a large amount of the Yamaha SR500 street version of the XT and TT.

I was amazed to see the number of Honda Interceptor sport bikes that accompanied all the Kawasaki Ninjas, as well as a fleet of more than two dozen Suzuki GSXR series sport bikes. There were also a vast number of Yamaha sport and cruiser bikes.

I noticed the address of the seller appeared to be used many times with different names. Two peculiar addresses which were repeated often were 470 Filmore Street and 370 Franklin Street in San Francisco. The names that accompanied these addresses appeared to be made-up names. I wondered if Charlie made up the names and used phony addresses throughout his entire books.

I was angry when I noticed one Kawasaki 750 Ninja the book stated I sold to Charlie's shop while I was recorded as living at Garg's building even though I never sold a Ninja 750 to Charlie or ever lived at Garg's building. I saw some scooters were sold to Charlie's shop with Bernard listed as the seller even though I knew he never sold the shop any scooters. Some of the VIN numbers I couldn't decipher but later I would find they were two stroke sport bikes that were not sold in the United States and I believed these bikes were the Arty black market bikes. Most troubling was the fact that some of Arty's bikes were listed in Charlie's book with my cousin from Illinois listed as the seller and not Arty. I grew angrier when I noticed a few of Arty's black market bikes were listed in the book after the time Bert took over the shop even though I told him I wouldn't do his paperwork deals for him. I knew Charlie was doing it for Arty behind my back.

Charlie recorded dozens of motorcycles using his name as the seller and his home address as the place where the seller lived when he sold the bike. I remembered many years ago Charlie was raided by a DMV agent who complained to Charlie that he couldn't legally sell a motorcycle to himself when he owned the business. It appeared Charlie continued to sell bikes to himself anyway.

The particular area of the books which pissed me off the most was the time between Bert taking over the shop from Charlie on October 1, 1997 leading up to the end of the books, when he crashed and broke his leg in July 1998. There were nearly 200 motorcycles Charlie wrote through the books during that time period.

Another thing that bothered me was at the time Bert took over the shop, we experienced a very hard winter, and it rained most of the months. I couldn't figure why Charlie wrote in the books that so many motorcycles came through the business because on most rainy days virtually no one came through the shop selling or junking out a bike.

I remembered when Bert took over Charlie's shop, she asked Charlie to let her do the DMV books, and he made her feel bad by saying, "Taking care of the books has always been my job in the shop. You're busy running the shop and your hair business as well." Then Charlie would play the sympathy card by saying to Bert, "Well, if you do the books for your shop, what will I do around here, just sit and be useless? How am I supposed to feel about taking a salary from you if I don't even have a job to do in the shop?"

I now could see why Charlie never wanted Bert to have control of the books in the first place and why he gave her the shop all together. He was busted with Dave and Ed and needed to escape the clutches of the law.

Once I deciphered the books, I was astounded to see over 3,000 motorcycles which were processed through Charlie's books from 1983 to 1998, with most written in the books under suspicious circumstances.

I wondered where Charlie acquired so many bikes. I knew of his alliance over the years with Dave and Verna, and Charlie always did paperwork deals with Dave in the office. I didn't believe all those motorcycles in Charlie's books came from the Bostroms alone. Or did they? After all, I read Ben stated in an interview his parents owned a string of motorcycle dealerships in the San Francisco bay area in the past. I wondered how many dealerships made up this so-called string.

As I sat at my desk and stared at the open books, I thought about how Charlie gave Bert the shop because of what Pat called the 'Ed Woo thing.' Charlie needed to retire in a hurry back in July 1997. I thought Ed Woo and his Porsches was most likely the reason why Charlie retired quickly and transferred the business to Bert.

I couldn't remember what Charlie and Ed were up to back in 1997, but I did remember Charlie told me he was helping Ed get his Yamaha back near the end of the year 2000. I wondered whether Ed may have been in trouble with his race bike all the way back in 1997. Charlie was probably involved with Ed and the police; that might be why he gave Bert the shop and retired.

Then I remembered when I over-heard Charlie and Pat talking in the office, Charlie said to Pat if I ever heard the truth from him, I would want to kill him.

One evening, I said to Bert, "I wish I could remember the name of the sergeant who called me and asked me questions about the burned Yamaha FJ1200 and Ed Woo a few years back."

Bert said, "I remember Ed bragged in his yard in Oakland he and Dave had that sergeant and the San Francisco Police Department eating out of their hands."

I laughed and said, "Yeah. I do remember when Ed talked about that because he said the name of the cop a few times."

She said, "I think I remember his name now. Ed kept saying he and Dave had that Rocporti eating out of the palms of their hands."

I said, "Yes that's it. Ed said he was a cop named Rocoporti. Maybe I can track him down and ask him what went on with Ed and Charlie. I'll try to find Sergeant Rocoporti, and if I do, you'd better get ready for something big because there's no telling what Charlie and Ed were up to."

The next day I took a gamble and called the San Francisco Police Department auto theft unit and asked the person who answered the phone if I could speak to a Sergeant named Rocoporti. The clerk at first didn't know who I was talking about and said there was no Sergeant Rocoporti there. Then he said to me, "Oh, you must be talking about Sergeant Dave Roccaforte. He retired from the police auto theft unit a few years ago."

I said, "Is he still around? Do you know how to get in touch with him?"

The man said, "Yes, he's still around, and he works as an investigator now in the bay area. If you want to leave your name and telephone number, I'll see he gets it the next time we hear from him." After giving the man my information, I hung up the phone and walked in the other room to talk to Bert.

"I found him!" I said excitedly.

She said, "Wow, when do you think he will call back?"

I said, "I hope soon because he'll be able to tell me what Ed and Charlie were doing with the Porsche cars and maybe even that exotic race bike as well."

Three days later, the phone rang. "Hello. This is Sergeant Dave Roccaforte, returning the call of the person who left me a message," the man said.

I introduced myself, and he remembered speaking to me a few years back. I said to him, "You called me a couple of years ago and asked me about a guy named Ed Woo and a Yamaha motorcycle. I would like to know what was happening with Ed at the time and why you called me."

Sgt. Roccaforte said, "A long time ago, before I retired, I was in charge of a case concerning Ed Woo and stolen Porsches. We were tracking Ed for some time, and when a Porsche was reported stolen next door to Charlie's shop in South San Francisco, we knew Ed must have had something to do with it, because other Porsches were stolen in areas Ed Woo was known to frequent. We had a two-year investigation from 1995 to 1997 on Ed and stolen Porsches, he was later charged with twenty three felony counts on nineteen different stolen cars. We knew Ed was hanging around Charlie's when he registered one of the Porsches to Charlie's shop under the false name of James Brown."

The news about Ed was coming at me too quickly. I interrupted the sergeant and said, "I think I was there the day Ed stole that car, because I saw Ed frantically trying to start a Porsche. When he couldn't start it, his friend showed up with a tow truck and pushed the car away. Charlie and some other guy made me believe Ed was trying to start his own Porsche on the side of the building, and Charlie was even helping Ed out."

He said, "I thought it might have been Ed Woo from the very beginning, but he was supposed to be locked up until the year 2002. Ed was released early on his conviction for trafficking cocaine back in 1986. He was sentenced to 15 years for selling a briefcase full of cocaine to an undercover officer. We assumed Ed would be in prison until 02, but when many Porsches came up missing in the bay area, we thought of Ed Woo and when we checked, we saw Ed was released early around 1992 from San Quentin State Prison."

I said, "It doesn't surprise me you suspected Ed, because when Charlie first opened his shop, Ed would come by with Porsche cars he said he built himself."

Sgt. Roccaforte said, " When the Porsches went missing Ed was our first guess because he was a known Porsche thief in the San Francisco bay area for years, and he has been in trouble with the law since he was fourteen years old. We expected to find some stolen Porsche cars or parts when we raided Charlie's salvage shop back in July of 1997. Ed was using the address of Charlie's shop to mail DMV titles for Porsches under phony names like James Brown."

"You raided Charlie's shop looking for Ed's Porsche stuff?" I asked. "Charlie told me you guys were looking for an old scooter that was reported stolen."

Sgt. Roccaforte said, "We raided Charlie's shop around the same time we raided Ed's house on Union Street and storage yard in Oakland. We seized a total of fifteen cars from three locations. Some were located at Ed's yard on Louise Street in Oakland, his house on Union, and the rest of them were located in a building on 9th street in a large garage Ed occupied. There were so many Porsches in the garage the people who lived in the building had to park their cars on the street. We also found and seized an exotic racing motorcycle there Ed recently attempted to register at the DMV using documents from Charlie's salvage shop. I asked Charlie in an interview if he wrote out the verification form Ed used for the registering of the race bike, and Charlie told me the signature on the form wasn't his. That was how we knew Ed forged the documents while attempting to register the ROC Yamaha race bike, and therefore, we seized the bike as well."

Surprised I said, "ROC Yamaha? Is that why you asked me if I ever heard of a Rock motorcycle when you called me in 2000?" He answered yes. I now knew without a doubt the race bike in Ed's garage was a genuine ROC YZR500 and wondered why it wore Marlboro colors.

I said, "I guess you were right. Ed must have stolen all those cars since I saw him steal the Porsche next door from Charlie's shop, but what does ROC race bike have to do with Ed buying a Yamaha from me? Why did you call me?"

He said, "Ed stated he bought a Yamaha from you after Charlie transferred the salvage shop to your wife. Ed was in trouble for stating the Yamaha he bought from you was involved in a large house fire, along with a ROC Yamaha race bike we seized from Ed in the raid back in July of 1997. Ed testified that a house burned down, and the motorcycles were both destroyed together in the house fire in Oakland."

"That's impossible," I said. "That burned up Yamaha FJ1200 frame and engine was already destroyed in a fire a long time ago before I bought it and sold it to Ed. He took the burned up frame and engine and another wrecked motorcycle out of my shop and never told me what he was using them for, or that he was in any trouble."

When I was finished speaking, Sgt. Roccaforte said, "We had experts who testified the ROC Yamaha was never destroyed in a fire.

Our fire specialists stated Ed's ROC was never exposed to any sort of heat more than a sun burn."

I laughed as he said, "The DMV employee stated to me, the day Ed tried to register the ROC race bike in 1997, he told her the motorcycle was in a house fire in which the whole house burned down and destroyed the ROC. Ed stated to the DMV employee the value of the burned ROC Yamaha was only $200 because it was in this so-called fire. Ed attempted to register the race bike for street use under his own name. I went to the DMV one day in 1997 checking on things with Ed's Porsche investigation. When I spoke to the supervisor about Ed, one of the clerks overheard me and told me a man named Ed Woo was just there ten minutes ago. She presented me with the documents Ed submitted in order to register the ROC for road use in California, with a $200 value. After the DMV clerk handed me Ed's papers, I looked at the VIN number, and it read ROC on the paper. I thought to myself, what the heck is a ROC? After checking databases, I was surprised because I didn't find a record of any vehicle called an ROC ever imported or sold in the United States."

He continued, "Ed also submitted a verification of vehicle form from Charlie's shop, with Charlie's signature, which stated Charlie did the inspection of the frame and engine number of the ROC at his shop."

I interrupted the sergeant, "Do you mean Charlie claimed to be the one who sold Ed the ROC from his shop in South San Francisco?"

He said, "No. Charlie was interrogated about the paperwork only. Ed claimed he acquired the ROC from a guy named Rick Davis, who lives in Naples, Florida."

I asked him, "Where did Rick Davis get a ROC race bike to sell Ed, and how much did Ed say he paid for the ROC race bike? How did Ed know that this Rick Davis was selling a ROC race bike if Rick lived in Florida?

He said, "Ed claimed he found an ad from Rick selling the ROC in a magazine called *Racing World*."

I asked, "Did Ed say he drove all the way down to Florida from California to buy his ROC race bike?"

Sgt. Roccaforte said, "No, Ed claimed he traded one of his built-up Porsches for the ROC and Rick towed the ROC on a trailer from Florida to California. Once Ed and Rick Davis finished the trade,

Ed claimed Rick then put the Porsche from Ed on the trailer and towed the car back home to Florida. Ed wanted us to believe this ROC, together with a Yamaha FJ1200 he purchased from your shop, was destroyed in a house fire after he acquired it from Rick. Ed even showed me the burned FJ1200 he bought from you, to prove to me there was a fire I always suspected had never happened."

"Sir," I said. "There could be a possibility Ed never acquired the ROC race bike from a guy named Rick Davis, because racing teams don't sell that kind of bike. Those race bikes are only owned by internationally famous race teams. Where would Rick Davis get a machine like a ROC Yamaha? Even if Rick Davis did have a bike like this for sale, why would he trade it to a guy in California like Ed Woo in exchange for a used built-up salvage Porsche? I remember years ago when Charlie installed a large rack and tow bar on his motor home before he left for a trip to Florida. He also said he needed to carry a loaded gun because he was towing valuable cargo with him and needed to protect it from being stolen. Its possible Charlie towed the Porsche to Florida, and Rick Davis never drove across the country towing an exotic ROC Yamaha YZR500 on a trailer. A few years ago, after you called me, Charlie told me his friend Dave Bostrom saved the day when it came to Ed getting his Yamaha back. What did Dave Bostrom have to do with a ROC Yamaha race bike and Ed Woo?"

Sgt. Roccaforte said, "Dave Bostrom was one of Ed's key witnesses in Ed's felony case. Dave Bostrom testified he helped Ed re-assemble and rebuild the ROC race bike after it was destroyed in the fire."

I said, "So Dave Bostrom lied to the cops? That's crazy. Do you know who Dave Bostrom's sons are? They are Ben and Eric Bostrom, two of the most famous motorcycle road racers in the world."

Sgt. Roccaforte said, "Ed Woo had a long list of people who were prepared to testify they witnessed the ROC rebuilding process from a burned wreck to restored condition. Dave Bostrom said some employees from Mission Motorcycles in Daly City witnessed him buy all the parts and pieces from their Yamaha dealership, in order for Ed and Dave to rebuild the burned ROC Yamaha together."

I said to him, "I remember when you asked me during the investigation on the phone about polishing an aluminum frame that was destroyed in a fire to restore it back to its original condition."

The Sergeant said, "Dave and Ed produced a witness named TJ, who ran a polishing-powder coating shop. He stated the three of them together polished the burned ROC race bike frame back to the original condition after it was destroyed in the fire."

I said, "That's astounding news. I don't think any of that actually happened."

He answered, "I knew Ed's ROC Yamaha was never involved a fire, but after four years of Ed and Dave manipulating the court system, Ed was able to receive his property back after he was allowed to plea bargain in the case. With all the witnesses Ed had, his lawyer was able to convince the courts there actually was a fire, a reconstruction of the race bike and an actual sale or trade of the ROC race bike between Rick Davis and Ed.

I said, "It's hard to believe Rick drove all the way here to trade his ROC to Ed for a used salvage Porsche. Don't they have used Porsches for sale in Florida with clean titles?"

He said, "We did trace one of Ed's Porsches to a guy named Rick Davis in Florida, and then we had a team of experts inspect the car. We found the Porsche was purchased in California as a piece of salvage by Ed and reconstructed before Rick Davis took possession of the car."

I said, "Why didn't Rick, after he found out he traded his exotic ROC Yamaha race bike for a re-assembled junk Porsche from California, become angry at Ed and want his ROC Yamaha back?

The Sergeant said, "I wondered the same thing too. Near the end of the case Rick Davis was in the process of being summoned to California to testify in the case before it went to trial. He was difficult to contact because it appeared as if he was always on vacation. Shortly afterwards, Ed Woo was able to plea bargain so it wasn't necessary for Rick to appear in California."

I said, "After Ed Woo acquired the ROC back from the police, I saw it in his garage, and he never for a moment told me anything about the bike except it was the one I helped him get back. When I saw the race bike in Ed's garage, I knew it was something very special, and I attempted to read the serial number on the frame but I didn't get a chance to do so. Do you have any way of getting that VIN number of Ed's ROC race bike?"

Sgt. Roccaforte said, "Oh, I have that memorized. I worked on Ed's case for almost six years. The serial number was ROCGP19209.

The ROC stands for the brand, the GP1 stands for Grand Prix racing, 92 is the year model, and 09 is the number of the bike itself. At first I didn't know anything about the bike but I knew the bike was a Yamaha because the engine number was YZR500E-9209. I also found no records in the database for that engine number so eventually I called Yamaha Motor Corporation and spoke to someone about the ROC race bike in the racing department there."

He continued and said, "Near the end of the case, Ed wasn't supposed to get any of those Porsche cars or the ROC race bike, but after a four-year battle in the courts, the DA decided to let him have his vehicles back when Ed agreed to plea bargain to forgery and was only charged with running a chop shop for cars. Originally Ed was charged in two separate cases with seven felony counts on the ROC Yamaha case and twenty three felony charges on Porsche case.

I said, "I can't believe Ed, Dave and Charlie really pulled it off without me even knowing a damn thing about it. I can't believe they got away with it, I should go down to Charlie's house right now and let him have it for what he did to Bert."

Sgt. Roccaforte said, "Well like I always say, I guess good police work stops at the courtroom door."

My pulse was racing for the last hour, listening to the story the sergeant told me. I said, "I still wonder about the ROC race bike. Do you mind if I call you back at some point after I research it more?" The sergeant told me I could call him back any time I had more questions. We talked another thirty minutes about Ed's ROC case.

I was numb when I walked in the other room. I said to Bert, "Charlie fucked us when he cut and ran from the shop in 1997 with Ed and the Bostroms after they were busted with stolen Porsches and the exotic ROC race bike we saw in his garage. Charlie gave us the shop and made us think he wanted to retire around the time when Grandpa died. What really happened was the shop was raided and Ed and Charlie were in trouble for registering Porsche cars and that ROC race bike through the shop. The Sergeant just told me the most unbelievable story I've ever heard. This part will blow you away. He told me Ed was raided and arrested on July 12, 1997, which is our wedding anniversary and also Sgt. Roccaforte's birthday."

Bert said, "That was the weekend Charlie went to the Laguna Seca races to see Ben and Eric race. The next day he came to us and said he wanted to retire and go to the races more with the Bostroms."

Bert was intrigued with the story.

I said, "I told you Charlie and Dave were up to no good with Ed so I'll keep looking to see just how special that ROC race bike in Ed's garage really is. The weird part is the cops didn't even know to look for Ed at a place on 9th street until a parking ticket that was issued on Ed's small truck went unpaid while parked on 9th and that's how the cops found him there. The Sergeant said the cars and the ROC were stuffed away in the garage in a hurry and he also found a briefcase full of different types of DMV documents along with a few forged bills of sale from Rick Davis to Ed that looked like they were used for practice signing by Ed."

Bert said to me, "How do you think Ed knew to hide all his good vehicles and his race bike at the address on 9th street?"

I said, "I bet you somebody tipped Ed off that Sgt. Roccaforte and the cops were asking questions about a ROC Yamaha Ed was trying to register through a salvage yard. The Sergeant said he called an acquaintance of his who owns a motorcycle dealership in San Francisco who told him a ROC was a grand prix race bike. He called Yamaha Motor Corporation and talked to someone there in the racing department and he also called AMA Pro racing and talked to someone there looking for information about the race bike and the ad that ran for its sale. He said he called the seller of the race bike named Rick Davis in Naples Florida because he had one of Ed's salvage Porsches and said he traded the race bike for the car. It could've been any one of them to tip Ed off. That would be enough for Ed to hide the ROC and all his cars quickly thinking he was in trouble."

Bert and I sat down to dinner, as I said, "Sgt. Roccaforte told me his 155-page report on Ed Woo's ROC and Porsche case is available for anyone to obtain at the courts. I will try to find the records because when I asked him if he could remember the names of the people he talked to at AMA Pro Racing and Yamaha Motor Corporation, he told me the names are in the original report, but he just couldn't remember them since it was so many years ago."

With dinner over I said. "I really do feel like calling Charlie and Ed on it because they fucked you and me on their deal with the cops. Sgt. Roccaforte said Ed wrote me down as one of his witnesses in his case for the ROC without ever telling me I was involved. Ed never even said he was in any trouble when he came and picked up the burnt Yamaha FJ1200 after Charlie broke his leg. I'm really mad at Dave too, because after they were busted, Dave and Eric came in the shop while Dave must have known Ed was in trouble on a ROC race bike, and they didn't say a fucking thing about it. Hell, I think Dave and Eric are part of the cover-up." I decided to check the facts further before calling Charlie.

I said confidently, "I don't believe the ROC came from a guy in Florida. Maybe it came from the Bostroms or even those big boys Ed Woo is always talking about. Only a professional motorcycle racer would have access to a race bike like a ROC. Let's check together on the Internet and see if we can find out who the famous racer was who owned or raced the number 09, 1992 ROC Yamaha YZR500."

Bert became upset but she was also infuriated Ed penciled us in as witnesses and lied to us for years. She couldn't believe Charlie would cut and run and stick us with the shop so he could devote his time to working with Dave and Ed to get the Porsches and ROC back from the cops. She said, "We loved Charlie like our own father, and he stabbed us in the back for the Bostroms and Ed?"

When I saw Bert's eyes fill up with tears, I couldn't believe how badly I felt. I knew she was right.

Charlie, the guy I knew to be my dad, fucked us.

We spent the next few months on the Internet, diligently trying to find out as much information about a ROC Yamaha YZR500. We ordered many books about the ROC and read about racers who raced the ROC Yamaha with different international grand prix road racing teams. I read up on information about Serge Rosette, who built the ROC. I was alarmed to see the 1993-94 edition of a Motocourse motorcycle racing book showed some pictures of what appeared to be the same motorcycle Ed had in his garage. The book listed a motorcycle, showing the exact same tail section that Ed's ROC Yamaha wore, as being a Marlboro ROC Yamaha YZR500. It stated the only team who owned these Marlboro bikes was known as the Evil Empire.

I ordered other books on the Internet, including the autobiography of Wayne Rainey, who stated in his book he raced and won international grand prix races on a Marlboro ROC Yamaha before he was paralyzed on one. I wondered if that same bike could be the one in Ed's garage and thought most likely Ed never bought the ROC from Rick Davis.

After the summer months came to an end, we received an email from Charlie's oldest daughter. It was more than a year since I talked to anyone in my family, and I wasn't too happy to hear from her. Charlie's daughter wrote that she, along with Charlie and my mother, just returned from Hawaii—Charlie's youngest daughter just celebrated her wedding there. She wanted to know in her email what was up with me and Bert and said she didn't believe all the crap Charlie was saying about me. I didn't know what she was talking about since I wasn't on speaking terms with Charlie.

After reading her email, I was pissed. I emailed back that Charlie should've been in jail with his friends instead of tanning his ass in Hawaii. I wrote that her father and his famous motorcycle friends fucked me, and I should write a book about them.

A few nights later, there was a message on our phone from my mom. She was angry because she heard I mentioned I might write a book about Charlie. Her message said I better not write a book about anyone in the family. I said to Bert, "I wonder if my mom knows what Charlie, Dave and Ed did to us and does she know why Charlie had to give us the shop when he retired around the time her father died? I also wonder if she knows who Sgt. Roccaforte is and if she has ever heard of a ROC race bike."

With the Christmas season approaching, Bert and I received another strange message. This one was from Charlie, who spoke in a panicked voice. He said, "Okay. There's a Porsche and a Ducati that my friend TJ owns, and we think Ed stole them. If you know where Ed's hiding out with the stuff, you can claim a $5,000 reward."

After the message finished playing, I said to Bert, "Charlie and Dave just finished their Christmas dinner, and I think they're planning to set us up by saying we know where Ed is, after Ed ripped off some guy. Charlie and Dave can find Ed Woo anytime they want, playing with Ben and Eric right out at Bostrom Ranch."

I thought since Ben and Eric could be found hanging out with Sensei Woo how could they possibly not know or maybe even be involved with all of the things Ed and Dave were mixed up in for the last twenty five years. After all, I recently read Eric was quoted in the press saying he came from a very 'tight knit' family.

2005

A few weeks passed since I received the message from Charlie about his friend TJ's stolen Porsche and Ducati motorcycle. I knew something was out of the ordinary because how could Ed steal a motorcycle and a car at the same time? I also thought it was strange since Sgt. Roccaforte already told me this TJ guy was one of Ed's witnesses. He helped Ed and Dave convince the courts they polished and restored the ROC frame from a burnt condition to a shiny like new state, even though we believed the ROC was never damaged in any fire.

I decided not to call Charlie back about TJ. I felt I was being set up by Charlie and his friends; they would have known where Ed was in the bay area, and they should turn Ed in themselves, instead of calling me to do it for them if Ed was really in trouble.

I called Sgt. Roccaforte to ask him a few questions about the case against Ed and his ROC Yamaha. I told the Sergeant, "A few weeks back, Charlie called me and said I could collect a $5,000 reward on Ed because he stole vehicles from his friend TJ."

He said, "That's strange because TJ recently called me and said Ed stole his property and he asked me if I could help him out. I never knew this TJ in the past, he was just another one of Ed's witnesses who claimed the ROC was destroyed in a fire and he was part of the repair process; I was surprised he called me at all because I'm retired."

I said to him, "It's strange this TJ would call you back, knowing he put one over on you with Ed and Dave concerning the fire on the ROC. Now he calls you to let you know Ed stole his property? I bet while TJ spoke to you about his vehicles, he didn't say anything about the ROC never destroyed in a fire. Its peculiar TJ wouldn't just deal with the local police on the issue instead he went through all the channels to find you, long after you retired from the police force. Charlie and Dave know exactly where Ed is so why is Charlie calling me and assuming I would know where Ed is hiding out with TJ's stolen Porsche and Ducati? I've never met TJ but I wonder if his car and bike were never stolen.

I changed the subject and said to the Sergeant, "I researched the ROC Yamaha online, and I bought books that show pictures of the international road racing scene at the time the ROC was first built in 1992. Originally there were only fifteen ROC race bikes built, in '92. They were built in France by an engineer named Serge Rossett. Ed had number 09 of only fifteen ROC race bikes produced in the entire world for that year. It's not possible for Ed to have legitimately purchased or traded for this race bike from a guy named Rick Davis, in my opinion."

Sgt. Roccaforte said, "The guy at Yamaha Motor Corporation in the racing department I called should have told me this information about the ROC being so exotic, and that it would not be possible for an average citizen to own and sell as if it was just a regular race bike."

I said to him, "He should have told you that because it would be the same as if Ed had a Marlboro Ferrari Formula One Grand Prix race car in his garage with all the stolen Porsches."

I told the sergeant that the ROC was only available to professional race teams who competed in the 500cc World Championship motorcycle Grand Prix. Even more interesting was the fact the paint scheme on Ed's ROC matched the two ROC race bikes pictured on page 143 of the road racing publication Motocourse for the year 1993-94. I said the picture featured two ROC Yamaha race bikes competing against each other in the British grand prix in 1993 with one of them winning the race. The ROC race bikes were painted red and white, with the Marlboro paint scheme. The team was the factory Yamaha team run by Kenny Roberts.

I also told the sergeant about the other book I recently read, which was the autobiography of Wayne Rainey. It stated in the middle of the 1993 racing season Wayne Rainey complained so much that his YZR500 factory Yamaha handled so poorly the team later acquired ROC Yamahas for the racers to replace the ill handling factory Yamaha race bikes. His book stated after Wayne Rainey won a couple grand prix races on a ROC Yamaha, riding for the Kenny Roberts Marlboro 500cc race team, he was paralyzed and his career was ended by a ROC. It was likely Wayne Rainey and even his team mate won at least two grand prix races each on the bike known as the Marlboro ROC Yamaha YZR500.

I said to the sergeant, "Looking at all these facts; it's hard to imagine the ROC Ed has in his garage could be one of only two

Marlboro ROC Yamahas known to exist in the entire world and could even be a grand prix winner. If the ROC in Ed's garage is one of the famous ROC race bikes, then that ROC is supposed to be in a museum, not seized with a bunch of stolen Porsches by the San Francisco police department with Ben Bostrom's father in the center of the conspiracy."

I asked Sgt. Roccaforte, "How's a person like Rick Davis from Naples, Florida, supposed to get his hands on a ROC? Did Rick have a title from Florida for his ROC he traded a junk Porsche for?"

He answered, "No, Rick Davis didn't have a title for the ROC. Ed only produced a handwritten bill of sale made out on the back of a torn envelope from Rick to Ed."

I laughed and said, "I can't believe a torn piece of paper was used for the bill of sale on an exotic racing bike. There is the possibility Ed's ROC could be one of the greatest pieces of American motorcycle road racing history in the entire world. I checked around for a magazine called *Racing World*, where you stated the advertisement for the sale of the ROC was listed by Rick. I couldn't find any magazine under that name, so I'll continue to search around and I'll let you know if I find some kind of match."

He said, "I used to have a copy of my 155-page report which stated all the names of Ed's witnesses and the people I talked to at Yamaha, AMA Pro Racing and the owner of *Racing World* magazine. The magazine owner stated to me in an interview the ad ran in his magazine back in summer of 1996. I will try to find the report when I have time. I may also have, stored away in my paperwork, pictures of the actual ROC we seized from Ed's 9th street garage. It was photographed as part of the case in deciphering whether or not it was really destroyed in a fire."

I said, "Wow. You have to try and find those pictures because if they match the pictures of the bikes in my books then Ed may have a Marlboro ROC Yamaha race bike in his garage, which will be one of only two known to exist in the world. Where would this Rick Davis get something like that? Let me try to get this straight. You seized fifteen cars between 9th street and Ed's yard in Oakland. What did you see when you raided Ed's house on Union Street?"

The Sergeant said, "The whole house was full of car parts in many areas. I noticed various pictures of Porsche cars and a van scattered around and in the background of the photos I saw trails and ruts cut in the mountainside."

I said, "That's wild news because what you saw in the pictures could be this mysterious place called Bostrom Ranch where Charlie and Ed Woo were known to hang out with the Bostroms in the past. I have a set of Charlie's books I believe may contain the VIN numbers of a fleet of motorcycles that may have been stored there in the country. This might be the same place where the pictures you found at Ed's house were taken. Can you run VIN numbers in your police computers and tell me the history of which dealerships the bikes were originally sent to?"

He answered, "Yes I can. I can also tell if a motorcycle has been reported stolen or if it was exported."

I gave the sergeant a VIN number for a BMW that was in Charlie's book. I wondered about it because the engine number seemed different than usual. In a moment he returned to the phone and said, "This isn't a motorcycle VIN number. This is the VIN number of a black BMW convertible automobile, which shows it was purchased from an insurance salvage auction. Then the record shows it was delivered to Charlie's motorcycle salvage shop, located on Antelope Drive in Sacramento."

I was shocked and said, "That's impossible! Charlie only had one salvage yard, in South San Francisco."

He said, "Nope. No mistake. He must have had another yard in Sacramento on Antelope Drive, because that is where the BMW went."

I asked the sergeant to give me the address and told him I would drive out to Sacramento the next day and take a look around. Charlie never told me, in over twenty years, he ever had a salvage business in Sacramento.

I said to him while looking in Charlie's books, "Most of these VIN numbers didn't come through Charlie's shop, only through his books. Can I give you a few VIN numbers and will you tell me where they were originally shipped to in the past?"

I gave him some VIN numbers and told him I would call again after he checked out the numbers.

I hung up the phone and walked in the bedroom to talk to Bert. I said, "I think Charlie and Ed built salvage cars together at a place called Antelope Drive in Sacramento. Sgt. Roccaforte told me a black BMW convertible was sent to an address with Charlie's shop name being registered there in Sacramento. The weird part is a long time ago Ed came to the shop in a black BMW convertible, with his wife and baby, and told me his wife could afford to drive a nice car because she had a great job that paid good money. Ed is a liar. He built that car his wife was driving from a salvage wreck at a secret shop in Sacramento."

The next day, Bert and I left early for the drive to Sacramento. We found Antelope Drive and I was filled with a feeling of déjà vu. "I've been here before in the past with Charlie," I told Bert. "Something feels really strange about this area."

As we approached the address, I said, "This is the exact place Charlie brought me around twenty years ago. He said he wanted to open another salvage yard in Sacramento, when he saw the rundown condition of this place, he told me he didn't want to rent any space and disregarded the idea of opening a second shop."

When we drove past the building, I recognized the garage doors and said, "Those are the doors where a man showed Charlie and me a unit, so there is no mistake. This is definitely the place Charlie brought me to twenty years back. Only now I find out Charlie and Ed did business here together."

We headed back to the freeway as I said, "I still can't believe Charlie lied to us like he did, he must have rented a spot here with Ed and never even said a fucking thing about it. We're finding out a bunch of lies Charlie told us, and I'm telling you right now Charlie's old VIN number books we found will tell a huge story when I get together with Sgt. Roccaforte and run all 3200 VIN numbers."

Bert said, "It breaks my heart Charlie would lie to both of us. What I think is unforgivable is when Charlie was in trouble with the police and Ed with that special ROC bike, he conned us into thinking he was getting old and was worried when Grandpa died. He said he wanted to retire and enjoy his old age by going to the races, then Charlie put his shop in my name and changed the license number over to me and continued to use the license illegally, he never retired. How could he do that to me?"

Later that evening, while in the office at home, I said to Bert, "Lets search the Internet for the names and the addresses in Charlie's DMV book." Bert turned on the computer, and we began to search. We checked many names in the book that came back phony. We then searched the name Bostrom on the net to see if we could find the place I thought Ben and Eric grew up on known as Bostrom Ranch. After reading through many web sites about Ben and Eric's racing careers, I saw something that read the name Paul Bostrom on my search, I told Bert to click that link up.

I was shocked when the link took us to a web page for an insulation company located at the same address as Charlie's old shop in South San Francisco. The web site said Paul Bostrom worked at the location for twenty five years. I looked at Bert and said, "Charlie knew Paul worked right in the yard at the old shop for twenty years and never said a fucking thing about it. What the fuck is that about? Charlie used to tell me he needed to walk to the opposite side of the yard and visit the landlord once in a while. I bet he was visiting Paul Bostrom and never said anything."

Bert said, "We shouldn't jump to any conclusions until you find out if that's Dave's brother. It could be another Paul Bostrom working there."

I smiled and said, "I doubt I have the wrong Paul Bostrom. I'm calling this insulation company in the morning, and I'll ask to speak to Paul."

Early the next morning, I called the number on the web site, looking to speak to Paul Bostrom. A man answered the phone and after I asked to speak to Paul, said to me, "Oh, you mean Paul Bostrom the motorcycle guy? He retired a while ago after working here for many years."

I hung up and said to Bert, "It was Charlie's Paul Bostrom in the yard the whole time. I recall seeing a guy while riding laps in the yard years ago. I bet he was Paul Bostrom, hiding out in the yard the whole entire time Charlie's shop was open."

I immediately wanted to go back on the Internet to do more searching. I checked other names and addresses in Charlie's DMV books and searched the address for Dave's old Honda-Yamaha dealership on Mission Street.

In less than one second, a long list of names appeared on the screen. Halfway down the list I saw the name Verna Ober. I said to Bert, "That's Ben Bostrom's mother's name."

When we clicked on the name Verna Ober, another list popped up, with all the addresses Verna Ober was associated with in the past. There was one address in Oakland listed as Oakland Honda and another which read 1471 Marshall-Petaluma road in Petaluma. I said to Bert, "That has to be it. The Bostrom Ranch is located somewhere in the countryside of Petaluma."

On the list of names from the Petaluma property, along with Verna Ober, was the name Torsten Bostrom. I realized this property was probably the place because Torsten was Ben and Eric Bostrom's brother. What seemed strange was the name Verna Ober was spelled at least five different ways and the address of 1471 Marshall-Petaluma road was changed around as well. The next name we entered into the computer search was Dave Bostrom. I noticed Dave's address was correct at 301 Harold Drive in Brisbane, but the odd thing was Dave's birthday was listed as 9-1. Ed Woo told me in the past Dave's birthday was in March. I saw Torsten Bostrom's birthday was listed as 9-1 as well.

I then put Charlie's name in the search, and we found some interesting results. A few of Charlie's children from his first marriage were also listed with birthdays on 9-1, except the ages of his children were many years off from the ages they actually were.

I said to Bert, "It's very strange how everyone's birthday is listed as September 1st, and I know I'm not searching the wrong people because the addresses are correct."

Then we saw under Charlie's search some of the investments Charlie made in Arizona and Nevada at addresses on the internet. Strangely the name Dave with Charlie's last name appeared on the search with an address in the Blairsden-Graeagle area at the exact same location where Charlie took me on a ride to Reno years ago when he stated he was using my brother Garg's name in his 'real estate association.'

I then said, "This must be a small glimpse into what Charlie used to refer to as the 'Name Game.' I guess more than twenty years ago, when Charlie and his friends were playing the 'Name Game,' they had no idea all this information would one day show up on the Internet where anyone could see it for themselves."

After Bert and I spent a few more hours searching, we were shocked to see some of Charlie's friends were listed as being 106 years old, even though they were only in their early seventies. Charlie had two friends listed as living in a few houses, along with several other people, even though the houses showed on the records they did not exist and were never built.

Once Bert and I searched some of the spouses and girlfriends of Charlie's friends and children, who also turned up with the birthday of 9-1, I said, "You know I can't believe Charlie. I don't even know who the guy is after having him as a father for the past thirty years. What the fuck?"

Bert said, "I know who he is. Charlie is a big fat liar."

I was angry and said, "I think the whole fucking shop was a lie for twenty years and Charlie only opened the place so all his friends could tank their dealerships. I bet Charlie's books will prove the place was a lie since I know I never saw those bikes come through the business. Besides, half the names in the book check back phony."

I said, "Let's search Ed Woo's house in San Francisco on the computer. I bet we'll find some funny stuff going on there as well."

I found some people with the birthday of 9-1 living at Ed's.

I said to Bert, "I've heard there are satellite websites we can go to which will show an aerial view anywhere in the world, so let's try and find the addresses listed for Ed and the Bostroms and maybe we can finally find Bostrom Ranch."

After Bert and I researched the address at 1471 Marshall-Petaluma road, we found the road started on the coast in the town of Marshall and traveled west inland to the city of Novato in Marin County. I said to Bert, "I bet the Bostrom Ranch is right in Marin County, somewhere along this Marshall-Petaluma road."

As we continued to look for what I believed to be Bostrom Ranch on the satellite website, Bert and I couldn't locate an actual property at the address of 1471. I said to Bert as we looked at the monitor, "Those twisting lines you see all over the hillsides may be dirt bike trails so this area could be very close to Bostrom Ranch. Those trails all over the mountains look like race tracks, so this must be near the place."

As Bert zoomed in, I suddenly said, "Look at that, it looks like two giant barns in a small valley. That is how Pat described the place in the past. Look, there's a lake near the barns. Maybe they are tucked away, back in the valley where no one can find them. Let's take a drive out to the Marin County coast tomorrow morning and we'll see if we can find the place after all these years."

The next day we headed out to the coast through Santa Rosa and soon we were traveling south along the coastal California highway. It was a beautiful drive as we came to the small town of Marshall. Bert said pointing, "There's a sign ahead for Marshall-Petaluma road, so we should turn left on the next road."

After turning left, I drove up a short hill and was surprised to see a small red church. I said to Bert, "I've been here before with Charlie on a ride. We waited for Pat right down the hill from this church. Pin Head told me years ago he would hide behind a red church along the Sunday morning ride route in the town of Marshall when he needed to ditch the police every time they chased him."

She said, "Well, I guess this must be the famous Pin Head red church then."

We followed the Marshall-Petaluma road inland, which took us up very steep coastal mountains. Our truck nearly occupied the entire narrow, pothole-filled road, which appeared more traveled by livestock than it did automobiles. The road winded through open cow land on top of the mountains and then descended into a few lush valleys. After we traveled nearly five miles on the road, we saw addresses for large dairy farms along the road that were close to the number 1471.

After we passed a farm with an old dilapidated cable car parked in the open field in front of the house, we came across a locked gate that appeared to lead down another road. We stopped the truck in front of the gate as I noticed a plywood sign next to the gate spray-painted with one of the names that was listed on the Internet for the property of 1471 Marshall-Petaluma road. The number 1471 was spray-painted under the name, with an arrow pointing in the direction of the locked gate.

I said to Bert, "This has to be the place. They must be located far back in this valley, where no one can find them. I read a long time ago in a motorcycle newspaper Dave was hooked on buying land and he owned a 400-acre piece of property somewhere. These ranches around here all look like dairy farms dating back 100 years. Dave's place must be on an old farm if it's around here. Pat bragged about two large barns at Bostrom Ranch that held all of their trophies and a large cache of motorcycles. When I was on a ride with Charlie and we waited for Pat in the town of Marshall, Pat suddenly came blasting down the hill on his motorcycle past the red church and told us he just rode from Oakland to Marshall in thirty minutes. I think Pat never rode from Oakland that morning, and he only came down the hill from a ranch around here. He looked as if he just woke up, and he didn't even have any socks on his feet."

Since the gate was locked, I couldn't get through to drive any further. I backed the truck out of the driveway and explored the area. I noticed a private dirt bike riding park and wondered if the Bostroms owned it or whether it could be a part of their property. We continued inland on Marshall-Petaluma road until we came to a small intersection, not too far from the locked gate. I said to Bert as I stopped the truck, "This is the exact spot where Charlie and Cal told me one day many years ago that I should go home one way as they were going out to the coast to go home a different direction."

Bert said sarcastically, "Maybe after ditching you, they just went right back up the road to the Bostrom Ranch for the night and ate a home-cooked meal with Ed."

I said, "What a bunch of dicks."

When we drove east into Novato, it was beginning to get dark. I saw a diner and noticed the name right away. It was called Stars.

Bert said, "I bet that's where Pat was eating dinner when he always bragged about dining at Stars."

I laughed and said, "He wanted you to think he was eating in a high-end San Francisco restaurant, when he was really eating here at a hamburger joint. I bet Bostrom Ranch is indeed hidden away back in that valley behind the locked gate."

As Bert and I were driving home I said to her, "In every interview I have ever read on Ben Bostrom, the only thing he says about himself is that he was born in Redding, almost 200 miles from Marin County. What's even stranger is for as many years as Ben and Eric were famous I never one time saw Dave out there in front of the cameras doing the father and son thing with Ben and Eric on the TV for the whole world to see."

Bert said, "You mean, you haven't read anything about the Bostroms raised in this area near the coast?"

I answered, "No, not a word. No one knows Ben and Eric Bostrom are probably from Marin County and may have been raised on a secret ranch, hanging out riding and training with Ed Woo on a giant fleet of missing bikes."

A week later, I was able to get in touch with Sgt. Roccaforte. I said to him, "I recently searched Ed Woo's home address on the Internet, and I believe there are many phony names listed on his property. I also found a place that may be where the pictures you found in Ed's garage might have been taken, a place called Bostrom Ranch, located near the Marin County coast. I found an address where I believe the Bostrom Ranch is located, but what's strange is when I search the names of Ben and Eric Bostrom on the Internet, they appear with incorrect birthdays and ages, several years older than they really are." I told him I called the search company to verify the accuracy of their records, and they assured me the records are accurate.

Sgt. Roccaforte said, "I'm well aware of the different names on Ed's address. We had evidence Ed registered many cars at his home address, as well as Charlie's shop, under phony names like James Brown and Larry Wong."

I said to the sergeant, "Ed told me twenty years ago he lived in Cupertino, and when I search his name there, he came back on an address of a $3 million house in Cupertino with his wife, and what also appears to be phony names living at the address as well. How in the hell are you supposed to afford a house like that in Cupertino when the only job you ever had was being a Porsche thief?"

The sergeant said, "You're probably right about Ed living in Cupertino as well as San Francisco because one day when I was driving on the freeway through Cupertino, after I retired, I noticed a Porsche 911 on the freeway in front of me. I recognized the license plate because it was one of the plates involved in Ed's case."

Sgt. Roccaforte changed the subject and told me he recently ran some of Charlie's VIN numbers on his computer. He said some of the bikes were showing they were shipped to different dealerships in the San Francisco bay area over the years from the factories. He said, "I also see some of the bikes in Charlie's books were originally shipped to dealerships located in Arizona, Louisiana and Nebraska."

I was shocked because those specific VIN numbers I gave him were high-line sport bikes that were written in Charlie's books and sold by a phony name or by Charlie, selling the motorcycle to himself as the buyer and seller.

I said, "These books I have are an amazing twenty year record of a few thousand bikes I believe never came through Charlie's business. Many of these VIN numbers are old dirt bikes I believe were built into flat track race bikes. They may have been used to train Ben and Eric with Ed ever since the Bostrom boys were very young. After

Charlie was in trouble with Ed back in 1997, Charlie gave my wife the shop, and I believe he continued to run 200 bikes through the books of the business without letting us know. I want you to check those 200 bikes also."

I read out one particular VIN number for a motorcycle Charlie wrote through the books when Bert owned the shop. Sgt. Roccaforte said, "I show this bike was originally sent to a dealership in San Francisco and then exported out of the country."

Surprised, I said, "Over the years Charlie had customers who came into his shop from Europe. Charlie would always be very happy to see them, even though they never spent any money buying from his salvage yard. There is the possibility many of these bikes in Charlie's books could still exist because they may have never been dismantled and could now be located all over the world." I told the Sergeant I would be in touch with him again and he agreed as we hung up the phone.

I knew I had to be right about Charlie's import customers from Europe because the biggest clue is when they came to the shop they always collected as many of the California model igniter boxes as they could find. Why would they need all those boxes for California bikes in Europe when the igniter box was different for the European model?

I also wondered why Charlie was so mad at me when I finally closed down the salvage operation and let the salvage license go and why he needed to ask me twice to confirm it. Was he still using my dismantling license up to 2004 behind my back with his friends and maybe even Ed Woo?

2006

After the last six months attempting to collect court records from Ed Woo's ROC Yamaha case, I finally received some official records in the mail from the courts. I reviewed the documents, which showed Ed Woo was in trouble with the law in 1997 and charged with twenty three felony counts concerning nineteen different stolen Porsche automobiles. I also received court documents stating Dave Bostrom as the number one witness for Ed in the ROC Yamaha case, in which Ed was charged with seven felony counts. Ed's court documents showed the VIN number, and I confirmed the number was ROCGP19209; it was the same ROC VIN number Sgt. Roccaforte gave me.

I now furthered my research on the ROC and found there could most likely be only two Marlboro ROC Yamaha YZR500s ever built. I also read there were only fifteen 1992 model ROC Yamaha race bikes ever constructed, and most would be in museums or private collections. I knew immediately Ed couldn't legitimately trade a built-up salvage Porsche for this race bike.

I figured the race bike being returned to Ed must have been so important to make Charlie and Dave lie to the police for a period of four years, almost the entire time during which Ben and Eric became famous. I thought to myself, what could be so important that Dave would lie with Ed to the police and gamble the entire careers of his sons, and possibly the entire sport of motorcycle road racing as well. Obviously Ed's ROC must be one special race bike.

When I added Charlie screwed over Bert by giving her the shop when he and Ed were in trouble with Dave on the ROC back in July of 1997, I thought Ed's race bike most likely could be a genuine Marlboro ROC Yamaha YZR500. The biggest clue I had was Charlie and my mom didn't speak to me in years. I knew Charlie was hiding out with Dave and Ed so I decided to call the Sergeant again.

I told him about the court documents I recently received. I said, "I found half of the court documents on Ed's case with the Porsches and the ROC, but I didn't find the names of the people you spoke to at AMA Pro Racing and Yamaha Motor Corporation, or some of

Ed's other witnesses. I did find a document that lists Dave Bostrom as Ed's first witness on the fire we know didn't happen. I have a document from Ed's lawyer here which states she tried to not allow Ed's past conviction for cocaine trafficking as evidence at his trial with the stolen Porsches and ROC."

Sgt. Roccaforte said, "Yeah. Ed's cocaine trafficking arrest was a federal case back in 1986, when Ed was arrested for selling a briefcase filled with cocaine to a undercover officer and sentenced to prison for 15 years. We wanted to have Ed's cocaine arrest allowed as evidence in his case, but his lawyer fought hard to keep his prior convictions out of the courts."

I said, "For the last few months I checked around, and didn't find anything called *Racing World* magazine. I thought you were talking about a magazine called *Road Racing World,* so I took the liberty to order the summer issues of 1996. There is an advertisement for a ROC race bike by guy named Rick in the classified section of *Road Racing World* magazine for August of '96."

I told the Sergeant about the ad that read 'For Sale 1992 ROC 500GP raced one year in Europe, own a piece of GP history, fastest race bike in the US $39,500 serious inquires only, call Rick 941-352-2692.'

I continued to say, "When I saw the ad I called the number, and there was no Rick at that number. I don't believe the sale is real just because there's an ad. Where are all the people who would've called to buy this famous bike for only thirty nine grand? Are we to believe out of everyone in the world Ed Woo is the only one who called the ad and convinced Rick Davis to trade away his 'piece of GP history' for a rebuilt salvage piece of shit Porsche instead of the cash?"

He laughed as I said, "I believe Ed may have had the bike all the time in California. He was injured on what he called a Yizzer back in the spring of 1996 before the ad ran or Rick Davis had enough time to take the 4000 mile road trip to California. I believe Ed had the ROC all the time and the whole thing might just be an elaborate scheme to title the race bike after a phony sale from Florida since the ROC race bike has no VIN record in Florida or California. Maybe they needed to show the DMV it was purchased legitimately outside of California. There would have been a very long line of rich people to buy this bike, so there is no clear reasoning as to how Ed stepped up after there was no buyer and traded the ROC for a junk car. Hell where was the owner of the magazine? Why didn't he step up to buy the ROC when he saw the ad in his magazine. I heard he's a racer. His son is a racer as well and what club racer wouldn't love to own a ROC after reading the ad in their own magazine. They or their friends would have been the first ones to call Rick; instead, it's Ed Woo. Right...That's sheer lunacy sir."

The Sergeant laughed again and agreed.

I said, "I have a document here that states Ed walked into the DMV the weekend of Dave's birthday on March 2nd of 1997 to register the ROC Yamaha. One thing that seems strange to me is Dave could convince the people at Mission Motorcycles to tell you they ordered many parts for the ROC after the so-called fire, even though I think they never ordered anything. You can't get parts for a ROC YZR500 race bike of any sort over the counter from a Yamaha dealership and you can't order any parts for an YZR500 engine either. I can't believe Dave can get everyone to lie for him. It's also hard to believe anyone at AMA Pro Racing and the Yamaha Company itself didn't further explain to you how important a ROC Yamaha really is and how it wouldn't be possible for anyone in the general public to own one. Why didn't either person jump at the chance to tell you as much information as they could or ask you some other questions about it?"

Sgt. Roccaforte said, "What's funny is everyone I talked to on the case always seemed to say the same thing. They all thought they heard about something like a ROC for sale out there somewhere."

I laughed and said, "What appears bogus is after Rick Davis supposedly towed his ROC race bike on a trailer all the way across the United States from Florida to California, he didn't get mad or demand his ROC race bike back when he realized he traded it for a previously wrecked salvage title built up Porsche and was ripped off by Ed. I remember you told me this Rick Davis is a pilot, so why didn't he fly right back to California to rectify the situation with Ed? Why would he tow the ROC all the way to California when he is the seller, especially since he supposedly didn't know Ed before Ed answered his ad? Who is this Rick Davis from Florida who traded away a famous ROC race bike for a junk Porsche?"

I also asked him, "Are we supposed to believe the ROC is then destroyed in a mysterious fire and then Ben Bostrom's father assembles the burnt race bike and repairs it back to new with Ed, the big Porsche thief? That must be why they call Dave Mr. Clean, because he burned my ass and maybe the entire system as well."

Surprised, the Sergeant said, "Is that what they call Dave Bostrom? Mr. Clean? Well, he didn't burn me because I always knew the ROC was never destroyed in a fire."

He repeated, "We had paid experts who testified the race bike never saw any more heat than a sun burn while we had the race bike impounded for over four years."

Laughing I said, "Recently during my research on the internet, I visited Ben Bostrom's official web site and I was surprised to see in his photo gallery along with family and racing photos, an interesting picture of an Italian bottle of the cleaning product '*Mr. Clean*.' It read on the label '*Don Limpio*' which is Italian for *Mr. Clean*. I think Ben knows his father is called Mr. Clean and has known it for years."

The Sergeant said, "I am surprised to hear the entire sale from Rick on the ROC may be a fabrication."

I said, "Why wouldn't the whole thing be a lie since they lied on the fire in the first place for years. We need to find out which ROC is the one sitting in Ed's garage, now registered to him through a salvage yard, because I need to know if it's a piece of international road racing history. It could be a grand prix winner or possibly even the ROC that paralyzed Wayne Rainey and ended the Kenny Roberts Yamaha Evil Empire."

Sgt. Roccaforte said, "It's been so many years, I have a difficult time remembering some of the details, but you're helping me to recall things now. Ed was able to claim the ROC back from the courts just around the time I retired from the police force, right before the World Trade Center terrorist attacks on 9/11.

I said, "Ed winding up with what could be one of the greatest motorcycles in the world is definitely of historical interest, especially since Ed's ROC should be in a museum in France. It could be one of the only non-factory race bikes to ever win races in the 500cc World Championship. If Ed's ROC is what I think it is, then it is truly a great race bike and the pride of all France. Ed doesn't even deserve to have that ROC because I believe he never acquired it legitimately. What would have happened if Ed and Dave's plan didn't work and Ed and Dave were caught lying and were sent to prison? What would have happened to the ROC?"

Sgt. Roccaforte answered, "The ROC was stored in a secret impound area for nearly four years during Ed's case, and if he was convicted, the ROC eventually would have been sold at a police auction to the general public, the same way the police department liquidates all vehicles that are confiscated in crimes."

I changed the subject and talked to Sgt. Roccaforte about the bikes listed in Charlie's DMV books. I told him I found what I believed to be hundreds of high line bikes, as well as a fleet of twenty four Yamaha YSR50 mini-road racers which may have been used to train Ben and Eric while they were mentored by Ed.

I said, "I drove to the coast and found what I believe to be the place called Bostrom Ranch. I think it's located on the shores of Arroyo Sausal reservoir, at the end of a long dirt road that intersects Marshall-Petaluma road. I can see from the satellite images two large barns near a lake, which is how the property was described to me in the past."

I spent the next hour on the phone with Sgt. Roccaforte, asking him more questions about the case. When we finished, he told me he would try to find the pictures he took of the ROC at the time it was seized. I said I would get in touch with him again.

After I got off the phone, I sat down with Bert and went over the information. When I told her about the ROC selling at auction to the general public if Ed was convicted, it made me think of my friend Dark Ninja down at the police auction years ago, trying to buy bikes for himself and other kids in his neighborhood.

I said to Bert, "What's wild is one of the greatest race bikes in the world could've been sold to one of Dark Ninja's buddies from the neighborhood for only a few hundred bucks if Dave and Ed were thrown in jail. Some kid from Dark Ninja's hood would've made the biggest score in the world. If Dark Ninja was alive today, he would laugh his ass off at the story of what Charlie and Dave tried to get away with on that ROC with the cops and Ed Woo."

I said, "At first Sgt. Roccaforte didn't know how famous Ben was internationally. I told him Ben had his own Race Replica Ducati named after him and each of the 155 Ben Bostrom Replica motorcycles were signed by Ben himself, and the Sergeant was impressed."

We walked in the office and I grabbed Charlie's VIN books and said, "I think we have the records of what could be considered the real Bostrom Replicas because there's a possibility the bikes here in Charlie's books actually might still exist. Finding them all could be the world's greatest scavenger hunt. Average people all over the globe would want to know if they own what I call a special Bostrom Salvage Series Replica because it would be more valuable than an average bike. We should publish a book with all Charlie's VIN numbers because some could be Bostrom Replica Salvage Bikes. Even better, I guess, I should get to work on a book on how Ben and Eric set the motorcycling world on fire after honed and fine-tuned by Sensei Ed Woo, the greatest Porsche thief and ROC Yamaha liar in the history of the planet. It would be the world's largest motorcycle crime conspiracy."

Knowing the value of Charlie's VIN number books I made copies and put the originals in a bank vault for safekeeping. I knew one day I would get together with Sergeant Roccaforte and run all 3200 VIN numbers and we would finally get to the bottom of the secret meetings between Cash Register Charlie and Dave Bostrom. I know it will be enough explosive information to write a second book.

On September 1, 2006, I began to construct and write the book that I would call *The Bostrom Conspiracy*.

I was saddened to receive a letter from Charlie the day after 9-1. The letter stated because I didn't return any of his phone calls he no longer considered me one of his children. I reflected on all the years and all the roads we traveled down together in life and how easy it was for Charlie to write me off in the end.

Deeply angered remembering the times he lied and fucked me for the past thirty years as a so called father, I couldn't help but think the only father Charlie really wanted to be, was the father of Ben Bostrom and Eric Bostrom, the famous American motorcycle racing brothers.

After all, Charlie achieved what he always wanted; Ed and Dave pulled off the biggest scam in motorcycle history and the Bostrom brothers became the most talented and internationally known pair of racing brothers the United States ever produced.

Three weeks later on the day of Charlie's birthday, when Ed and Charlie would have been at a party with Dave and their friends, I received a message on my phone from Ed Woo.

I did not return the call.